# Wireless
# Security

# Wireless Security

Merritt Maxim
David Pollino

**McGraw-Hill**/Osborne

New York   Chicago   San Francisco
Lisbon   London   Madrid   Mexico City
Milan   New Delhi   San Juan
Singapore   Sydney   Tokyo   Toronto

**McGraw-Hill**/Osborne
2600 Tenth Street
Berkeley, California 94710
U.S.A.

To arrange bulk purchase discounts for sales promotions, premiums, or
fund-raisers, please contact **McGraw-Hill**/Osborne at the above address.
For information on translations or book distributors outside the U.S.A.,
please see the International Contact Information page immediately following the index of this book.

**Wireless Security**

1234567890 CUS CUS 0198765432
ISBN 0-07-222286-7

| | |
|---|---|
| **Publisher** | **Acquisitions Coordinator** |
| Brandon A. Nordin | Emma Acker |
| | |
| **Vice President &** | **Technical Editor** |
| **Associate Publisher** | Carlton Davis |
| Scott Rogers | |
| | **Composition and Indexing** |
| **Acquisitions Editor** | MacAllister Publishing Services, LLC |
| Jane Brownlow | |
| | |
| **Project Manager** | |
| Jenn Tust | |

This book was composed with QuarkXPress™.

# Dedication

This book is dedicated to the two people that have been the most supportive in all aspects of my life: my wonderful wife Michelle Pollino and my father Paul Pollino, Sr.

*—David Pollino*

To Demetri and Cassandra.

*—Merritt Maxim*

# Contents at a Glance

# Contents

# Acknowledgments

I would like to give special thanks to the following individuals who have been extremely important people for their tremendous support to my career and personal life, making this book possible: DC Cashman, Henry Chung, Mat Hughey, Aaron Keaton, David Kim, Theran Lee, Andrew Mehren, Jay Mehren, Farrah and Paul Pollino Jr., Eric Rafanan, Gilbert Ribét, Steve Roge, Shelah Ryan, Mike Schiffman, Lois Spencer, Sean Stinson, Joanna Tandaguen, and Joel Wallenstrom. I cannot forget the following for their help with my wireless security research: Brian Hassick, Michael Oh, Michael Stokes, and Sri Sundaralingam.

—*David Pollino*

While only two names only appear on the front cover of this book, countless other individuals played an integral role in the successful completion of this book. Thankfully, this section provides a vehicle to recognize those individuals whose collective advice and support helped sustain the project and enable it to proceed smoothly.

First, I would like to recognize the individuals at McGraw-Hill/Osborne who steered me the multi-step process of producing this book. Emma Acker and Jane Brownlow both ensured that project deadlines were met and provided useful advice and encouragement throughout the entire process. Bettina Faltermeier helped with promotional and marketing activities. Lastly, credit is due to unnamed individuals in the art department who successfully translated my scribbled drawings into the diagrams presented in this book.

In addition to the McGraw-Hill/Osborne people, several other individuals deserve mention. Fellow author Carlton Davis provided useful technical reviews of the chapters and Beth Brown also assisted in the page layout and review process. Courtney Flaherty at Brodeur Worldwide was also instrumental in procuring the necessary product images of the Blackberry devices.

Last, but certainly not least, special gratitude is directed towards my extended family who provided valuable support and, in some cases, necessary nourishment. The most significant supporters for this project were my wife Lefki and our two children, Demetri and Cassandra. Despite the growing demands of running her own business, Lefki was a beacon of inspiration and encouragement for me and made the entire book writing process proceed without a hitch. While my children are still too young to appreciate what writing a book means, I hope they find this book useful someday as their generation will undoubtedly witness amazing transformations in wireless technologies in the coming decades.

*—Merritt Maxim*

# About the Authors

**David Pollino,** Director of the Wireless Center of Excellence at @stake, Inc., conducts leading research into wireless security issues. He is a respected information security consultant with an extensive networking background. His wireless and network security expertise is published in magazines and books. David speaks on security issues at several industry events.

**Merritt Maxim** is an experienced information security professional. He has spoken at numerous industry events on wireless security. He provides security consulting to commercial clients on numerous security topics and was previously a product manager for wireless security at RSA Security Inc.

**Carlton Davis** is doing research in wireless network security for his Ph.D. degree in Computer Science at McGill University, Montreal, Canada. Before returning to McGill, he held a number of IT-security-related positions, which provided hands-on experience with various system and network security applications and tools. These positions included Senior SE for Network Associates (Santa Clara, California), Unix System Manager for Bell Canada (Montreal, Canada), and System Administrator at the School of Computer Science, McGill University (Montreal, Canada). Mr. Davis is also the author of *IPSec: Securing VPN*, published by McGraw-Hill, April 2001.

**Brian Hassick** is currently the founder of Consilium-III, a research prototype house that explores various fields of wireless networking, decentralized networks, and advanced antenna design. Previously, he was one of the founding researchers of @stake, Inc., and one of the principle developers of the Wireless Center of Excellence. Prior to that, he spent five years at Bolt, Berenak, and Newmann, where he worked on the GP1000, the TC2000, the NASA ACTS Gigabit Satellite Network, the Gigabit SuperRouter, and the Safekeyper. He is also one of the founders of BAWIA, the Boston Area Wireless Internet Association, and has been active in building community-based wireless networks since 1995. He has given talks on secure hardware design, and wireless networking, and written articles on wireless threats and countermeasures.

**Michael Oh,** MCSE, MCT is a technical instructor and consultant with ten years experience in a wide area of information systems technologies. He has a strong focus on messaging, networking, and Internet security systems such as firewalls, VPN's, IDS, and monitoring systems. His current research interests are in networking, wireless LAN's, and Linux.

# Foreword

Welcome to *Wireless Security*. This book is part of a continuing series of titles published by RSA Press, the publishing arm of RSA Security Inc.. While I believe all our publications are valuable and relevant to organizations seeking to bolster the security of their e-business infrastructures and electronic resources, this book is different because the wireless world is different. Wireless has distinct capabilities and also presents distinct challenges from a security perspective.

For this reason, I am proud that *Wireless Security* is the first book entirely devoted to wireless security that has been written specifically for IT professionals and other users. I think you will find the mix of historical background, technical discussion, and market insight extremely useful as you begin to plan and implement a security strategy for your wireless systems and technologies.

The very term wireless denotes something untethered and unconstrained. This contributes to the sense of freedom and mobility that wireless technology brings to users. At the same time, wireless also connotes something difficult to control and protect. All of these associations are valid. Wireless does help people break through the geographical boundaries of the wired world; yet it can also make information transmitted through wireless networks vulnerable to unauthorized access or attack.

This is why organizations need to understand the range of security threats endemic to wireless technologies, including eavesdropping, wireless denial-of-service attacks, and various encryption issues. *Wireless Security* was created to help IT professionals address these challenges. The magnitude of potential problems that wireless may pose is discussed in detail in Part 1, Chapter 2: "Wireless Threats." The broad characteristics of various cellular networks and long- and medium-range wireless data network technologies are examined throughout Part 2: "Wireless Technologies & Applications." This kind of valuable information helps IT professionals appreciate the challenge of making wireless devices and networks secure.

Of course, there are currently a number of wireless security protocols in use. An overview of these technologies, including Secure Sockets Layer (SSL), Wireless Transport Layer Security (WTLS), and Secure Internet Protocol (IPSec), is provided in Part 1, Chapter 3: "Introduction to Wireless Security Protocols & Cryptography." The capabilities and limitations of these security methods, and the strategies for deploying them in a cohesive and comprehensive wireless security system, is discussed in Part 3: "Wireless Deployment Strategies."

Encompassing the historical and technological evolution of wireless communications, from Marconi's first wireless radio transmission in 1894 to today's wireless Internet, *Wireless Security* will help you deploy secure wireless technologies throughout your organization. Using this book as a guide, you will be able to enjoy all the benefits of wireless, the freedom and the flexibility, while strongly mitigating its inherent security risks. Mastering this information can help you control and protect your wireless networks, and the critical information they transmit.

We hope that readers will benefit as much from this book as from the other acclaimed titles previously released by RSA Press. We always welcome your comments and your suggestions for future titles. For more information on RSA Security Inc., please visit our website at www.rsasecurity.com; to learn more about RSA Press, please visit www.rsapress.com.

Scott T. Schnell
Senior Vice President
Sales, Marketing, and Corporate Development

# PART 1

# Introduction to Wireless

# CHAPTER 1

# Welcome to a Wireless World

Ever since Guglielmo Marconi transmitted the first wireless radio signal through the Italian hillside in 1894, wireless technologies have transformed how people communicate and receive information. From the amplitude modulation (AM) radio sets of the 1920s to the multiple wireless devices of the twenty-first century, wireless technologies have evolved dramatically, defining new industries in the process and spawning a host of new products and services.

As the twenty-first century unfolds, wireless technologies have become an increasingly important technology area and a vital catalyst for economic growth. Unfortunately, these new wireless technologies have been coupled with confusion. Today's business and technology press are replete with a myriad of terms and abbreviations including Code Division Multiple Access (CDMA), Global System for Mobile Communications (GSM), Time Division Multiple Access (TDMA), 802.11, Wireless Application Protocol (WAP), third generation (3G), General Packet Radio Service (GPRS), Bluetooth, i-mode, and so on. The sheer number of new technologies can be daunting to consumers and enterprises alike. Will these technologies coexist? Are they mutually exclusive? Are they globally available?

The sheer number of new wireless technologies and services indicates that this is just the beginning of the wireless revolution. Wireless devices and services are projected to experience high growth rates in the foreseeable future. By 2004, over 1 billion people worldwide are expected to carry a cellular phone, a 105 percent increase from 2000 (see Figure 1-1).

The market projections for other wireless technologies such as wireless local area networks (LANs) and Bluetooth are equally impressive. According to market researcher International Data Corporation (IDC), the wireless LAN equipment market grew 80 percent in 2000 and is expected to continue robust growth into the future as wireless networking is installed in airports, hotels, academic settings, and corporations (see Figure 1-2).

The forecast for Bluetooth, a new short-range (less than 10m) wireless technology for interconnecting devices and peripherals like printers, personal digital assistants (PDAs), keyboards, and cell phones is impressive as well (see Figure 1-3). By 2005, nearly 1 billion Bluetooth-enabled devices will be shipping worldwide, according to Cahner's In-Stat Group. Collectively, this means that even with the astonishing advances in wireless technology over the last 20 years, further technological advances will still occur in the future.

**Figure 1-1**

Worldwide wireless phone users

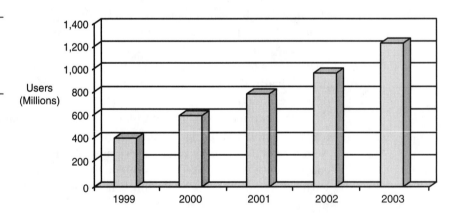

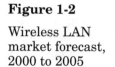

**Figure 1-2**

Wireless LAN
market forecast,
2000 to 2005

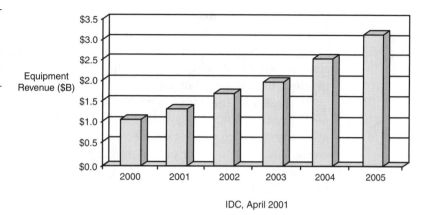

IDC, April 2001

**Figure 1-3**

Bluetooth market
forecast, 2000
to 2005

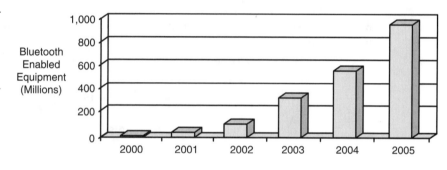

Calmers In-Start Group, April 2001

# History of Wireless Technologies

In order to understand where the wireless market is headed, it helps to understand from where the wireless industry has come.

Wireless technology started in the late nineteenth century with the development of Marconi's wireless telegraphy. Patented in 1896 in England, this technology enabled the transmission of wireless radio waves across great distances. However, Marconi's technology could only send the dots and dashes of the Morse code; it was not capable of sending voice waves. Thus, its initial user was limited to applications like ship-to-ship and ship-to-shore communication.

Once Marconi's invention demonstrated wireless' potential, individuals and companies raced to develop technology to send voice waves through the air. Following Marconi's success, American inventor Reginald Fessenden completed the first true radio broadcast in 1906 and the wireless revolution commenced in earnest.

By the 1920s, companies such as General Electric (GE), AT&T, and the newly created Radio Corporation of America (RCA) were aggressively creating the first real wireless industry: the AM radio. The results were staggering and eerily similar to the growth of the Internet 70 years later.

"Overnight, it seemed, everyone had gone into broadcasting, newspapers, banks, public utilities, department stores, universities and colleges, cities and towns, pharmacies, creameries, and hospitals, among others."[1]

As radio content grew, so did the consumer demand for radio. By 1929, over 6 million radios were in use in the United States, providing consumers with a new mechanism for receiving content and information. In just over 20 years, radio technology had reached 25 percent of the population. At that time, it was the fastest adoption of any mass-market technology (see Figure 1-4).

Wireless technologies expanded despite the global depression of the 1930s, as other new technologies such as frequency modulation (FM) radio and television were developed. The advent of World War II further accel-

**Figure 1-4**

Comparative adoption of mass-market technologies

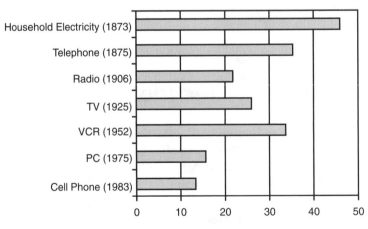

Years to Reach 25% of US Population

---

[1]Tom Lewis, *Empire of the Air*, New York: Harper Collins, 1991, 162–163.

erated wireless development as the military provided significant resources to further product development.

Following World War II, the development of new mass-market wireless technologies stalled. The Soviet launch of the Sputnik satellite in 1957 changed everything. Overnight, the United States and the former Soviet Union raced to put a man on the moon, throwing massive amounts of human capital and money into new space-related technologies. Communicating with spaceships required advanced wireless communication systems, and vendors raced to develop new wireless systems. These efforts generated information that would prove useful to the design of future wireless systems.

## The 1970s—The First Wireless Networks

The first wireless phone systems appeared in the United States in the 1970s. Based on technology developed at AT&T's Bell Labs in the late 1940s, these systems were analog, operated in a limited frequency range, and could only handle a low volume of simultaneous calls. Initial uses were in law enforcement and public safety. A key limitation of these systems was that they did not support communication continuity during movement from one cell to another.[2]

Demand for mobile voice grew during the 1970s, requiring the development of methods to support more users in a single cell and mobility between cells. Using cell sites of less than 1km in diameter, operators designed systems that, for the first time, enabled calls to be transferred from cell site to cell site, enabling true mobile voice. The first system of this type to be installed was AT&T's *Advanced Mobile Phone Service* (AMPS), which was deployed in Chicago in 1979. Similar systems were installed in Europe and Japan in the early 1980s. These systems are now referred to as first-generation networks.

The first-generation networks were hardly indicative of the future potential of wireless technology. Demand for mobile telephony started to outstrip available network bandwidth, leading to dropped connections. In 1981, the New York City system could only handle 24 simultaneous calls and the network operators limited the total subscriber base to only 700

---

[2]Sami Tabane, *Handbook of Mobile Radio Networks*, Boston: Artech, 2000, 206.

users![3] The limited capacity restricted mobile phone usage to an elite group of people. Plus, the early mobile handsets were large and heavy. Nevertheless, demand and interest in the mobile phone only increased. Network operators eagerly upgraded networks to meet the growing demand.

The biggest hurdle to further network development was the wireless radio frequency. Previously, governments allocated radio spectrum primarily for military and law enforcement purposes. Government regulation of wireless spectrum was not a highly visible public policy issue. Faced with these emerging wireless technologies, governments around the world needed policies and procedures to allocate additional wireless spectrum in an appropriate manner.

In the 1980s, the United States and the rest of the world took divergent policies to promote the development of new wireless networks. In Europe and Asia, the policy thrust was driven toward the development of a single wireless voice standard (GSM), while there were competing standards in the United States. These will be discussed in more detail in the next section. At the time, these differences did not warrant much attention from policy makers and technologists alike. Only in the twenty-first century would these differences manifest themselves. By this time, the wireless market had evolved and growing interest had created the need for a true global wireless network. Unfortunately, these differences would prove to make that dream difficult to achieve in the short term.

## The 1980s—Wireless Markets Start to Evolve

Following the success of the AMPS systems, pressure grew on the U.S. government to allocate additional radio spectrum for wireless communication. The Federal Communications Commission (FCC) was tasked to regulate the market, through licensing new radio spectrum. In the spring of 1981, the FCC announced its intention to allocate 40 MHz of spectrum in the major metropolitan markets in the United States. This was a significant step forward in capacity. This spectrum enabled 666 channels for cellular communication in each major metropolitan market. Compared to the 44 channels that had been previously allocated to cellular service, this was a quantum leap in capacity.[4] The FCC's initial focus was on the

---

[3]James B. Murray, *Wireless Nation*, Cambridge, Mass.: Perseus Publishing, 2001, 19.
[4]Ibid., 25.

largest cities in the United States, but ultimately, spectrum would be allocated for the top 300 metropolitan areas in the country.

To promote competition, the FCC awarded each market two licenses: one license to the local phone company (otherwise known as a Baby Bell) and another license to a nonwireline company. Most importantly, the FCC was technology agnostic—winners of the spectrum auctions could deploy any wireless network technology. The technology-independent policy was indicative of the laissez-faire policies of President Ronald Reagan's administration, but it was also influenced by the U.S. government's breakup of the AT&T phone monopoly.

To promote more competition in the telecommunications market and avoid creating a national cellular monopoly, the FCC wanted two carriers in each market. Since the AT&T breakup was announced in the midst of the initial wireless spectrum auction in 1982, it was clear that a host of new players, not AT&T, would be creating the wireless voice market. AT&T even downplayed the value of cellular service and did not participate in the first spectrum auction, leaving the market wide open for other new entrants. When AT&T finally entered the cellular market through the 1993 acquisition of McCaw Cellular, it would cost AT&T over $12 billion.

In 1983, the FCC began awarding spectrum licenses in the major markets. In October 1983, Ameritech, one of the seven Baby Bells created by the AT&T breakup, launched the first commercial system in Chicago and quickly signed up 3,000 subscribers.[5] Although these early systems were analog, the FCC's technology-agnostic policy meant that little attention was paid to developing compatible networks.

In Europe, the mobile phone market developed quite differently. In the early 1980s, European administrators were developing policies for a European wireless market. At the time, the European telecommunications market differed from the U.S. market in several key dimensions, which ultimately led to very different policies than those of the United States, as explained in the following list:

■ **State-owned telephone monopolies**   In most of Western Europe, state-owned telephone monopolies provided local and long-distance phone service. Competition was minimal. Although privatization efforts were underway (notably in the United Kingdom), most countries only had one phone carrier. This contrasted sharply with

---

[5]Ibid., 70.

the United States, which was breaking up the AT&T phone monopoly and promoting a new wireless voice market without AT&T. The European market limited competition, which meant that incumbents were the only players with the capability and capital to develop these new wireless systems.

- **Geography** Western Europe is a much smaller area than the United States and has a much higher population density. This means that the physical cost of developing networks would be considerably less than in the United States.

- **Mobile population** The creation of the European Common Market encouraged the creation of Pan-European commerce and trading. Europeans traveled to other countries with much greater frequency than Americans. The population's mobility placed a premium on crossborder compatibility between wireless networks.

In 1982, the Conference of European Posts and Telecommunications Administrations (CEPT), which consisted of the telecommunications administrations of 26 nations, convened to establish a European wireless telecommunications market. The CEPT made two important decisions. First, the CEPT decided to create a single European wireless technology standard and established a task force to define that standard. Second, the CEPT agreed to allocate wireless spectrum in the 900-MHz band in each country for use with this new wireless network.

In an instant, the CEPT had achieved what the FCC had yet to accomplish: the creation of a technology standard and the allocation of sufficient radio spectrum. Although it would still take ten years before the first European standard-based GSM system would commence operation, the CEPT's early decision helped create a successful and robust wireless marketplace.

While the CEPT member nations worked on developing the GSM standard, individual nations like the United Kingdom, France, and Germany launched analog-based wireless systems. However, these systems were very similar to AMPS; they were high-priced and had poor coverage and signal strength. Nonetheless, these early systems still generated interest and demonstrated the capabilities of wireless technologies.

By the late 1980s, the CEPT had developed the GSM standard, and mobile operators from 13 European countries signed a *Memorandum of Understanding* (MoU) that outlined the specifics of the GSM standard. Importantly, the GSM standard settled on a digital system instead of analog. Selecting digital proved to be a very prescient choice. Digital offered better spectrum allocation, better signal quality, an easy interface with ISDN-based landline services, and most importantly, better security.

## The 1990s—Wireless Networks Mature

During the 1990s, wireless technologies finally burst into the mainstream. In the 1960s, Intel cofounder Gordon Moore predicted that the number of transistors that could fit on a single chip would double approximately every 18 months. Over time, Moore's prediction proved remarkably accurate. By the 1990s, the benefits of Moore's Law resulted in rapidly faster and cheaper silicon chips for PCs and wireless phones, and component prices for handsets fell considerably. In addition, networks continued to expand, improving call reception and signal reception. What was once a $3,000 status symbol was now a device suitable for the mass market. Wireless subscribers continued to grow at healthy rates around the world.

In 1991, the first commercial GSM networks began offering service, starting in Scandinavia. A year later, Australia became the first operator to offer GSM service outside Europe. GSM and the other network standards (TDMA, CDMA, and Personal Digital Communication [PDC]) are known as second-generation (2G) networks. See the following illustration:

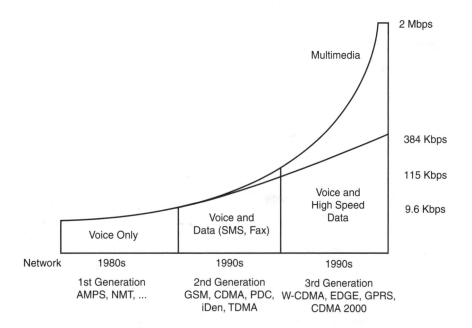

In 1992, the first international roaming agreement between two European carriers, Vodafone and Telecom Finland, was signed enabling transparent roaming between Vodafone and Telecom Finland's customers. Other roaming deals soon followed. In adopting a universal technology standard, Europe was able to offer the ability to travel and place calls throughout Europe from a single mobile phone, something that would not be realized in the United States for another six years. The result was a steady increase in GSM subscribers in the mid-1990s, as shown in Figure 1-5.

Even though Europe's policies favored the incumbent phone monopolies, competition still existed and proved to be a powerful catalyst in enabling a broader deployment of wireless services. Consider the situation in Poland in the late 1990s. As the Soviet bloc crumbled in the late 1980s, many former Warsaw Pact nations embraced capitalist ideals and immediately attracted deep-pocket Western companies willing to partner and profit in these growing markets. Despite the rapid move toward free market policies, the migration toward new technologies and services was still slow. In 1997, the average wait to install a new wired phone line in Poland was over 4 years and Poland had less than 13 fixed phone lines per 100 people compared to over 50 fixed lines per 100 people in the West.[6] In this environment, wireless services had huge potential—there were no lengthy waits for services and complete mobility. The result was that many Poles simply went wireless and did not even bother installing fixed service at home.

**Figure 1-5**

GSM subscribers, 1993 to 2000

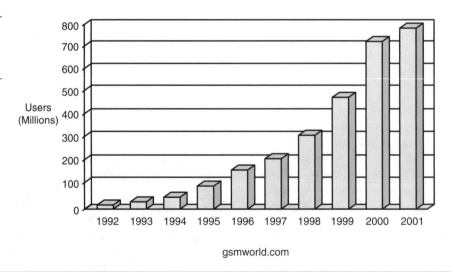

gsmworld.com

[6]European Bank for Reconstruction and Development, *Poland Country Guide*, 1997.

| | Date | Carrier | Promotion |
|---|---|---|---|
| **Table 1-1**<br><br>Promotions and Discounts in the Polish GSM Market, October 1996 to March 1997[7] | September 1996 | Era and Plus GSM | GSM services launched |
| | October 1996 | Plus GSM | 601 free minutes with service activation |
| | January 1997 | Era GSM | Free Philips phone (valued at $320) with service activation |
| | February 1997 | Plus GSM | $100 off activation |
| | February 1997 | Era GSM | Phone and service activation for $200 |
| | March 1997 | Plus GSM | Service activation for only $1 |

Although the Polish government only licensed two GSM carriers in Poland (Era GSM and Plus GSM), these two carriers competed aggressively for subscribers. Table 1-1 shows the effects of the competition in just the first six months of GSM service being available in Poland. Initial services required purchase of a mobile phone ($300+) and an activation fee ($300+). Within six months, the activation fee had dropped to $1, phones were heavily discounted, and tens of thousands of users had signed up.

By contrast, in America, nationwide roaming was difficult to implement. The FCC's policies created a cellular market comprised of different technologies and competitors in each major market. Unlike GSM, where interconnecting networks was relatively straightforward, U.S.-based cellular networks used different hardware and switches, making interconnection a lengthy and complicated process. Furthermore, local wireless carriers failed to see the benefits of roaming and were more interested in protecting the local market than offering nationwide service. It was not until the late 1990s when the service plans offered by AT&T Wireless and Sprint PCS provided customers with a nationwide footprint and roaming, nearly six years after the GSM counterparts first offered roaming.

## The Mid-1990s—Other Wireless Networks Emerge

In addition to growth in wireless voice, the 1990s also saw the emergence of numerous data-only wireless networks such as paging systems. Paging

[7]Information provided by Era GSM executives in a March 1997 interview with the author.

systems had been in existence since the 1960s, but usage was limited to certain vertical markets such as law enforcement and health care. These systems were only one directional and were only capable of sending a signal (a beep). Beginning in the early 1990s, operators worked on improving these networks' functionality, adding features such as two-way paging and the ability to send alphanumeric messages. In striking parallels to the mobile voice market, the paging market quickly diverged into two competing standards: one for Europe (Ermes) and another for outside Europe (FLEX). The main difference was that Ermes was conceived in a very GSM-like fashion with collaboration from numerous operators throughout Europe, while FLEX was conceived and developed by the U.S. wireless heavyweight Motorola.

Paging grew substantially in all markets. Paging hardware and service plans were considerably less than wireless voice-making pagers, which were very attractive in regions with lower incomes. In certain vertical markets such as transportation and construction, pagers soon became a needed accessory.

Other wireless data-only networks appeared in the 1990s. In 1992, the Baby Bells pooled resources to create a new packet-based wireless data network called *Cellular Digital Packet Data* (CDPD). The CDPD networks offered relatively high throughput (up to 19.2 Kbps) and were based on Transmission Control Protocol/Internet Protocol (TCP/IP), making compatibility with the Internet relatively straightforward. More importantly, CDPD was designed to run on the legacy AMPS network hardware, meaning that the infrastructure costs for CDPD were quite low. By the end of the twentieth century, CDPD networks covered the 50 largest metropolitan areas in the United States and possessed over 10 million subscribers, mainly for uses such as transportation, messaging, and inventory control.

Besides these long-range wireless data networks, efforts also progressed on developing medium-range (less than 100m) and short-range wireless standards. By the end of the 1990s, these results manifested themselves as wireless LANs and Bluetooth.

The wireless LAN standard started in 1990 when the Institute of Electrical and Electronics Engineers (IEEE) started the 802.11 committee to define a wireless LAN standard. The standard was not finalized until 1997, but computer manufacturers such as Intel, 3Com, Cisco, and Lucent were soon producing and marketing wireless LAN products for applications in universities, home networking, and corporate networks. Unfortunately, as Chapter 7 describes, the security specifications of the IEEE

802.11 were considerably weak, leading to some significant weaknesses that have left the future of wireless LANs uncertain.

For near-range (less than 10m) wireless networks, the Bluetooth Special Interest Group (SIG) was founded in May 1998 by Ericsson, IBM, Intel, Nokia, and Toshiba. Taking its name from Harald Bluetooth, a Viking warrior from the tenth century, the Bluetooth SIG created a mechanism for enabling wireless devices to communicate with each other in a world without wires. By 2001, the Bluetooth SIG counted over 1,800 members and the first Bluetooth-enabled products started appearing on the market. However, Bluetooth is by far the newest wireless technology, and considerable questions remain about it, particularly in the economic model (Bluetooth chips are quite expensive), compatibility between products, and security.

Collectively, these assorted wireless technologies started to reach critical mass by the year 2000, providing consumers with a wealth of choices in wireless products and services.

## The Late 1990s—The Wireless Internet Emerges

In the midst of this wireless revolution, another disruptive technology—the World Wide Web—exploded onto the scene. Initially commercialized by Netscape Communications Corp., the Web unleashed a consumer fervor never before witnessed in documented history. The Web's popularity was driven by the ability to easily uncover a vast amount of information and communicate with people around the globe, but it was also designed with a high-powered PC in mind.

No sooner had the Web started to explode than people considered the possibility of harnessing the power of the Web with the ubiquity of a wireless device. An early pioneer was Unwired Planet, which was founded in 1995 and by December 1995 had been awarded a U.S. patent for the concept of accessing the Internet from a wireless device in an interactive manner.

Unwired Planet's vision was simple. Just as Netscape made the Web accessible to millions through its browser, Unwired Planet planned to do the same with its Unwired Planet browser. Within two years, Unwired Planet had succeeded in convincing the mobile heavyweights Nokia, Ericsson, and Motorola to create the WAP Forum and commercialize the concept of accessing the Web from a mobile device. By the end of 1997, over 90 companies had joined the WAP Forum. The WAP Forum was not a standards body, but an industry trade association whose goal was to promote and encourage the development of the wireless Internet. The initial specification, WAP 1.0, was released in late 1997 and finally ratified in mid-1998.

Much like their wireless voice counterparts ten years earlier, the wireless Internet was very slow to attract customers. AT&T Wireless was an early adopter of WAP services with their PocketNet service, but consumer uptake was very slow. WAP-based services also suffered from a chicken-and-egg dilemma. Because the new WAP services required new handsets and infrastructure, handset vendors and network operators were reluctant to invest in WAP unless there was sufficient demand to justify the investment. However, demand was hard to predict since consumers were unlikely to try these new services unless they possessed the new handsets.

In 1999, operators began slowly launching WAP services. They consisted of basic information services such as weather, news, and airline flight timetables. Users needed to purchase new handsets and pay an incremental monthly fee for service.

Despite the considerable hype and press coverage, the wireless Internet experienced slower than expected adoption. There were some exceptions (notably Japan and the Nordic region), but in the North American market, new WAP services failed to achieve significant numbers of new users. In 2000, the major wireless operators in the United States spent over $10 billion on sales and marketing expenses to promote wireless services and attract new customers. Although this money drove demand for new mobile voice services, interest in the wireless Internet remained low.

At the end of the year 2000, it was estimated that there were only 1 million wireless Internet users in the United States, which was less than 1 percent of the total wireless phone users in the nation. Forecasts for other wireless technologies like Bluetooth and wireless LANs were equally unimpressive. Bluetooth and 802.11 technologies suffered considerably. Bluetooth-enabled devices were few and far between and carried high prices, while some very public security flaws were exposed in the 802.11 specification. These weaknesses especially worried corporate customers who were afraid of the interception of wireless LAN signals and therefore decided to postpone major investments in wireless LANs.

So why has the uptake of WAP, Bluetooth, and wireless LANs been slower than expected?

■ **Economics** As with any new technology, the price points for new wireless technologies have not been attractive for mass adoption. For example, wireless-Internet-capable cell phones are often quite expensive and require additional monthly service charges. In January 2001, an AT Kearney/Judge Institute poll of 1,600 wireless customers showed that only 16 percent of them actually owned a wireless-Internet-capable phone. With Bluetooth, the new chipsets are still quite expensive, leading to high prices for Bluetooth-enabled devices. These price points will eventually decrease, but in the interim, many of these services will only be attractive to a limited set of individuals.

■ **User experience** For many, the initial wireless Internet experience was underwhelming. Users accustomed to full color displays on high-speed PC-based connections were subjected to four-line black-and-white displays over very slow connections. Content providers were also slow to optimize existing wired content for delivery over a wireless network. Customers tried these services, but quickly decided that the value and convenience was not worth the extra cost.

■ **Security** Although the security requirements for wireless services like weather and sports scores are minimal, value-added services like stock trading, wireless access to corporate networks, and transactions require a much higher level of security than the current infrastructure could support. Users were not left with many alternatives, and the entire mobile commerce effort stalled. In the same AT Kearney survey in January 2001, only 12 percent of wireless users indicated a willingness to conduct transactions from a wireless device, which was down from 32 percent in June 2000. Likewise, several significant weaknesses in wireless LANs were uncovered in 2000 and 2001, further dampening enthusiasm for this technology.

It is worth noting that the wireless Internet market is still evolving and like any new market, it takes time for compelling products and services to be built. Look at America Online (AOL) in the mid-1990s. AOL was widely criticized for poor customer service, constant busy signals, and poor content. However, AOL learned from the mistakes, fixed them, and by the end of the decade, had grown to become the world's largest Internet service provider (ISP). There is no reason to believe that the wireless Internet market will not follow a similar path. As the industry learns from its mistakes and starts building products and services that consumers value, there is no doubt that the wireless Internet will rapidly grow throughout the world.

The wireless Internet still faces some serious obstacles. For one, there are some significant physical differences between the client devices. As Table 1-2 indicates, the differences between a standard PC and a wireless-Internet-capable cell phone are dramatic.

Obviously, some of these drastic differences are intentional; mobile devices were not intended to serve as PC replacements. The emphasis on voice, size, weight, and battery life involved trade-offs for the cell phone. The physical differences between these devices means that the wired Internet must account for these new wireless users.

The wireless user interface is especially important. Because of the slow throughput of wireless networks, wired Internet content must be modified for wireless users. This means fewer graphics and simpler displays. Content providers must understand that the wireless devices possess little to no local file storage or processing capability, thereby pushing the processing burden to the web servers.

The good news is that these limitations have been identified. The bad news is that the worldwide macroeconomic downturn in 2000 and 2001 exacerbated the problem as companies (both on the wireless demand and wireless supply side) delayed or cancelled planned capital wireless investments or service offerings.

The problems that needed to be addressed were accompanied by a reluctance to invest heavily to fix the problems. As financial problems

| **Table 1-2** | **Category** | **PC** | **GSM Cell Phone** |
| --- | --- | --- | --- |
| Hardware Differences Between PCs and Cell Phones | Processor speed | 1 GHz | 50 MHz |
| | Memory | 512MB | 32KB |
| | Storage | 50GB | 64KB |
| | Battery life | 3 hours | 100+ hours standby |
| | Display | 15-inch Super XGA+ | 5-line monochrome |
| | Operating system | Windows 2000 and XP, Linux | Proprietary operating system |
| | Bandwidth capability | 1 GBps | 14.4 KBps |

plagued everyone from Nokia and Ericsson to network operators like Vodafone and British Telecom, advances and improvements in the wireless Internet were postponed or cancelled. Through the first six months of 2001, the Chicago-based outplacement firm Challenger, Gray, & Christmas reported that 175,350 jobs had been cut in the telecommunications sector in the United States, up from only 6,848 layoffs in 2000. The result was considerable uncertainty about the future of the wireless Internet.

Amidst the uncertainty, however, were pockets of optimism. Certain services such as short message service (SMS) and wireless banking demonstrated promising early results. Operators remained optimistic about other future services such as location-based commerce, micropayments, and streaming video on mobile devices. The net result is that the economic downturn of 2001 delayed, but did not destroy, enthusiasm for wireless services. Furthermore, market projections indicate that significant growth in mobile commerce is still several years out as operators upgrade networks, improve services, and consumer demand returns.

In fact, the mobile commerce market forecasts from Jupiter Research indicate that significant volumes in mobile commerce revenues will not materialize until 2003 through 2004 (see Table 1-3). This study included everything from retail transactions, receiving subscription content services (finance and messaging), and revenues from advertising.

The optimistic forecast means that wireless vendors willing to address these problems today can expect improved customer retention, incremental revenue, and a platform on which to launch new value-added services into the future.

| **Table 1-3** Worldwide Mobile Commerce Revenues, 2000 to 2005 ($ billion) | **Region** | **2000** | **2001** | **2002** | **2003** | **2004** | **2005** |
| --- | --- | --- | --- | --- | --- | --- | --- |
| | Asia | $0.4 | $1.3 | $2.6 | $5.0 | $7.4 | $9.4 |
| | Latin America | $0.0 | $0.0 | $0.0 | $0.1 | $0.2 | $0.5 |
| | North America | $0.0 | $0.1 | $0.2 | $0.7 | $1.8 | $3.5 |
| | Western Europe | $0.0 | $0.1 | $0.5 | $1.7 | $4.6 | $7.8 |
| | Rest of the World | $0.0 | $0.0 | $0.1 | $0.2 | $0.4 | $1.0 |
| | Total | $0.4 | $1.5 | $3.4 | $7.7 | $14.4 | $22.2 |

Source: Jupiter Research, 2001

# History of Wireless Security

Ironically, developments in wireless technologies were accompanied by equivalent developments in tools to intercept those wireless signals. As World War II commenced, the Allies and Axis powers increasingly relied on wireless radios to communicate with their geographically dispersed military forces. Yet, the increased traffic also increased the probability of interception. Even though signals were encrypted, they were still being intercepted. In some cases, the ability to intercept and decrypt wireless signals provided significant advantages. Consider the case of the Battle of Midway.

---

## Note:

*In early 1942, the U.S. Pacific campaign against Japan was in a critical state. Still reeling from the loss at Pearl Harbor, the U.S. Navy was mismatched against the Japanese in resources, ships, and planes. Given the mismatch, the U.S. Navy demanded good intelligence about Japanese naval movements. Under the direction of Laurence F. Safford, the Navy's OP-20-G group attacked JN-25, the Japanese Navy's operational code.*

---

Capturing the transmissions was simple, quickly proving the insecurity of wireless transmissions. Deciphering JN-25 was another story. JN-25 contained over 45,000 five-digit numbers, with each number representing a word or phrase. Prior to transmission, the five-digit numbers were encrypted by adding a number to the five-digit number, using values from a predetermined table. To crack the code, Safford's team had to subtract the value and then determine these values by analyzing the frequency of their usage over time.

Owing to the efforts of OP-20-G, the U.S. Navy was able to intercept and decrypt enough of JN-25 to determine the Japanese navy's movements and learn of the Japanese intent to attack the Pacific island of Midway. Using this information, the U.S. Navy was able to move toward Midway, prepare for the Japanese attack, and strike a decisive victory against the Japanese.[8]

---

[8]Excerpts from http://www.nsa.gov/docs/history/AFWater.html.

Forty years after the Battle of Midway, radio signal interception was still relatively straightforward. Early advertisements for wireless services in the United States even claimed that wireless service was as secure as an office phone.[9] Unfortunately, that was far from the case. People flocked to Radio Shack to purchase basic radio scanners. These simple devices were capable of eavesdropping on cellular conversations at will.

## Eavesdropping and Jamming

The relative ease of intercepting transmissions with these devices even led some state governments to consider banning radio scanners and for mobile operators to begin testing encrypted voice and data.[10] The eavesdropping fear consisted of two dimensions. One dimension was that curious citizens could listen in on random conversations. The second and more sinister dimension was that government agencies such as the CIA and FBI could intercept conversations at will in the name of law enforcement or national security. The specter of Big Brother concerned consumer advocates who called for greater protection of personal privacy.

Ironically, regulations protecting citizens from eavesdropping were first introduced before eavesdropping even became a major issue. The Communications Act of 1934 specifically made it illegal to disclose the content of radio transmissions and to monitor traffic for personal gain. With the dawn of the cellular age, Congress added the Electronic Communications Privacy Act in 1986. This legislation prohibited eavesdropping on cellular conversations and also prohibited the manufacture and use of scanning equipment to intercept wireless calls.

In addition to eavesdropping, wireless signals can also be jammed. First pioneered for military applications, jamming technology enabled cellular networks to become inoperable in a limited geographic area by sending a high volume of radio signals. Although these devices are prohibited in the United States, there are many overseas manufacturers of this equipment and it is still imported illegally into the United States. Besides jamming an individual phone, it is also possible to jam an individual cellular tower, thereby taking down an entire geographic area.

---

[9]James B. Murray, *Wireless Nation*, Cambridge, Mass.: Perseus Publishing, 2001, 82.

[10]Ibid., 125.

As ZDNet pointed out, wireless networks are susceptible to the following possible breaches:

- Interception of law enforcement data on specialized mobile radio, private radio, or CDPD networks
- Interception of credit card authorizations over wireless networks
- Stealing of cellular airtime
- Interception of e-mail messages on wireless Internet connections
- Physical breach of security at unmanned base stations or other communications centers

Despite the eavesdropping concerns, demand for wireless services grew in the 1980s. Although eavesdropping concerns were prevalent in non-U.S. markets, the GSM standard's reliance on digital signals and secret-key encryption helped alleviate these concerns. In the GSM world, the security concerns were more related to fraud as criminals developed mechanisms to clone cellular phones, enabling them to make calls on the network at the operators' expense.

Despite the migration from analog to digital networks in the United States, eavesdropping concerns were still prevalent in the 1990s. Eavesdropping became a national issue in 1997 when a cellular conversation between U.S. Speaker of the House Newt Gingrich and his aide was intercepted, recorded, and released to the public. Although the perpetrators were caught and plead guilty to wiretapping, the incident clearly raised awareness about the insecure nature of cellular networks.

## The Wireless Internet—Wireless Security Moves into the Mainstream

With the introduction of the wireless Internet, security issues rose to the forefront. During the meteoric growth of the wired Internet, security and privacy issues were important issues. Vendors like Netscape and Microsoft supported Secure Sockets Layer/Transport Layer Security (SSL/TLS) encryption over Hypertext Transfer Protocol (HTTP) in web browsers and web servers. Commerce providers like Amazon quickly realized the importance of security and privacy in designing e-commerce sites. In the wired Internet, SSL became the standard security mechanism for transmitting sensitive information from a PC to a web server. SSL significantly aided in the acceleration of e-commerce by providing a universal secure method to conduct business and transactions. As users approached the wireless Internet, demand and awareness for an equivalent level of security was high.

Unfortunately, a similar SSL standard was lacking in the initial wireless Internet. The WAP Forum provided an SSL-like alternative called *Wireless Transport Layer Security* (WTLS), but this architecture was widely criticized because it did not provide end-to-end encryption. The WAP approach required two protocols: WTLS from the wireless handset to the WAP gateway and SSL from the WAP gateway to a web server on the Internet. During the protocol conversion from WTLS to SSL, data was unencrypted and reencrypted, leaving data temporarily in an unencrypted form. This so-called WAP Gap created a level of concern about wireless security that delayed consumer adoption. See the following illustration:

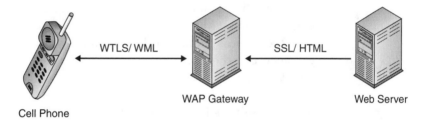

WTLS was designed specifically because the low-bandwidth and hardware limitations of cellular handsets made implementing wireless SSL technically challenging. Rather than waiting for the hardware and networks to get more powerful, the WAP Forum moved ahead with WTLS to get the wireless Internet off the ground. WTLS was never intended to be a static concept and was designed to evolve to a more SSL-like architecture. Unfortunately, the WAP Gap forced many content providers to focus initial WAP services on information that did not require security like weather and news. Plans for real mobile commerce services where end-to-end security was needed were scaled back.

## Wireless Value Chain

Although the initial WAP experiences exposed security weaknesses, immediate remedies to the situation were not forthcoming. While the WAP Forum improved the specification, the specification approval process and long product development cycles meant that improved solutions were often more than two years away. However, to understand the wireless security issues, one needs to understand the wireless market itself. Owing to the various powerful parties involved, views and attitudes on security vary considerably, meaning that future security solutions will require compromise between these players.

The wireless value chain (for example, those vendors that compose the wireless market) can be divided into five different sectors. Some vendors operate in multiple sectors and some firms are almost 100 percent wireless focused, whereas others trace their roots to traditional wired networking products. Table 1-4 contrasts the different players in the wired and wireless worlds.

### Device Vendors

This sector is responsible for designing, manufacturing, selling, and marketing myriad wireless devices available to consumers worldwide. Voice-oriented devices (namely cell phones) compose the vast majority of this category, but there are also wireless data devices from Compaq, Palm, Handspring, and Research in Motion.

This sector experienced tremendous growth during the ramp-up of wireless services in the mid-1990s. Large volumes of new users enabled manufacturing economies of scale and more functional phones at very aggressive price points.

| | | **Wired** | **Wireless** |
|---|---|---|---|
| **Table 1-4** Wired and Wireless Market Segments | Device vendors | Dell, Compaq, HP, Toshiba, NEC, IBM, and Apple | Nokia, Motorola, Ericsson, Siemens, Palm, Compaq, and Handspring |
| | Network operators | AOL, AT&T, Prodigy, and Earthlink | Verizon, Vodafone, DoCoMo, and Sprint PCS |
| | Hardware providers | Intel, Cisco, Lucent, Sun, IBM, and EMC | Texas Instruments, Ericsson, Alcatel, Siemens, and Cisco |
| | Content providers | AOL, eBay, Amazon, Yahoo, and MSN | Yahoo, airlines, and Weather.com |
| | Application providers | Microsoft, Oracle, SAP, Lotus, IBM, and BEA Systems | Openwave, iAnywhere, CellPoint, and Jinny |

Because this sector provides the end-user device, it is heavily dependent on the macroeconomic environment as well as changes in consumer tastes and preferences. The 2000 through 2001 global economic downturn, coupled with consumers' fickle attitude toward new value-added services like WAP, forced many handset vendors to scale back product plans and lay off significant numbers of employees.

Within this sector, Finland-based Nokia remains the dominant player. As Figure 1-6 demonstrates, Nokia was the dominant worldwide market share leader in mobile handsets in 2000. Although Nokia is not as powerful in certain markets (notably Japan), Nokia has established a powerful global brand for wireless and is now using that position to establish beachheads in other wireless categories like software and services.

One final point about the handset vendors is that like the PC market, the handset vendors must sell wireless products twice. First, the handsets must be sold to the wireless network operators who then offer these handsets to consumers. Once the operator purchases the handsets, the handset vendors need to generate demand on the consumer side, usually through advertising promotions highlighting the brand. These so-called push-and-pull marketing efforts (push the handsets to operators and generate consumer demand to pull the handsets off the retail shelves) has proven quite successful, but it still requires careful coordination and planning to ensure that the proper product mix is available at the retail level.

**Figure 1-6**

Worldwide wireless handset market share, 2000

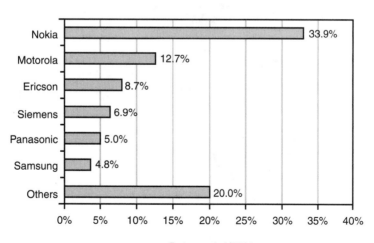

Dataguest, 1/2001

**View on Security** The handset vendors are quite aware of security issues. During 1999 through 2000, many vendors offered high-end WAP handsets that offered various security features. However, some of these security features were usually provided by third parties and bundled with the handsets. The handset vendors do have significant influence over security through their large brand building advertising efforts, which can highlight security issues and thereby generate demand.

## Network Operators

The network operators are responsible for building, maintaining, and promoting wireless networks. Many network operators (such as Verizon and British Telecom) began as wired operators and used that position to expand into wireless services. Within the wireless value chain, they are the most powerful segment. This is a very capital-intensive segment, and the operators rely on a steady stream of consumers to generate positive cash flow that can be used to finance these activities.

In the early days of wireless voice, there was little differentiation among network operators. In many countries, the wireless carrier was merely a subsidiary of the local phone monopoly, leaving consumers with few competing alternatives from which to choose. Table 1-5 lists some of the major mobile operators in the world, based on the number of subscribers.

Gradually, many markets opened the wireless sector to new entrants, creating more competition. This created additional problems for operators, particularly in the area of *churn* (customers leaving one operator to subscribe to another). Given the relatively high cost of acquiring a net

| **Table 1-5**<br><br>Major Global<br>Wireless<br>Operators | **Operator** | **Markets Served** | **Subscribers as of 2001 (in millions)** |
|---|---|---|---|
| | Vodafone | United Kingdom, Germany, and Japan | 96 |
| | China Mobile Telecom | China | 89 |
| | T-Mobil | Germany | 42 |
| | NTT DoCoMo | Japan | 38 |
| | Verizon | United States | 28 |
| | Telefonica | Spain and Latin America | 25 |
| | Telecom Italia | Italy | 22 |

new wireless customer (between $300 to $600 each), reducing customer churn was a high priority for carriers. Operators looked at customer service and network coverage as key areas to reduce churn and invested heavily in these areas.

As interest in wireless data rose, operators viewed these services as a differentiator and another mechanism to reduce churn. In the United States, Sprint PCS aggressively promoted its wireless web services in 2000 through 2001, targeting mobile professionals who needed real-time access to wireless information. In the earliest examples, many operators adopted a "walled-garden" approach. This strategy provided wireless data users with access to a limited number of content providers (Yahoo, eTrade, Weather.com, American Airlines, and so on). These same content providers paid the carriers so-called slotting fees to be listed on the initial menu. This helped generate incremental revenues for the operators, but did not always impress consumers who were accustomed to being able to visit any web site they chose.

Unfortunately, the push to promote wireless data services was accompanied by the global economic downturn, so interest in these services was slow.

**View on Security**   Although the network operators were largely successful at addressing the wireless voice security issues, wireless data introduced a new series of issues. Specifically, the WAP architecture meant that WAP Gap was often located on the operator's WAP Gateway. For many enterprises and security-conscious services like banking, this was not acceptable. Because the WAP architecture did not offer many immediate alternatives, this proved to be a serious obstacle to realizing wider usage of mobile commerce. Some operators tried to bridge the gap by offering to serve as a payment provider (and have charges added to the subscriber's monthly bill), but these were not always met favorably. The role of the operator in the security scheme continues to be one of biggest challenges for the industry. Do consumers want to trust the operator, or someone with whom they already have a trust relationship (such as a financial institution)?

## Hardware Providers

This sector is almost invisible to consumers, but it is a critical supplier to the network operators and handset vendors. These firms provide the hardware (chips and CPU) for the handset vendors as well as the network-switching infrastructure for connecting wireless networks. There is some overlap between the handset vendors and this segment. For instance, Ericsson, Siemens, and Alcatel are all major hardware providers in addition to being handset manufacturers. This sector is getting increasing focus because of the migration to faster wireless networks. Given the network operators' desire to offer new revenue-generating services on higher-speed networks, the hardware providers are under considerable pressure to deliver products that can fulfill these needs.

**View on Security**   This sector does not have a direct influence on security. However, security is relevant to the new high-speed wireless networks that are being built. Because security services like encryption, authentication, and digital signatures function much better at higher speeds, the new network hardware will help in the adoption of security.

## Content Providers

This sector is responsible for generating and distributing information that can be served up on a wireless device. Not surprisingly, many of the leading wired content providers like AOL, Yahoo, MSN, Amazon, and eBay all announced wireless versions of their content in 2000. Owing to the unique structure of the wireless industry, distributing content was not easy. In the wired world, the content providers served as a portal—any user from any geography using any ISP could browse a site. In the wireless world, to a large extent the operators determined what content subscribers could or could not view. If content provider X did not have a distribution agreement with network operator Y, network operator Y's subscribers could not view that content.

Despite these issues, the content providers still aggressively promoted wireless services. They were especially interested in location-based services. Newer networks and handsets could give content providers the location of a specific subscriber to within a city block, creating many new potential uses. Is a user near your restaurant? Send him or her an SMS message offering a 10 percent discount on dinner if he or she comes in immediately. Yet location services still face the same challenges as other content. Since the network operator will possess the location data, content providers will have to cooperate with operators to access this data and use it properly. Location-based services also raise interesting privacy and security questions about subscriber's willingness to let his or her current location be made available.

**View on Security**   Security is very important for the content providers, especially those engaged in commerce as opposed to pure information distribution. Content providers suffer from the same WAP Gap issues facing the network operators. Content providers are reluctant to offer services that are not completely secure because of potential breaches, loss of consumer confidence, and erosion of brand equity. This segment's continued push for improved security will have a positive impact on the growth and development of wireless security and mobile commerce.

### Application Providers

This sector is divided into two categories: traditional independent software vendors (ISVs) that have modified existing wired applications for wireless environments and software vendors that have developed exclusively for wireless environments. In 2000, all the major software vendors including Oracle, IBM, Microsoft, and SAP announced plans to make existing applications wireless ready. The same year saw the emergence of certain wireless pure-play vendors like Phone.com (now called Openwave), CellPoint, and Jinny Software. These vendors can coexist in wireless environments, particularly in scenarios where a wireless device needs to connect to a legacy application or database.

**View on Security** Application providers possess a good awareness of security. Those firms with roots in the wired Internet have already dealt with many of the security issues and are aware of the need to maintain this in the wireless sector. The pure wireless ISVs are equally aware of security issues and have already started to build security functionality into their products.

# State of the Wireless Industry, 2001

Now that a wireless industry overview has been provided, it is necessary to review the current state of the wireless industry as of 2001. Table 1-6 gives a sense of the ubiquity of wireless technologies throughout the world.

This overview is split into four geographic regions because the wireless market has evolved quite differently across the globe. The following are the four geographic regions to be reviewed:

- North America
- Europe
- Japan
- Asia

| Indicator | Year End 2000 |
|---|---|
| Monthly churn | 2.56% |
| SMS messages sent per GSM subscriber per month | 30 |
| World's largest cellular market | USA (130 million subscribers) |
| World's fastest growing cellular market | Morocco (629% increase in subscribers versus 1999) |
| World's largest GSM market | China (73 million subscribers) |
| World's largest CDMA market | United States (55 million subscribers) |
| Highest penetrated market (percent of population with mobile phone) | Iceland (77.4%) |

**Table 1-6**

Key Wireless Indicators in 2000 (EMC World Cellular Database)

## North American Wireless Industry, 2001

Following frenetic growth during the early 1990s, the North American wireless industry entered a more mature phase. Where there were once hundreds of firms vying for the FCC's wireless licenses, there are now a handful of well-funded players. Where there were once dozens of wireless firms focused just in regional markets, there are now six dominant national brands (AT&T Wireless, Cingular, Nextel, Sprint PCS, Verizon, and Voicestream) that control 90 percent of the U.S. wireless subscribers. Where there were once all analog networks, there are now four different and incompatible digital network standards (CDMA, GSM, TDMA, and iDEN)—see Table 1-7. Where there were once only a handful of device and calling plans, consumers now have a tremendous variety of devices (cell phones, wireless PDAs, and interactive two-way pagers) and calling plans.

Table 1-8 summarizes some key figures for the U.S. wireless industry.

Although the United States is the largest cellular market in terms of subscribers, the adoption rate of cellular services (40 percent of the population owns a cell phone) still lags behind other regions of the world where adoption rates exceed 60 percent of the population. Based on this comparison, there is still a significant upside for wireless industry.

The North American market divides into two segments: consumer and enterprise. U.S. wireless carriers market wireless services in a variety of manners. For instance, Nextel focuses exclusively on the corporate mar-

**Table 1-7**

U.S. Network
Operators

| Carrier | Network Technology | Subscribers as of Dec. 2000 (in millions)[11] |
|---|---|---|
| AT&T Wireless | TDMA | 16 |
| Cingular | CDMA and GSM | 21 |
| Nextel | iDEN | 8 |
| Sprint PCS | CDMA | 13 |
| Verizon | CDMA | 28 |
| Voicestream | GSM | 5 |

**Table 1-8**

U.S. Wireless
Market Metrics
(2000 CTIA
Semiannual
Wireless Industry
Survey,
Dec. 2000)

| Metric | Value |
|---|---|
| Subscribers (as of Dec. 2001) | 131,000,000 |
| Direct carrier employees | 185,000 |
| Cumulative capital investment | $89,000,000,000 |
| Total year-2000 cellular service revenues | $4,900,000,000 |

ket, offering special handsets that enable Nextel users to communicate with each other like a walkie-talkie, instead of placing an actual call. Other carriers, such as Sprint PCS and AT&T Wireless, focus on the mobile professional, promoting their nationwide networks and flat-rate pricing. Service plans are very similar. Users pay a nominal fee for a handset (sometimes it is free) and sign up for a certain "bucket" of monthly minutes. Because of the high cost of attracting a new customer, carriers need to retain subscribers for several months to break even. This is why operators are keen to offer new services (such as wireless data) that will increase customer satisfaction and retention.

In 2000, several new wireless gadgets appeared on the North American market. Palm Computing Corporation, the makers of the popular Palm PDAs, introduced the Palm VII, a wireless device that could retrieve information and browse portions of the Internet. The Palm VII attracted a

[11]Subscription numbers provided by www.hoovers.com and company annual reports.

loyal following, but subscription numbers remained small for three reasons. For one, the Palm VII hardware and service was pricey. Second, the Palm VII adopted a walled-garden approach, meaning that users could only view content with providers who had distribution agreements with Palm. Third, Palm VII suffered from the same proxy architecture as WAP, leading to persistent security concerns.

The other major device was Research in Motion's (RIM) Blackberry interactive pager. Nicknamed Crack Berry by *USA Today* because of its addictive nature, this pager interfaced directly with corporate e-mail systems like Microsoft Exchange and Lotus' cc:Mail, enabling Blackberry users to receive e-mails sent to a traditional corporate e-mail inbox and forwarded to a wireless device. These pagers quickly became a must-have accessory for mobile executives.

Owing to the variety of wireless devices, American consumers demonstrated a surprising willingness to carry multiple wireless devices. Unlike other regions, where the GSM phone satisfied most consumers' needs, U.S. consumers looked to other devices like PDAs and pagers to supplement a wireless phone. A February 2001 survey of 1,023 Americans conducted by Yankelovich Partners revealed the following:

- When asked which wireless device they wanted to carry if cost was not an issue, 53 percent responded that they wanted multiple devices.

- Of those who wanted multiple devices, 37 percent chose a two-way e-mail device like the RIM Blackberry, 32 percent chose a PDA, and 31 percent chose all three devices: phone, PDA, and e-mail device!

Although the vast number of wireless subscribers is in the consumer segment, the most profitable segment is the enterprise segment. In 2000, enterprises were extremely attracted to wireless data services because they viewed wireless data as an important strategic tool that could address three areas:

- **Improved productivity**   Enabling employees real-time access to enterprise information would allow for quicker information distribution and allow employees to obtain important business information faster than before.

- **Improved customer service**   Wireless data services enabled mobile users to get immediate reports on customer relationships or issues and respond to those issues in a very fast manner, thereby improving customer satisfaction.

■ **Competitive advantage**   As more companies adopted wireless technologies to maintain contact with customers, partners, suppliers, and employees, many companies realized that wireless connectivity was a necessity.

Enterprises were quick to move ahead with wireless plans. As Figure 1-7 indicates, many companies quickly moved from wireless pilots into production environments that went companywide. Security often emerged as a barrier to deployment, but in many cases, senior management put security issues aside in order to realize other business benefits like better productivity, customer service, and so on.

Early services that attracted consumer interest were financial services and other general informational services such as weather, traffic, and news. Messaging services were slow to catch on, partially because of the network incompatibility (a Voicestream subscriber could not send an SMS message to a Verizon subscriber and vice versa). In many cases, the wireless Internet was bundled with wireless voice service so that subscribers often did not perceive any real value in the wireless Internet and were reluctant to try it. Furthermore, the operators' walled-garden approach meant that users could often not view the same web sites that they were accustomed to viewing from a PC.

On the consumer side, the wireless Internet generated consumer interest, but that interest did not always translate into high volumes of revenue-generating users. Sprint PCS, one of the most aggressive marketers of wireless data services in the United States, claimed over 500,000 wireless Internet users in 2000, but it was unclear how many of these users generated significant revenue to the carrier and how many were just trying the service as a novelty or for a single-use trial. Nonetheless, Jupiter Research's analysis shows dramatic growth in U.S. wireless Internet users. By 2005, 33 percent of all wireless subscribers will be using wireless data services (see Figure 1-8).

**Figure 1-7**

*InformationWeek* survey of enterprise wireless deployments, 2000

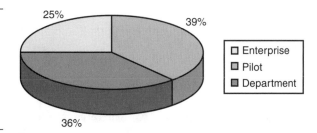

**Figure 1-8**

U.S. wireless
Internet users,
2000 to 2004

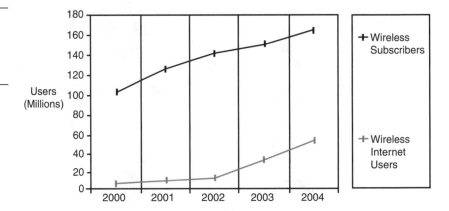

Jupiter Research, 1/2001

Other wireless technologies appeared in the North American market in 2000. Several high-profile wireless LAN announcements were made. First, coffee retailer Starbuck's announced intentions to equip their retail outlets with wireless LAN kiosks to enable users to surf the Web and read e-mail while sipping on a cappuccino. In addition, American Airlines and Delta Air Lines also announced plans to provide wireless LAN connectivity from the business-class lounges in major U.S. airports.

Even the industry giant General Motors entered the wireless fray with the creation of MobileAria, a joint venture between GM parts supplier Delphi Automotive and PDA vendor Palm Computing to create and design Internet-capable wireless devices that could be built into future vehicles.

Although these announcements generated significant buzz, there was little substance behind them. First, several major security vulnerabilities were uncovered with wireless LANs, placing that technology under very intense scrutiny and delaying product rollouts. Other technologies such as Bluetooth were still treated with skepticism and questions.

In order for these new wireless services to succeed in the United States, two things must happen:

- *Fix security.* It is imperative that the security weaknesses in wireless LANs be addressed. If the wireless LANs cannot provide solutions immediately, organizations need to adopt a best-practices security policy to minimize risk, but still allow the technology to be deployed.

- *Develop compelling apps.* American consumers can be a skeptical bunch, which is why new wireless technologies like Bluetooth and wireless LANs must have well-articulated benefits that consumers can understand. If consumers do not see the value of a new technology, they are unlikely to adopt it. If Bluetooth provides a world without wires, what is the benefit of that? How it is compelling?

Looking ahead, the U.S. wireless voice industry faces three crucial issues:

- Mobile Party Pays
- Spectrum allocation
- Technology divergence

## Mobile Party Pays

In the United States, wireless phone users pay to place and receive calls on their handsets in what is called Mobile Party Pays. In every other region of the world, users only pay to place a call in what is called Calling Party Pays. Mobile Party Pays has been widely criticized and viewed as a potential barrier to wider wireless adoption. U.S. wireless operators have been very interested in moving to Calling Party Pays as they believe it will lead to greater usage. In 1998 through 1999, the FCC formally began the process of establishing rules around Calling Party Pays. To date, some carriers have offered Calling Party Pays, but attempts to adopt a nation-wide Calling Party Pays policy have largely failed.

## Spectrum Allocation

As the United States plans to promote future 3G-based wireless voice and data networks, it is becoming obvious that operators need additional wireless radio frequencies to support higher throughput. This is a result of previous policies that limited the amount of spectrum available for mobile communications. As James Murray points out, the FCC has allocated only 189 MHz of radio spectrum for mobile communication, compared to 300 MHz in Japan and 364 MHz in the United Kingdom.[12]

Unfortunately, the frequencies best suited for 3G are currently occupied by two important constituencies: the U.S. Department of Defense and UHF-TV stations. This leaves the FCC in a difficult bind. Because

[12]James Murray, *Wireless Nation*, 317.

spectrum is a finite resource, the FCC has to determine the relative benefits of each constituent, and if appropriate, reallocate spectrum in a manner that maximizes economic benefit. Any reallocation will take considerable time and likely involve intense political lobbying. As a result, the future viability of 3G remains uncertain in the United States.

The only alternative to the spectrum issue is to design handsets, devices, switches, and other networking hardware that can more efficiently use the existing radio spectrum. This is still possible given the ongoing innovations in silicon chips, but it will also take time.

## Technology Divergence

The tangled assortment of wireless technologies in the United States complicates matters and slows down innovation. While the government is not going to adopt a national standard like GSM, the different networks hurt the U.S. wireless market in four ways:

- **No global roaming**   With only one GSM provider (Voicestream) operating within the U.S. borders, American consumers can only roam internationally if they possess a GSM phone. This does not help business users who travel abroad.

- **Supplier customization**   Handset vendors and hardware suppliers eager to serve the American market must develop products according to the multiple network standards. The customization means that suppliers for CDMA handsets cannot enjoy the economies of scale that a GSM handset manufacturer can because the CDMA market is much smaller than GSM. Many of the device innovations are often introduced in a GSM version first to attract the broadest market possible. Some major handset vendors (Siemens & Philips) do not even provide phones to the American market. In fact, some leading handset vendors in America, like Samsung and LG Group, are Korean because Korea is another major CDMA market.

- **Network compatibility**   The lack of a single network standard hampers data services between subscribers of different networks. The previously cited example of sending SMS messages between CDMA subscribers and GSM subscribers is a perfect example. Operators can promote SMS, but only within their subscriber base.

- **Network infrastructure**   The network issues manifest themselves in other manners. Consider the seemingly mundane issue of constructing cellular towers and antennae. Currently, in the United

States there are over 100,000 cellular towers. Unlike Europe, where only one GSM antennae is required, in the United States a given metropolitan area might require four different antennae—one for each network technology. In Europe, the tower-siting approval process is quite straightforward. In the United States, there are state and local ordinances that must be addressed, leading to a drawn-out approval process. Because the network build-out for 3G services will require at least three to four times as many antennae as are currently deployed, network operators can expect a lengthy process to achieve 3G networks.

In summary, although the United States has made tremendous strides in building a successful wireless industry, it faces some significant obstacles that must be resolved if the market is to continue to grow and prosper. Some of these obstacles will have to be solved politically (through legislation or policies), whereas others will likely be decided by the market itself.

# European Wireless Industry, 2001

Europe's early decisions on wireless technology (adopt a standard and allocate sufficient spectrum) have created a very robust and growing wireless market. Attitudes toward wireless technologies remained very optimistic in Europe during 2000 and 2001. While North American struggled with multiple standards and incomplete network coverage, every European country used the same mature network standard (GSM) and enjoyed very good coverage, enabling Pan-European roaming. The result was a culture steeped in wireless technology with extremely high adoption rates of cellular phone usage. Owing to Europe's much larger population, the European wireless market is considerably larger than North America's wireless market, as indicated in Table 1-9.

In 2001 European operators enjoyed several benefits over operators in other regions:

- **Stable universal network infrastructure** The GSM network was complete in Western Europe with over 110 GSM networks online. Plus, the single network standard avoided the American headaches of having to install three to four different antennae in a given cell area, making incremental additions to the network much easier.

| | Metric | Value |
|---|---|---|
| **Table 1-9** | Subscribers (as of Dec. 2000) | 281,000,000 |
| European Wireless Market Metrics (www.gsmworld.com) | Direct carrier employees | 470,000 |
| | Cumulative capital investment | $120,000,000 |
| | Annual year-2000 cellular service revenue | $215,000,000 |

- **Relatively high cost of wired Internet access**   The national phone monopolies continued to keep the cost of dial-up Internet access much higher than that in North America. This, combined with the high costs of PCs, led to a slower adoption of Internet access than that in North America. This situation made the European market more attractive to the wireless Internet because users would not be supplementing their existing wired Internet access; the wireless device would be the only access mechanism to the Internet.

- **Healthy nonvoice revenue stream**   European operators were highly successful in marketing SMS in 2000, generating significant revenues, and reducing reliance on voice calls only. In some regions, it is estimated that SMS traffic accounts for up to 20 percent of an operator's revenue. Plus, the GSM standard enables Pan-European SMS messaging.

- **Protected incumbent carriers**   European operators still enjoyed a relatively protected local market. Although many state phone monopolies had been partially privatized in the 1980s, these same players were still the dominant telecommunications players in 2001. Vodafone was one of the few to attempt a crossborder merger when they acquired German-based Mannesmann in 1999, but this was the exception. The local markets remained very much the territory of the local phone monopoly.

The marketing of cellular service in Europe was similar to North America with one major exception. Whereas North American operators heavily subsidized the handset costs, European carriers' subsidies were considerably less. This meant that consumers had to purchase the handset outright. Service plans were very similar with the exception that SMS was widely promoted as an additional service.

In the late 1990s, Scandinavia quickly emerged as a hotbed of wireless innovation and activity. Owing to the local presence of two wireless giants

(Sweden-based Ericsson and Finland-based Nokia), interest, activity, and investment in wireless was significant. Many global companies (Motorola, Microsoft, and EDS) established wireless research centers in Helsinki and Stockholm to capitalize not only on the superior wireless skill set in these countries, but also to utilize the region as a test market for new products and services.

In 1999, the Nordic mobile operators (Sonera, Telia, Telenor, and Tele-Denmark) began aggressively promoting WAP services. Airline flight timetables, weather, stock quotes, and sports scores were just some of the initial services offered. Consumer uptake was slow, but the hype was furious. The media was full of stories about users paying for parking spaces, soft drinks, and movie tickets from a mobile phone. Although these stories made great headlines, many services were just pilot projects that served as proof of concept.

Despite the optimism, Europe still faces some significant challenges in 2001:

- **3G debt loads**   European operators do not suffer from a spectrum shortage, but the development of 3G networks in Europe has come at a staggering cost because of the high license fees paid to governments for the right to build 3G networks. In the United Kingdom and Germany, operators spent over $75 billion just on the spectrum. These licenses have put the carriers heavily in debt at a time when wireless revenue is down. Plus, the operators still have an equivalent investment required just to build the networks themselves. Because the operators will not have a high volume of 3G subscribers for a few years, the operators will have to service the massive debt load, without having any new services to help pay for them.

- **Subscriber saturation point**   The tremendous success of GSM has resulted in many Western European countries reaching adoption rates between 60 and 70 percent. At this saturation rate, there are not many remaining eligible new subscribers (the remaining 30 percent of a population is either too old or too young for cell service). In order for the operators to grow revenue further, they need to derive more usage from the existing user base. This can be difficult to sustain and raises the question of how much more growth plain wireless voice can generate.

- **Regulation**   Although the European market is widely applauded for its policies in promoting wireless markets, certain regions are still dominated by the incumbent phone monopoly. The result is limited competition and higher prices. In some regions, governments are conducting 3G spectrum auctions via so-called beauty contests in which spectrum is not allocated based on the highest bidder, but based on some qualitative measures that the government determines. This process favors incumbents. Ultimately, this will affect consumers in the form of higher prices for 3G services as operators try to recoup these massive investments.

Even with these problems, the European wireless market is still robust. It is a large market and home to some of the wireless industry's leading firms. The successful policies of the 1980s helped create a huge installed base on which operators can build new wireless services and technologies.

## Japanese Wireless Industry, 2001

When it comes to wireless technology, Japan is in a class by itself. Although Japan chose to adopt their own wireless voice technology in the 1980s (PDC), the Japanese market exploded into the mainstream in the late 1990s. The phenomenon was the i-mode wireless data service offered by NTT DoCoMo. DoCoMo (Do is the Japanese word for everywhere) is a subsidiary of Japanese phone monopoly Nippon Telegraph and Telephone (NTT). DoCoMo started offering traditional wireless voice in 1992 and quickly became Japan's leading mobile operator with over 35 million subscribers.

In August 1999, DoCoMo launched i-mode, a wireless Internet service. i-mode offered three distinct technology advantages:

- Service was a packet-switching network, not circuit-based network ("based" meaning that the service was always on).
- It was compatible with existing cellular networks infrastructure—no additional investment was needed.
- Service did not require significant modifications to existing wired web content.

The results of the i-mode service were astonishing. Within 18 months, over 20 million subscribers had signed up to the service and over 30,000 i-mode-specific content sites were available. To put it into perspective, it took AOL nearly 15 years to achieve the same number of wired Internet subscribers. i-mode's success dwarfed that of any other region, as Figure 1-9 demonstrates.

Economically, i-mode users paid an incremental $3 per month for i-mode service plus 0.3 yen for each packet of data transmitted. All the monthly rates and fees are presented on the subscriber's monthly voice bill. In some cases, i-mode growth was so rapid that DoCoMo suspended any marketing or advertising about DoCoMo for fear that excessive demand would cause severe network congestion.

Although the initial i-mode content was widely derided in the West as "consumer candy," it was still highly successful at attracting new users, particularly in the youth category. Popular content included downloads of ring tones, Pokémon characters, and games. i-mode's usage is displayed in Figure 1-10. It is worth noting that even in its earliest stages, i-mode managed to generate demand for transaction-based services, suggesting that future i-mode usage could include real mobile commerce.

Moving ahead, DoCoMo has already started the first trial of a 3G network and plans to launch the 3G service in 2002, well ahead of any other operator in the world. DoCoMo has also made minority investments in AT&T Wireless (United States) and KPN (Netherlands) and announced intentions to launch i-mode-type services through these partners in 2002. It remains to be seen whether the i-mode miracle can be duplicated outside Japan, but DoCoMo's remarkable success has proven to be a crucial validation point for the entire wireless industry. In fact, DoCoMo's success is helping keep the wireless Internet alive in the economic downturn of 2001 by serving as a positive proof point for this technology.

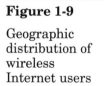

**Figure 1-9**

Geographic distribution of wireless Internet users

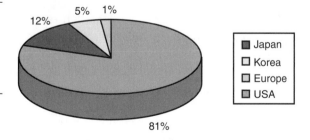

Eurotechnology, 12/00

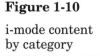

**Figure 1-10**

i-mode content by category

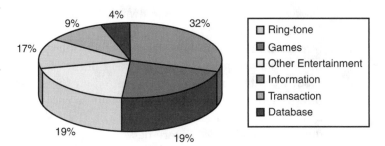

NIT DoCoMo, 12/00

So why has i-mode been much more successful than any other wireless Internet efforts? The following are some of the factors:

- **High cost of fixed Internet access**    In Japan, NTT still controls the local and long-distance phone market, making dial-up Internet access quite expensive. As a result, many Japanese consumers do not surf the Web from home-based PCs like their American colleagues. For them, i-mode was their first and only means of accessing the Internet. Some people have even suggested that NTT deliberately kept dial-up costs inflated to promote usage of i-mode.

- **Cultural**    Japan is a very mobile society. It is not unusual for people to have lengthy commutes on trains and public transportation. i-mode's service became an attractive means to pass time on the commute and fueled growth of the services.

- **Close collaboration with Japanese suppliers**    DoCoMo has nurtured its relationships with the major Japanese electronic manufacturers like Sony, Sharp, Matsushita, and others. By giving the hardware and handset vendors early access to new technologies and marketing plans, Japanese suppliers can design and deliver the appropriate hardware to match the DoCoMo services. Not surprisingly, the major non-Japanese-based handset vendors, such as Nokia and Motorola, have had difficulty gaining significant market share in Japan because they cannot leverage the same relationships that their Japanese competitors can.

- **Dominant incumbent phone monopoly**    Although Japanese regulators have tried to build a competitive phone market, NTT is still a very dominant market player. Companies like KDDI and

J-Phone have emerged, but they still lag behind NTT in terms of capital, cash flow, and presence. This situation only strengthens NTT and will provide ample resources to its DoCoMo subsidiary to deliver new services and cement its market-leading position.

In summary, Japan remains the benchmark for the emerging wireless Internet market. The rapid growth of the i-mode service has proved that consumers are willing to use mobile phones for something besides voice. The next crucial step is whether these services will migrate successfully into other markets. If the migration is successful, NTT DoCoMo is well positioned to reap the rewards of their aggressive pursuit of the wireless Internet market.

## Asian Wireless Industry, 2001

Outside of Japan, the rest of Asia's wireless industry varies from country to country. Macroeconomic conditions are closely linked to the relative state of each individual market. In countries with high standards of living like Singapore and Taiwan, wireless usage equals that of many Western European nations (above 50 percent). In countries like Indonesia and the Philippines, wireless subscribers are growing rapidly, but the technology is still out of reach financially for a large majority of the respective populations.

However, this economic gap presents some significant opportunities in developing countries. In countries where incomes and infrastructures will not support the traditional wired Internet business model seen in North America, consumers' only access to the Internet will be from a mobile device. This has led to the often cited point that by 2005, more people will access the Internet from wireless devices than from wired PC clients.

Obviously, the country that attracts the most attention as a future wireless market is China. Owing to its 1.2 billion people, wireless vendors are very eager to participate in the Chinese market. China is already the second largest wireless market (after the United States, in terms of subscribers), yet only 10 percent of China's population carries a cell phone. This low saturation rate suggests tremendous upside if the saturation rate can increase over time. Table 1-10 summarizes the key statistics for the Chinese wireless market.

Unfortunately, China is not as liberalized a telecommunications market, most others, and the Chinese government is actively involved in determining policy and establishing the ground rules for foreign

| | Metric | Value |
|---|---|---|
| **Table 1-10** | Subscribers (as of Dec. 2000) | 85,300,000 |
| Chinese Wireless Market Metrics (Courtesy of *South China Post* and *Business Weekly*) | Cumulative capital investment | $60,000,000 |
| | Annual year-2000 cellular service revenue | $16,000,000 |

competitors. For instance, throughout the 1990s, the San Diego-based CDMA pioneer Qualcomm aggressively courted Chinese regulators to adopt CDMA networks over GSM. Qualcomm had successfully convinced South Korea to choose CDMA over GSM in 1996, and Qualcomm was eager to duplicate its success in China. Senior U.S. government officials were engaged in lobbying the Chinese delegation and Qualcomm's stock soared 2,600 percent in 1999 as investors anticipated a major CDMA win in China. Yet for all the lobbying and negotiating, in December 2000, Chinese Communications Minister Wu Jichuan declared that China would not pay foreigners royalties for using wireless technology developed elsewhere. Ultimately, China chose GSM and plans to migrate to wideband CDMA (W-CDMA) for its 3G networks, leaving Qualcomm out in the cold. The entire process demonstrated the shrewd negotiation skills of the Chinese and the difficulty in successfully entering the Chinese wireless market.

Ultimately, the sheer size of the Chinese market will make it impossible to ignore. Owing to a relatively poor landline infrastructure, wireless technologies have tremendous promise. However, disposable income must continue to rise in order to generate incremental demand for wireless services. Attitudes toward the wireless Internet in China are still vague, but it is safe to assume that most consumers in China will not have a PC, meaning that if they are going to use the Internet, it will most likely be from a mobile device. Stay tuned.

# Conclusion

The primary aims of this book are to educate users and managers about the current state of wireless security, show them where the risks lie, and enable them to implement a wireless strategy that protects their organization's critical digital assets while simultaneously providing competitive advantage.

Wireless security cannot be assessed in a vacuum. Managers must understand the macroenvironment surrounding a particular technology. How mature is the market? Are there regional differences?

This chapter was meant to provide a basic understanding of the wireless market around the world. In many cases, security (or lack of it) remains an issue or impediment to further growth of a particular wireless technology. Because it takes time for new standards and security solutions to be implemented and developed, it is important to know what options exist today. Ultimately, a successful wireless security strategy and policy should combine an understanding of the issues and risks raised in subsequent chapters with the market context and data provided in this chapter.

# CHAPTER 2

# Wireless Threats

Tremendous advantages can be realized by using wireless technology. Wireless technology gives users the freedom of mobility, gives network designers more options for connectivity, and gives many new devices the capability to connect to networks. However, wireless technology brings significantly more threats than traditional wired networks. In order to design a secure wireless application, the threats or attack vectors that wireless technology gives attackers must be realized. Please note: Applications are never totally secure, but you should still investigate the potential risks of wireless technologies. Therefore, we must realize the potential attacks that exist, so we can design our networks to prevent the common attacks and prepare our processes to mitigate the uncommon attacks.

## The Uncontrolled Terrain

The major difference between wired and wireless networks is the anonymous, uncontrolled coverage areas between the end points of the network. In wide area cellular networks, the wireless medium cannot be controlled at all. Current wireless networking technology offers little to control the coverage area. This enables attackers in the immediate vicinity of a wireless network to perform a number of attacks that are not found in traditional wired networks. This chapter will review the threats that are unique to wireless environments, the equipment required by the attacker to successfully leverage the threats, the problems that occur when roaming from one cell to another, the covert wireless channels, and the cryptographic pitfalls prone to open medium communications.

# Eavesdropping

The most widely known problem with an open, uncontrolled medium like wireless technology is that it is susceptible to anonymous attackers. The anonymous attacker can passively intercept radio signals and decode the data being transmitted as shown in Figure 2-1. The equipment used to perform eavesdropping on the network can be as simple as the equipment used to gain access to the network itself. This equipment is sometimes given away with mobile phone activation. At the time of this writing, wireless networking cards can be purchased for under a hundred dollars. All wireless devices have the hardware required to send and receive on the wireless network. With little or no modification, the devices can be configured to capture all traffic on a particular network channel or frequency. The attacker must be in proximity to the transmitter in order to receive the transmission. These types of attacks are nearly impossible to detect and even harder to prevent. The use of antennas and amplifiers enables

**Figure 2-1**

Wireless attacker eavesdropping on wireless communications

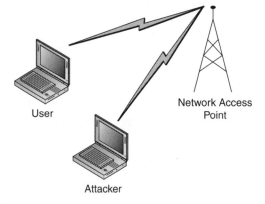

User

Network Access Point

Attacker

an attacker to be a considerable distance away from the target during an attack. Recent tests of 802.11 wireless networking equipment show that an attacker can be nearly 20 miles away from a target and still receive a signal, thereby eavesdropping on wireless network communications.

Eavesdropping is used to gather information on the network under attack. The primary goals of the attacker are to understand who uses the network, what is accessible, what the capabilities of the equipment on the network are, when it is used least and most, and what the coverage area is. This information is needed to launch an attack on the target network. Many commonly used network protocols transmit sensitive data such as username and password information in cleartext. An attacker may use captured data to gain access to network resources. Even if communications are encrypted, an attacker is still presented with the ciphertext, which can be stored and analyzed at a later time. Many password encryption algorithms such as Microsoft NTLM can be easily broken.

Active eavesdropping is possible when an attacker can connect to a wireless network. Active eavesdropping on a wireless local area network (LAN) normally involves *Address Resolution Protocol* (ARP) *spoofing*. This technique was originally designed to sniff a switched network. Essentially, this is a man-in-the-middle attack (MITM) (discussed later in the chapter) at the data link layer. The attacker sends out unsolicited ARP replies to target stations on the LAN. The target stations will send all traffic to the attacker instead of the intended destination and the attacker will then forward the packet to the originally intended destination. Therefore, it is possible for a wireless station to sniff the traffic of another wireless client that is out of signal range or a wired client on the local network.

## dsniff

dsniff is a suite of network utilities that may be used to sniff passwords, read e-mail, monitor web traffic, and perform active sniffing. For more information, visit http://monkey.org/~dugsong/dsniff.

# Communications Jamming

Jamming occurs when an intentional or unintentional interference overpowers the sender or receiver of a communications link, thereby effectively rendering the communications link useless. An attacker can apply jamming in several ways.

## Denial of Service (DoS) Jamming

Jamming the entire network can cause a denial of service (DoS) attack. The entire area, including both base stations and clients, is flooded with interference so that no stations can communicate with each other as shown in Figure 2-2. This attack shuts down all communications in a given area. This type of attack can require a significant amount of power if applied to a broad area. DoS attacks on wireless networks may be difficult to prevent and stop. Most wireless networking technologies use unlicensed frequencies and are subject to interference from a variety of different electronic devices.

**Client Jamming**   Jamming a client station provides an opportunity for a rogue client to take over or impersonate the jammed client as shown in Figure 2-3. Jamming also can be used to DoS the client so that it loses connectivity and cannot access the application. A more sophisticated attack may attempt to interrupt connectivity with the real base station to then reattach with a rogue station.

**Base Station Jamming**   Jamming a base station provides an opportunity for a rogue base station to stand in for the legitimate base station as shown in Figure 2-4. The jamming can also deprive clients of service or a telecom company from revenue.

---

**Figure 2-2**

Jamming attack on wireless communications

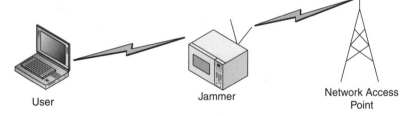

User

Jammer

Network Access Point

**Figure 2-3**

Jamming attack against client to hijack communications

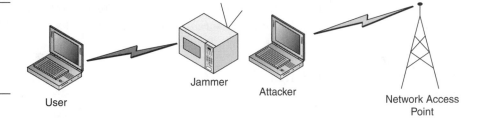

User          Jammer          Attacker          Network Access Point

**Figure 2-4**

Jamming attack against access point to hijack communications

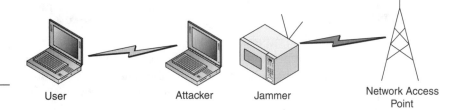

User          Attacker          Jammer          Network Access Point

As stated before, most of the wireless networking technologies utilize unlicensed frequencies. Therefore, many devices such as cordless phones, baby monitors, and microwave ovens may interfere with wireless networking and effectively jam the wireless communications. To prevent this kind of unintentional jamming, site surveys are recommended before spending significant money on wireless equipment. These surveys will help to verify that other devices will not interfere with communications and may prevent unneeded capital expenditure on useless equipment.

# Injection and Modification of Data

Injection attacks occur when an attacker adds data to an existing connection in order to hijack the connection or maliciously send data or commands. An attacker can manipulate control messages and data streams by inserting packets or commands to a base station and vice versa. Inserting control messages on a valid control channel can result in the disassociation or disconnection of users from the network.

Injection attacks can be used for DoS. An attacker can also flood the network access point with connect messages, tricking the network access point into exceeding a maximum limit, thereby denying authorized users access to the network. Bait-and-switch attacks or midstream insertion attacks are also possible if the upper-layer protocols (discussed in Chapter 3) do not provide real-time integrity checks in the data stream.

## Man-in-the-Middle (MITM) Attacks

Similar to injection attacks are MITM attacks. MITM attacks can take many forms and are designed to subvert the confidentiality and integrity of the session. MITM attacks are more sophisticated than most attacks and require significant information about the network. An attacker will normally impersonate a network resource. When a victim initiates a connection, the attacker will intercept the connection, and then complete the connection to the intended resource and proxy all communications to the resource as shown in Figure 2-5. The attacker is now in a position to inject data, modify communications, or eavesdrop on a session that would normally be difficult to decode, such as encrypted sessions.

---

### dsniff

Another use for the dsniff utilities is to perform testing of MITM attacks against Secure Sockets Layer (SSL) and Secure Shell (SSH). These tools can serve as a good auditing mechanism for these kind of attacks. Make sure users know what MITM error messages look like; many times users will just disregard the messages.

---

# Rogue Client

After studying a client in the field, an attacker may choose to mimic or clone the client's identity and attempt to gain access to the network and advertised services. The attacker may also be so bold as to steal an access device to attempt to gain access to the network. Securing all wireless devices may be very difficult, for convenience and mobility dictate that most wireless devices are very small. A common wireless security mechanism was supposed to use layer 2 access controls to limit access to

**Figure 2-5**

MITM attack

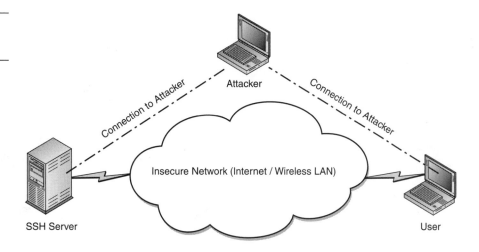

resources. This mechanism proved a failure when it was used by cellular phone companies to limit access to phone numbers by using an Electronic Serial Number (ESN). Then the failure was repeated by the 802.11 wireless LAN standard with Media Access Controls (MACs) that can be easily circumvented by a skilled attacker.

## Rogue Network Access Points

An adept attacker can set up a rouge access point to impersonate a network resource. Clients may unknowingly connect to this false access point and divulge sensitive credentials such as authentication credentials. This type of attack can be used in conjunction with directive jamming to block the ears of the legitimate network access point as shown in Figure 2-6.

**Figure 2-6**

Rogue access point

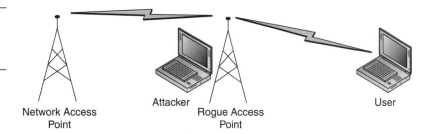

Users with access to the wired network may also install rouge access points, unknowingly opening up the network to attacks. Users may install a wireless access point seeking the convenience of wireless without knowing the security concerns. Currently, access points can be purchased at almost any electronic store for a minimal cost. These access points can serve as backdoors to the wired network because they are normally installed with the default configuration so they are wide open to attack. Attackers can easily connect to these access points and have the same access that a wired user would have. Most networks rely on firewalls for perimeter security and are not prepared for an attack from an attacker on the inside.

### Attack Anonymity

Complete attack anonymity can be achieved through wireless ventures. Without properly laid-out networks to determine locality and direction-finding equipment, an attacker can remain anonymous and hidden anywhere in the wireless coverage area. This can make locating an attacker and forensic work very difficult. I predict that Internet attacks will become increasingly more difficult to solve due to the wide availability of anonymous access through insecure access points. There are many Internet sites that publish the location of insecure access points that may be used for this purpose.

# War Driving

*War driving* is the process of searching for open wireless LANs by driving around a particular area. The name comes from the term "war dialing," which is an old attack method that involves repeatedly dialing different numbers to search for modems and other network entry points. There are many Internet sites devoted to war driving. For less than $300, an attacker can outfit a laptop with a wireless network card and a Global Positioning System (GPS) unit for war driving. War-driving software is freely available on the Internet at www.netstumbler.com.

It is important to note that many attackers are searching out networks not to attack internal resources, but to gain free anonymous Internet access. The access can be used for a malicious attack against other networks. If network operators do not take prudent steps to prevent malicious attackers from using their network, they may be liable for damages inflicted against other networks using their Internet access. Caution must be exercised.

## Client-to-Client Attacks

Once on a network, other network clients can be attacked directly. If successful, the attacker may gain the credentials required to gain further access into the corporate or telecom network. Most network administrators do not take the time to harden stations or install personal firewall software. Therefore, successful attacks on wireless-connected clients may reveal sensitive information such as the username and password that can be used to access other network resources. All Internet or wireless-connected stations need to be adequately hardened.

## Infrastructure Equipment Attacks

Incorrectly configured infrastructure equipment is a prime target for attackers and usually provides a means for attaining further penetration into the network. These are sometimes referred to as stepping stones and can be used to bypass access controls. Network devices such as routers, switches, backup servers, and log servers are prime targets. Many network administrators rely on layer 2 security mechanisms such as virtual LANs (VLANs) to keep wireless networks separate from wired networks. There are many documented attacks that can be used to bypass VLAN security. There are many attacks depending on the switch, but they break down into three main categories: switch attacks, MAC attacks, and routing attacks.

Switch attacks take many different forms. Some involve flooding the MAC or ARP table in the switch to cause it to fail open. This attack is often caused inadvertently by administrators choosing a low-quality switch. Other attacks against the switch involve manipulating the protocol that switches use to communicate such as spanning tree. MAC attacks include ARP spoofing and other physical layer attacks that can be used to fool network devices into sending the data to unintended recipients. Routing attacks are very difficult and normally involve participating in the routing protocol, such as Open Shortest Path First (OSPF) or Enhanced

Interior Gateway Routing Protocol (EIGRP), to change the flow of traffic for DoS or sniffing.

# Attacker Equipment

The equipment used by the casual attacker can minimally consist of a wireless network interface. This can either be a wireless Ethernet network interface card (NIC), a General Packet Radio Service (GPRS), or a Cellular Digital Packet Data (CDPD) cellular telephony handset connected to a laptop either as a Personal Computer Memory Card International Association (PCMCIA) card or through some communications link. Advanced attackers will sometimes employ this wireless interface in conjunction with jammers and specialized software. A sample is shown in Figure 2-9. Cellular network attackers will generally use a configuration as depicted in Figure 2-7 because the network coverage is understood and generally covers a large area.

On the other hand, wireless Ethernet networks generally cover a smaller area. Attackers will first detect the networks and determine the coverage area to find the best position to mount an attack. The preferred position is one that provides cover sometimes behind landscaping or in a

**Figure 2-7**

Attacker
hardware
configuration

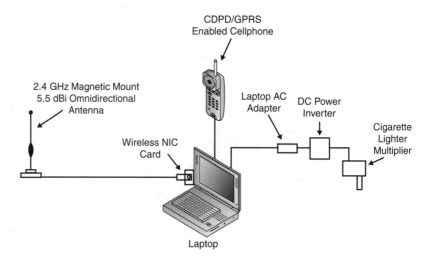

different building and optionally an easy escape route. The basic network discovery setup consists of a laptop, a GPS unit, an antenna, an amplifier, and a wireless Ethernet NIC. In order to perform long-duration sweeps, extra power can be obtained by using an inverter for converting 12V DC into 120V AC to power the laptop or any other equipment one may be using (such as a jammer or a low-noise amplifier [LNA]). Some attackers have been known to remove dashboard cigarette lighters and replace with DC inverters to provide power for an extended period of time. Once the basic coverage is determined, the attacker, utilizing various antenna apparatus, determines the best link from which to mount attacks.

Attackers will utilize various antenna types when mounting an attack, depending on the situation and the desired effect. Antenna types are generally characterized by the amount of gain or increase in received or transmitted signal strength and beam width. The beam width of an antenna indicates how electromagnetic radiation emanates. The three most common antenna types are the omnidirectional antenna, the yagi, and the parabolic.

The omnidirectional antenna has a beam width of 360 degrees and is usually deployed to survey or jam a wide area (see Figure 2-8). Electromagnetic radiation is received from all sides and therefore, unless in an array, direction cannot be determined with a single station utilizing an omnidirectional antenna. Omnidirectional antennas also have little to no gain, unless they are assembled in a collinear array where gain can be as high as 8 dBi.

**Figure 2-8**

Common omnidirectional antenna

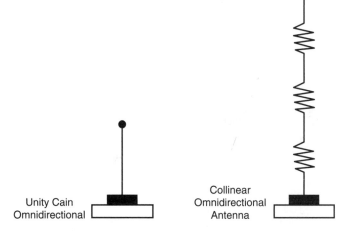

Unity Cain Omnidirectional

Collinear Omnidirectional Antenna

The yagi antenna has special properties that focus the electromagnetic radiation from a driven element into a directed pattern. A yagi antenna, shown below, typically exhibits a beam width of 10 to 20 degrees and a gain of 10 to 18dBi. The yagi is usually deployed when one cannot gain direct access to the coverage area using an omnidirectional antenna. A typical yagi antenna has a gain of 10 to 18 dBi. A yagi can also be used when the jamming of a particular device or group of devices sharing a geographical area is desired. Using a tripod designed for a camera or a telescope can prove effective for aiming a yagi in the field.

The parabolic antenna, shown below, has the narrowest beam width of all, typically between 4 and 10 degrees. The parabolic antenna is generally deployed when concealment is of concern and great distances are to be covered. The parabolic antenna is difficult to use due to the narrow beam width, but this characteristic can be used to determine location. This antenna can also be used to support jamming functions as well as very precise attacks, perhaps to avoid detection systems.

Survey software for collecting packet reception locations in a log file categorized by longitude and latitude is commonly used to discover the location and coverage of unknown wireless Ethernet networks. The longitude/latitude coordinates are supplied by a GPS device. Wireless coverage

**Figure 2-9**

Wireless assessment/war-driving hardware setup

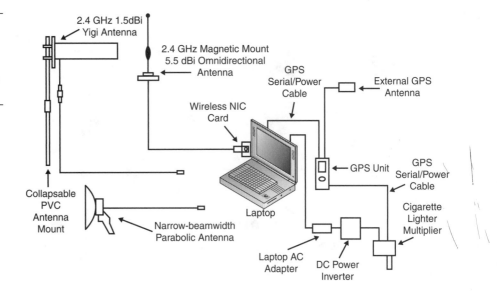

of a given area can then be clearly identified when plotted on a map. Typical attacker hardware configuration is shown in Figure 2-9.

An antenna is by far the most useful tool for a network designer or an attacker, but an amplifier can also be used to boost reception over a long distance. Amplifiers will increase the signal as well as the noise, so getting a good quality amplifier is important. Using amplifiers may violate Federal Communications Commission (FCC) regulations, so great care needs to be taken.

# Covert Wireless Channels

There is a final vector that wireless implementers must consider when evaluating or designing a wireless network. Due to the low cost of wireless access points and the ease of creating software-based access points consisting of a standard desktop or laptop computer and a wireless NIC, one must be vigilant in detecting incorrectly configured or unintentionally deployed wireless equipment on the wired network, such as the network backdoor shown in Figure 2-10. This equipment can poke very damaging holes in the fabric of the wired infrastructure, which will be exposed to attackers within several miles of a target network.

**Figure 2-10**

Access point
network backdoor

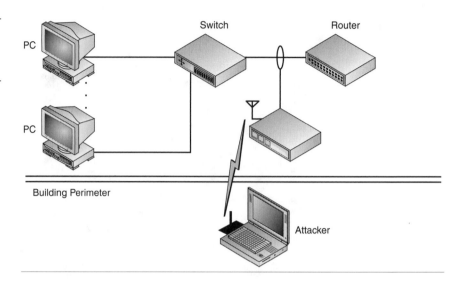

A similar configuration can also bridge air-gap networks via a wireless channel and funnel data from an air-gapped network outside a protective building by chaining access points together until the final leg of the link leaves the confines of the building as shown in Figure 2-11. This configuration can effectively increase the amount of coverage area to many miles. The equipment needed for this configuration is very inexpensive and may be purchased at most electronic stores.

# Roaming Issues

Another major difference between a wireless and a wired environment is end-point mobility. The concept of roaming on Code-Division Multiple Access (CDMA), Global System for Mobile Communications (GSM), and wireless Ethernet are all very similar. Many Transmission Control Protocol/Internet Protocol (TCP/IP) network applications require the IP address of the server and the client to remain static; however, when roaming among a network, you will undoubtedly be required to leave and join across subnets. This requirement is the drive behind mobile IP and other wireless network roaming mechanisms.

**Figure 2-11**

Attacker
extending range
by chaining
access points

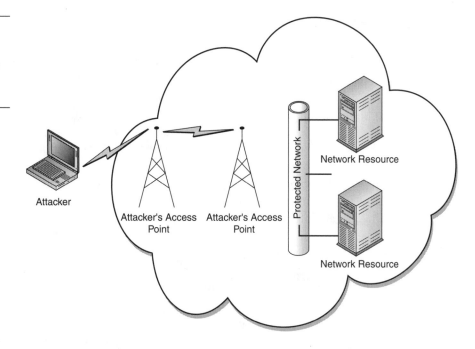

The basic idea behind mobile IP is location registration and packet redirection. A location-independent address is used to keep TCP/IP connectivity alive, while a temporary location-dependent address is used to provide connectivity to the local network resources. There are three other mandatory requirements of a mobile IP system. There is the mobile node (MN), home agent (HA), and the foreign agent (FA). The MN is the wireless user device, the HA is a server located on the MN's home network, and the FA is a server residing on the roamed-to network. When an MN roams to a network, it obtains a temporary location-dependent IP address and registers with a FA. The FA then communicates with the HA, notifying the HA that the MN is attached to it, and that all packets should now be routed through the roamed-to FA to be delivered to the MN.

There are some obvious problems with this schema. Replay attacks of the registration process can be performed by a rogue station in a different cell to attempt to capture outbound traffic from the network. One can also imitate a valid station and illegitimately obtain network service.

# Cryptographic Threats

CDMA and GSM cellular networks and wireless Ethernet networks have employed cryptographic mechanisms in order to deter eavesdropping and stymie unauthorized network usage. However, in both networks, oversights resulted in the compromise of communications and fraudulent use.

Wired Equivalent Privacy (WEP) is a cryptographic mechanism designed to provide security for 802.11 networks. Implementation flaws and key management issues have proved WEP almost useless. WEP was designed with a single static key that was to be used by all users. Controlling access to these keys, changing the keys frequently, and detecting compromises is nearly impossible. An examination of the implementation of the RC4 algorithm in WEP has revealed weaknesses that enable an attacker to completely recover the key after capturing minimal network traffic. Tools are available on the Internet that allow an attacker to recover the key in a number of hours. Therefore, WEP cannot be relied on to provide authentication and confidentiality on a wireless network.

Using these cryptographic mechanisms is better than not using them, but due to the known vulnerabilities, other mechanisms are needed to protect against the aforementioned attacks. All wireless communication networks are subject to the attacker eavesdropping on phases of contact, namely, connection establishment, session communication, and connection termination. The very nature of wireless communication eliminates out-of-band management and control, thus requiring protection. Key management, as always, presents additional challenges when being applied to roaming users and a shared open medium. We will discuss commonly used cryptographic mechanisms in the following chapter.

# Conclusion

Understanding the threats to wireless technology is the first step in securing wireless implementations. The advantages of using wireless are tremendous. Therefore, these threats need to be considered, but should not stop the deployment of wireless applications. Taking a few simple security measures can dramatically reduce the impact of many common attacks. The following chapter will help to show what steps can help to reduce wireless threats.

# CHAPTER 3

# Introduction to Wireless Security Protocols and Cryptography

With all the threats discussed in Chapter 2, you may think that securing wireless applications in any form is going to be a monumental task. Besides, it is probably going to take complex mathematical algorithms and months or years of custom programming. You may have already taken out the course catalog of the local university expecting to need further education on the topic or called your boss and told him or her to push back the deadline of the current wireless project. Securing your wireless application should not require any of these actions. In fact, the threats we face in a wireless environment are not substantially different from many of the threats we face when taking our business on the Internet.

This chapter is not designed to be a comprehensive implementation guide to any of the topics discussed, but rather it is designed to give the reader an overview of the tools that can be used to solve wireless problems. Further chapters will discuss additional design concepts.

## Removing the FUD

This chapter is going to attempt to remove the fear, uncertainty, and doubt, commonly referred to as FUD, in wireless security solutions. The fact of the matter is that some of the threats discussed in Chapter 2 are *not* unique to wireless. With the commercial Internet reaching a decade of age, information security professionals and academics have devoted large amounts of time and resources tackling these problems. Why reinvent the wheel? All we need to do is clearly identify the ways to mitigate threats, and this can be done by applying technology and applications that are already in use for other applications on the Internet and in the office.

We will start with a brief review of the Open System Interconnection (OSI) model so we can identify at what layer traditional security mechanisms are implemented. Then we will discuss common security technologies that can be used to secure a wireless network. Chapter 8 will discuss actual implementations and design concepts.

# OSI Model

The OSI model is a standard developed in the mid-1970s that defines a framework for developing networking protocols and is divided into seven layers as shown in Figure 3-1. Many technical classes will teach the OSI model to help students understand networking by breaking it down to smaller components. Not all protocols are based on the OSI model and in many cases a single application will perform the functions of many layers of the OSI model.

The following list describe the seven layers of the OSI model:

- **Application layer**   The application layer is the user's interface to network communications. Programs such as browsers, e-mail, and file transfer software are on this layer.

- **Presentation layer**   This layer negotiates syntax, so the applications communicating will be able to understand each other.

- **Session layer**   This layer is responsible for coordinating communications between applications as well as tracking what data belongs to what data connection.

- **Transport layer**   This layer primarily provides the organization for network communications. Reliability and ordering are primary functions of the transport layer. Portions of data in this layer are commonly called *segments*.

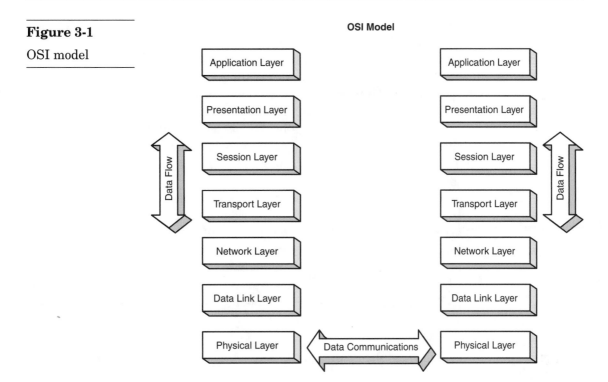

**Figure 3-1**

OSI model

OSI Model

- **Network layer (also called the Internet layer)**   On this layer, routing and logical addressing are handled. Portions of data in this layer are commonly called *packets*.
- **Data link layer**   Physical addressing such as the Media Access Control (MAC) address are part of this layer. Portions of data in this layer are commonly called *frames*.
- **Physical layer**   This layer is responsible for the actual communication, changing the zeros and ones into voltages for wires or radio signals for the air.

## OSI Simplified

In many large enterprises, different groups handle different networking functions. For example, let us examine the organization of a large financial institution from the perspective of the customer service application.

There is a telco group that handles network cabling. The desktop/server group is responsible for the network interface cards (NICs) in the end users' PCs and servers, as well as the hubs and switches. The network operations group is responsible for the routers in the network, assigning IP addressing, and operating the Domain Name System (DNS) on the network. The application development group handles the customer account program that runs over the network. The customer service representatives use the application and are responsible for inputting customer data. This particular organization maps to the OSI model rather well, as shown in Table 3-1.

This organization may seem overly complicated and you may think that troubleshooting the application can be difficult, but this organization actually makes troubleshooting easier. Pulling wires through a drop ceiling and debugging code are two very different disciplines. The separation of duties enables each group to become domain experts in their area of responsibility. Therefore, when groups are well coordinated, the specialized experienced groups solve problems faster.

| **Table 3-1** | **Application** | **Customer Service** |
| --- | --- | --- |
| Mapping to the OSI Model | Presentation | Application development |
| | Session | Application development |
| | Transport | Network operations |
| | Network | Network operations |
| | Data link | Desktop/server |
| | Physical | Telco |

# Internet Model

For many developers, the OSI model is too complex for practical use with regard to implementation. Therefore, another model has emerged: the Internet model. Sometimes referred to as the Transmission Control Protocol/Internet Protocol (TCP/IP) model, it is a simplification of the OSI model that more accurately reflects how Internet applications are built. However, since we will be talking about many intermediate protocols, the

OSI model will be used for this book. Just in case you learned the Internet model instead of the OSI model, I have included this section as a reference. Please refer to Table 3-2 for reconciliation.

# Wireless Local Area Network (LAN) Security Protocols

In developing 802.11, developers followed the OSI model. Wireless Ethernet was designed to be a drop-in replacement for wired Ethernet. Therefore, the entire protocol exists on the physical and data link layers of the OSI model. Although we have years of experience in implementing security on networks, very few implementations have ever been designed below the network layer. As a result, no specific security protocol could be directly implemented in the physical or data link layers. Therefore, new security mechanisms were created and, as discussed in Chapter 2, they were found to be less than effective. Many manufacturers and standards bodies are working feverishly to improve 802.11 security mechanisms. For certain applications, the existing security may be adequate, but most of today's applications will require using security protocols that exist in the network layer and above.

The following sections discuss commonly used security protocols that can be used to secure wireless applications. But before we get into the specific applications, we need to discuss the underlying concepts that make all of these protocols effective.

| **Table 3-2** | **OSI Model** | **Internet Model** |
|---|---|---|
| Equivalent Layers in the OSI and Internet Models | Application layer<br>Presentation layer<br>Session layer | Application layer |
| | Transport layer | Transport layer |
| | Network layer | Internet layer |
| | Data link layer<br>Physical layer | Network interface layer |

# Cryptography

Cryptography is commonly defined as the process or skill of communicating in or deciphering secret writings or ciphers. Cryptography has a history beginning long before the Internet and wireless technology. One famous historical example of cryptography is the Caesar Cipher, which was supposedly used by Julius Caesar to communicate with his army generals. It was based on a simple substitution of each letter in the encoded message with the letter that appears three letters to the right of the original message. For example, the message "BRING ME A SALAD" would be "EULQM PH D VDODG." Refer to the following for reference:

```
Plain text:  ABCDEFGHIGKLMNOPQRSTUVWXYZ
Cipher text: DEFGHIJKLMNOPQRSTUVWXYZABC
```

In more recent history, great strides have been made with cryptography that will help keep your data safe, not just from Julius Caesar's enemies, but also from determined attackers or even government agencies. In fact, much of the cryptography that is used today is based on research that was first done to keep government information safe during times of war. Different forms of cryptography can be used to solve our wireless security problems. However, cryptography is not a magic bullet that is going to solve all of our security problems.

To illustrate this, let's say that you have a treasure chest full of gold and you want to protect it from bandits. We might say that physical security is a primary concern. Due to the value of the treasure, you decide to spend a significant amount of money protecting it. Therefore, you construct a vault. The vault is made of steel reinforced with concrete six feet thick. The door of the vault is made from the strongest steel money can buy. Now your treasure is safe, right? Not necessarily—if you left the key to the vault in a place where the bandits could steal it, then all the additional security of the vault would be easily circumvented. Or maybe the lock on the vault could be easily picked or destroyed. Therefore, the storage of keys and the methods used to lock the valuables are equally as important as the protection scheme.

The same is true with cryptography. We can use cryptography to help solve some security problems, but the overall security will be impacted by choosing the correct process for encrypting or algorithm and by choosing the best protection for our keys. We are going to highlight some of the most common cryptographic methods that can be easily used with wireless technology to solve security problems.

There are three primary areas where cryptography is used to solve security problems:

- **Authentication**   This is used to reliably determine someone or something's identity. This is to prevent someone from impersonating a legitimate user or to prevent a device from impersonating a legitimate resource.

- **Encryption**   This is the process of encoding data and is used to prevent eavesdropping. The protection that encryption provides is also referred to as confidentiality service. This is supposed to keep data safe from unintended listeners. The two classes of encryption algorithms are symmetric (private key) and asymmetric (public key). When using a symmetric algorithm, both the sender and recipient use the same key for encrypting and decrypting the data, but this creates a problem for securely distributing the key between senders. This can be solved by asymmetric algorithms in which data encrypted with one key can only be decrypted with another key. Therefore, a key can be exchanged on an untrusted medium without worrying about eavesdropping. Asymmetric algorithms are typically used to establish a key for a symmetric algorithm because asymmetric algorithms are computationally expensive and not normally used for transferring large amounts of data.

- **Integrity**   This guarantees that data has not been modified. We need to make sure that the message that was received is the message that was sent.

# Secure Sockets Layer/Transport Layer Security (SSL/TLS)

Secure Sockets Layer (SSL) was originally designed to solve the security problems with web browsers. Back at the beginning of the Internet boom, the great commercial opportunity that the Internet offered was realized, but the security concerns of sending personal and credit card information in cleartext needed to be addressed because attackers could easily intercept this information and use it for evil purposes. Netscape was the first browser to offer SSL and made the Web safe for commercial transactions; thus, a secure channel could be provided for transmission of data. SSL is transparent, which means that the data arrives at the destination unchanged by the encryption/decryption process. Therefore, SSL can be used for many applications.

SSL and its successor, Transport Layer Security (TLS), are the most widely implemented security protocols on the Internet. Originally implemented by Netscape in 1994, SSL/TLS is implemented in nearly every browser and most e-mail clients. Due to the nature of the applications that necessitated SSL/TLS, it uses TCP as the reliable transport protocol and does not have any reliability mechanism built into it. SSL/TLS has been the basis for other security protocols including Microsoft's Private Communications Technology (PCT), Secure Transport Layer Protocol (STLP), and Wireless Transport Layer Security (WTLS).

SSL was originally a Netscape de facto standard, but was adopted by the Internet Engineering Task Force (IETF) as TLS. Unofficially, the IETF's task was to resolve the dispute between Netscape and Microsoft over the implementation. Despite the controversy, SSL/TLS remains the most used security protocol and it does not appear that any other protocol will claim that notoriety anytime soon.

SSL/TLS's primary application is for web traffic or the Hypertext Transfer Protocol (HTTP). The process is very basic. In normal HTTP communications, a TCP connection is made, a request is sent for a document, and the document is sent. With an SSL/TLS HTTP connection, the TCP connection is established, an SSL/TLS connection is established, and then the HTTP connection proceeds over the SSL/TLS connection. Two things to note—SSL/TLS relies on TCP for the connection and the addition of the SSL/TLS connection does not change the HTTP communication. To prevent confusing standard HTTP servers, HTTP over SSL/TLS is typically implemented over a different TCP port (443) than standard HTTP (80). Many of the applications that use SSL/TLS use different ports than the non-SSL/TLS standard protocol.

SSL/TLS is used to authenticate and encrypt a connection. This is accomplished by using a combination of different technologies that are based on symmetric and asymmetric algorithms. SSL/TLS has the capability to authenticate the server and client, but in most cases, only server authentication is actually preformed. The authentication is accomplished by using public-key cryptography and is referred to as a *handshake*. The actual communications using SSL/TLS use a symmetrical encryption algorithm. As mentioned before, the benefit of using a symmetrical algorithm over an asymmetrical is performance.

SSL/TLS can be used to secure many varieties of network communications. The most common implementations are based on known TCP communication, such as e-mail, news, telnet, and the File Transfer Protocol (FTP). In many cases, different TCP ports are used for the SSL/TLS secured communications.

# Secure Shell (SSH)

Secure Shell (SSH), much like SSL/TLS, was created out of a necessity for secure communication when the only protocols being used were unsecured protocols. SSH was developed in 1995 by Tatu Ylönen after his university network fell victim to a password-sniffing attack earlier that year. SSH was originally designed to replace some Unix programs such as telnet, FTP, remote login (rlogin), rshell remote shell (rshell), and remote copy (rcp). Besides replacing these programs, SSH can be used to secure otherwise insecure programs over a network. Due to its flexibility and ease of use, SSH is a highly used security protocol and comes with the standard installation of many operating systems.

SSH is much like SSL/TLS in operation from a high level. SSH uses a public-key exchange to secure the initial connection and negotiates a symmetric key for the data transfer during the session. SSH can also easily be configured to authenticate both the server as well as the client.

## Protocol or Program?

The most common implementation of the SSH protocol is the Unix ssh program. There are multiple SSH programs available: commercial ssh, OpenSSH, putty for Windows platforms, and F-Secure ssh. Each of these programs is interoperable with each other, but have their own unique features and configuration options. Some of these programs are open source and some are distributed for free. You will need to examine the features and support options to determine which program will be appropriate for your application.

## Terminal Access and File Transfer

The most common use of SSH is for replacing telnet. Telnet is a common application used to manage network hosts. Telnet sessions can be easily sniffed (revealing sensitive data), hijacked, or data can be injected (causing commands to be executed or preventing commands from being executed). If properly implemented, SSH eliminates these security concerns. If you are still using telnet for anything, please replace it with SSH immediately. Many device and operating manufacturers are starting to include support for SSH.

Most file transfer protocols such as FTP, the Trivial File Transfer Protocol (TFTP), and the Common Internet File System (CIFS) are very insecure. These protocols suffer from the same sniffing, injection, and hijacking attacks. SSH includes the capability to transfer files over an encrypted authenticated session.

## Port Forwarding

Some manufacturers are not supporting SSH as a telnet or FTP replacement. In these situations SSH can be used to secure otherwise insecure applications such as telnet, FTP, the Post Office Protocol (POP), or even HTTP. This can be accomplished by using the port-forwarding feature of SSH. Please see Figure 3-2. In the figure, the firewall is configured to only allow traffic from the insecure network to the SSH server. No traffic will be allowed to or from the e-mail server to the insecure network. In addition to using SSH for terminal access to the SSH server, port forwarding can be used to tunnel e-mail traffic over the insecure network to the SSH server. Then the SSH server forwards the packets to the e-mail server. From the e-mail server's perspective, the traffic would be coming from the

**Figure 3-2**

SSH tunnel

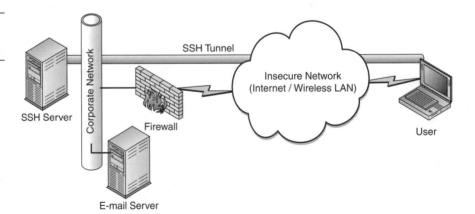

SSH server and packets would be returned to the SSH server for tunneling back to the user. E-mail is just one example of the many TCP protocols that can be tunneled over SSH. Other common applications for SSH include securing file transfers (Network File System [NFS], FTP and CIFS), web applications (HTTP), and thin client applications (MS Terminal Server and XWindows).

## A Word of Caution

Due to the flexibility and ubiquitous access that SSH enables, great care must be taken when implementing SSH. SSH is a tool that is commonly used by attackers. In our port forwarding example, we explained how SSH can be used to bypass firewall rules for accessing e-mail or other applications. This may be used by legitimate users or by malicious attackers. Therefore, make sure that SSH servers and clients are adequately secured and do not forget to secure applications behind the firewall.

# Man-in-the-Middle (MITM) of SSL/TLS and SSH

Some implementations of SSL/TLS and SSH may also be vulnerable to man-in-the-middle (MITM) attacks. Both SSL/TLS and SSH use a public-key algorithm for establishing symmetric keys for the data transfer. A malicious attacker could intercept the handshake and replace the public keys exchanged with counterfeit keys. The attacker would then be able to attack the SSL/TLS or SSH session. Implementing a Public Key Infrastructure (PKI) or holding *key-signing parties* are ways to prevent this type of attack. PKI uses complex mathematical algorithms to verify the authenticity of a key by checking it against information from a certificate authority (CA). Key-signing parties eliminate the need for a CA, but require all parties that would communicate to meet together and personally exchange keys. In either case, failure modes must be investigated. The error messages in many applications displayed during an SSL/TLS or SSH MITM attack may go unnoticed by users.

## Tech Challenge

dsniff (mentioned in Chapter 2) can be used for testing applications using SSL/TLS and SSH for MITM attacks. It is important to document messages displayed during these attacks, so users will be aware of abnormal behavior.

# WTLS

WTLS is based on SSL/TLS. WTLS is used by Wireless Application Protocol (WAP) devices such as mobile phone handsets and personal digital assistants (PDAs). The primary difference between SSL and WTLS is the transport layer. SSL relies on TCP for reliability functions, such as the retransmission of lost packets and out-of-order packets. The WAP devices using WTLS cannot use TCP for these functions because WAP devices only use the User Datagram Protocol (UDP). UDP is not a connection-oriented protocol, so these functions have been included in WTLS.

Three classes can be negotiated during the handshake process (refer to the "SSL/TLS" section for protocol details).

- **WTLS class 1**   No certificates
- **WTLS class 2**   Server certificate only
- **WTLS class 3**   Client and server certificates

In class 1, no authentication takes place and the protocol is simply used to set up an encrypted channel. In class 2, the client (typically a handset) authenticates the server; in most cases, the certificates are included in the firmware of the handset. In class 3, both the client and server are authenticated. This normally involves the implementation of a PKI. WTLS is similar to SSL/TLS in that it can be used to secure other protocols, such as Wireless Markup Language (WML). WML is much like Hypertext Markup Language (HTML), but it is specifically designed for WAP devices, such as mobile phones and PDAs.

# WEP

Wired Equivalent Privacy (WEP) is the security mechanism included in the 802.11 standard and is designed to provide confidentiality and authentication services. WEP is based on the RC4 algorithm, which is referred to as a *stream cipher*. Packets are encrypted by generating an RC4 stream with a combination of a 24-bit initialization vector (IV) and a shared key. The IV is used to make the RC4 stream generated with the shared key different for many of the data transmissions. The data is then XORed with the generated stream and transmitted in a WEP frame with the IV in the header so the receiver can generate the same RC4 stream to XOR the packet for decryption.

There are problems with the implementation of WEP. WEP can be used as a first line of defense, but cannot be relied on for security because weaknesses have been proven that can compromise the WEP key. At the time this book was written, a typical wireless network's WEP key can be compromised using software on the Internet in a few hours, so WEP can be used to slow attackers down, but it will not keep them out.

WEP also presents a number of key management problems. A common WEP key is normally used for all users on a given wireless network, which makes it very difficult to protect the key. WEP keys would need to be changed very frequently. Employees are constantly leaving the company or are losing wireless equipment such as laptops.

Some of the latest implementations of WEP, often bundled in 802.1x functionality upgrades (see the following section), negotiate a WEP key at the time of initial authentication. Advanced implementations also rekey during the session without the awareness of the end users. This nullifies many of the original WEP weaknesses that relied upon the unchanging nature of the WEP key or where a single WEP key was used to protect a fleet of wireless clients, rather than individual sessions.

# 802.1x

802.1x and its associated protocols are an attempt to increase the security of networks before layer 3 protocols (such as IP) are set up. The technology is not specific to 802.11 and can be used on Ethernet, Token Ring, and so on. 802.1x is a layer 2 protocol that can be used for a number of operations. At the time of this writing, 802.1x details for 802.11 are still in draft form, but the basic functionality is not likely to change.

The basic purpose of 802.1x is to authenticate users and can optionally be used to establish encryption keys. When a connection is established, only 802.1x traffic is allowed to pass. This means the other protocols such as the Dynamic Host Configuration Protocol (DHCP), IP, and so on are not permitted. Extensible Authentication Protocol (EAP) (RFC 2284) is used to authenticate the users. EAP was originally designed to solve some of the authentication issues with the Point-to-Point Protocol (PPP), but its main use will probably be solving wireless issues. EAP authentication packets are sent to the access point with user login information; in most cases, this will be a username and password. The access point can authenticate the user by any means the vendor chooses to support. In most cases, this will be via Remote Authentication Dial-in User Service (RADIUS). Once the user is authenticated and optional encryption is established, communication will be enabled and protocols such as DHCP will be allowed to pass. A high level overview of the process is shown in Figure 3-3.

# IP Security (IPSec)

IP Security (IPSec) was developed by the IETF working group and continues to evolve. The IPSec protocol is lower in the protocol stack than

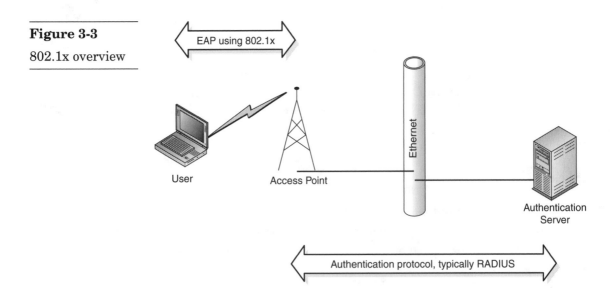

**Figure 3-3**

802.1x overview

SSL/WTLS, SSH, or WTLS. The security is implemented on the IP layer in the Internet model. The most common implementations of IPSec are using a tunnel mode that enables all IP traffic to be encrypted and optionally authenticated inside a single session. IPSec is the enabling technology behind most virtual private networks (VPNs) used on the Internet today. Due to the flexibility of IPSec and its broad range of application support, many choose to use it for securing their wireless applications.

IPSec has multiple implementation options that should be used based on the application. IPSec can be used to provide encryption by using Encapsulated Security Payload (ESP) or authentication by using Authentication Header (AH). AH may be implemented without ESP. This would not provide confidentiality against sniffing, but would prevent tampering with the data and damaging the data in transport, and positively identify the sender. ESP can be implemented without AH to provide confidentiality and basic authentication services of data, but many administrators choose to implement both AH and ESP.

IPSec has many different cryptographic algorithms that can be used for AH and ESP. The most commonly used encryption algorithms for ESP are the Data Encryption Standard (DES), Triple DES (TDES), and Advanced Encryption Standard (AES). AES is the replacement for DES and TDES, and the IPSec standard mandates that it be implemented in all IPSec implementations. The most commonly used authentication algorithms used for AH are Message Digest 5 (MD5) and Secure Hash Algorithm (SHA).

Two modes can be used by IPSec for encapsulating data. Transport mode is normally used when using IPSec to communicate between two hosts. Transport mode only encrypts the data of the IP packet and all the header information remains unencrypted. Tunnel mode encrypts the entire IP packet including the headers. Tunnel mode is more flexible for Internet applications because many enterprises utilize private network addressing, as described in RFC 1918.

The most common implementation of IPSec for secure communications is for remote-access VPNs over the Internet. Whenever a public network is used for private networking functions, it can be called a VPN. Using this definition, networking technologies such as Asynchronous Transfer Mode (ATM), Frame Relay, and X.25 can be considered VPNs, but most people exclusively use the term to refer to encrypted tunnels over the Internet. In this application, a gateway is installed on the perimeter of the corporate network, as pictured in Figure 3-4. Remote-access users will establish an IPSec tunnel to the gateway using tunnel mode with ESP and AH.

**Figure 3-4**

IPSec VPN
tunnel

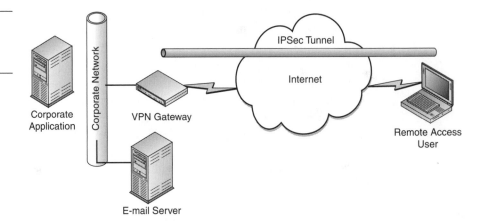

# Conclusion

This chapter was not designed to be a comprehensive discussion of any of
the aforementioned security protocols. However, after reading this chapter, you should be aware of some of the choices that exist for securing your
wireless application. Later chapters will discuss specific examples of how
these can be implemented. In order to effectively implement any of these
protocols, additional research is recommended because many times implementation-specific mistakes can significantly reduce the security of your
application.

# CHAPTER 4

# Security Considerations for Wireless Devices

Most wireless devices are designed to be small and mobile. Many times these devices are quite expensive. The security of these devices and the data contained on them is important. Keeping the devices secure can prevent theft or loss that may result in a needless expense or a compromise of a wireless application. Securely storing data on wireless devices can prevent information leakage or unauthorized access to wireless network resources. When designing a secure wireless network (details are discussed in Chapter 8), you should consider the possibility of the wireless devices falling into the wrong hands since this is likely to happen.

## Wireless Device Security Issues

This section considers the general security issues that are common to most wireless devices. If we examine many common wireless applications, we will find that the devices generally fall into four categories: laptops, personal digital assistants (PDAs), wireless infrastructure (bridges, access points, and so on), and mobile phone handsets. After examining the security issues that apply to all wireless devices, we will discuss device-specific issues in detail. Specific issues pertaining to each of these types of wireless devices will be discussed and possible solutions will be proposed.

# Physical Security

Mobility is one of the key enablers for wireless applications. However, because wireless devices are mobile, they are very easy to lose or steal. Therefore, the possibility of theft and loss of wireless devices must be an important factor when designing a wireless application. Taking some simple precautions for the physical security of the devices can drastically reduce the loss of wireless devices and thus reduce the overall cost of a wireless application.

## Be Aware

A little common sense goes a long way in protecting devices. People want to steal things. Laptops are common targets for thieves because they are very small and valuable. Laptops are also easy to sell on the black market or at online auctions because there is a large demand for them. Airports are a common place for laptop theft. Thieves are aware that many business travelers are equipped with laptops. Since the terrorist attacks of September 11, 2001, airport security screening has become more comprehensive. Many airports require that laptops be removed from their cases for screening. Some travelers simply forget that the laptop has been removed and leave it behind, whereas other travelers might accidentally pick up the wrong laptop. Thieves might also strike when a traveler is being questioned, when a bag is being searched, or when a traveler is required to repeatedly go through the metal detectors or be searched by hand-held metal detectors.

Airport restrooms are another common place where thieves often strike unsuspecting travelers. Some travelers will turn their back on their luggage while using the facilities. Some thieves have been known to grab bags out from under restroom stalls while the traveler is occupied. The thief may quickly disappear into a crowd before the victim can even see him or her. Be sure that your business travelers are aware of these threats so they can take reasonable precautions to prevent theft.

### Lock It Up

If you know that your wireless device is a target of thieves, which it probably is, then lock it up. Use airport lockers or check luggage with a trustworthy concierge when traveling with devices. If your environment is static and your devices cannot travel, then use device cables to lock them down. Banks even do this with their pens. You can also utilize security cameras to monitor hostile environments. Most laptops and PDAs can be secured with an inexpensive cable to a large object such as a desk or table. Infrastructure devices such as access points can be bolted down or locked in a container to prevent theft. A camera can also be used as a deterrent or a recovery mechanism for wireless devices.

Uniquely identifying devices may help with the inventory and recovery of devices. This can be done with labels, distinguishing marks, or asset tags. Checking out devices to employees or customers and making them financially responsible for the safety of the device is an effective way to make sure the devices are returned. Tracking the serial numbers of devices and keeping receipts may prove to be valuable aids in recovering equipment that has been seized by law enforcement.

## Information Leakage

Most wireless devices contain data storage capabilities. Some wireless devices are designed to store application data during intervals between wireless connectivity to the network. For example, laptops are commonly configured to store e-mail for offline reading and sending. The storage capabilities of wireless devices are constantly expanding and are capable of storing large amounts of very sensitive data. Reasonable steps must be taken to secure sensitive data. The loss of data may bring about additional expenses for recreating the data or recovering the loss of intellectual property to a competitor.

In order to make a decision of what reasonable steps to take to secure a wireless device, consider the amount of sensitive information that may be contained in the device. A single laptop with a small hard drive can contain large amounts of data including customer lists, employee information, intellectual property, source code, password lists, calendars, e-mail, or current projects. PDAs normally have an address book, calendar, and to-do list and can be used to store documentation or execute applications.

Cryptographic keys may also be stored on wireless devices. Many laptop users have been known to write passwords on a sticky note or use the Remember Password options common to many applications.

A good backup policy may reduce the amount of effort needed to recover from a lost device. Frequently, business travelers will not back up their data, which leads to a large loss when the data is lost, stolen, or destroyed.

## Device Security Features

We have already talked about the potential for information leakage from wireless devices. Some devices contain password-protection or lockout options that are supposed to keep data safe. These features may keep an unskilled attacker out, but most of them can be easily defeated when an attacker gains physical access to the device. The following are just a few ways that specific security mechanisms can be defeated.

Palm-OS-based PDAs have a password-protection feature that can be used in various ways to protect data. Research has proven that the password can be recovered by using a modified HotSync program to another PDA or desktop computer. Embedded debug features can even be used to retrieve that password out of a locked device.[1]

Mobile handsets normally have a lockout feature to prevent unauthorized access that uses a password or Personal Identification Number (PIN) code provided by the user. Many mobile handsets have factory or master passwords that can be used to completely bypass any security mechanism.

Many programs for PDAs and laptops are used for secure data or password storage. Security researchers have found problems with some of the programs that use poor encryption methods that enable the data to be retrieved by an attacker. In most cases, the data for these programs is unlocked by providing a password. If this password is easily compromised, for example, by the user writing it down or using it in other easy-to-compromise places, then the data may not be safe.

---

[1]www.atstake.com/research/reports/security_analysis_palm_os.pdf.

## Application Security

With client-side security, security features of a client/server application are enforced or enabled by the end user's client software. For example, consider an e-commerce site that uses a web browser for purchasing products. During the final checkout process, the client often submits information to the server, such as a credit-card number, shipping address, and other processing information. Sometimes the server will also pass the price to the client in a hidden field and rely on the client to submit the price back to the server for final payment processing because many times the checkout process may involve the use of many servers. If a malicious user wanted to modify the price to something lower, he or she would be able to do so. Therefore, the server can never trust data submitted from a client without some sort of data validation process.

Another common mistake that programmers make is embedding passwords or cryptographic keys into an application. This leads to many problems with the application. Malicious users may reverse-engineer the program to reveal the passwords or secret cryptographic keys. Network attacks may sniff a session to reveal embedded passwords that can be used for malicious purposes. (We already discussed how easy it is to sniff many wireless applications in Chapter 2.) A practical example of this is a network device that is administered with a Java client. The programmers embedded a password to the code that enabled a read-only user to have full read/write access.

Another fault in using client-side security is that the only thing required to access a sensitive application is the client software. In this case, a lost or stolen wireless device may be used to access an application. As a result, a complete rewrite of the application and distribution of the new application may be necessary.

# Detailed Device Analysis

This section will discuss specific details of the most widely used wireless devices. It is designed to provide solutions for specific problems and be a quick reference for wireless application designers needing information on specific devices.

# Laptops

Laptops are common wireless devices in corporate and Small Office Home Office (SOHO) wireless networks. The low cost of wireless network gear has made wireless laptops a common appearance in the corporate enterprise and in home environments.

## Problems

Physical security is a major problem with laptops. One of the key decision-making factors when purchasing a laptop is size. Generally, the smaller the laptop, the more it costs. The smaller the laptop, the easier it is to steal, and thus the greater the loss to the company.

The loss of data encryption keys, such as Wired Equivalent Privacy (WEP) keys, soft tokens, remembered passwords, or private keys (such as Pretty Good Privacy [PGP] keys), is a large problem that needs to be considered when creating an application. Once an attacker has obtained physical custody of a laptop, most security mechanisms can be circumvented. The attacker can install his or her own software on the laptop. Once the attacker controls the software, most software-based security mechanisms can be defeated.

The mobile nature of laptops also means that they are likely to connect to other networks that are not protected by the corporate firewall. These may be Internet connections, customer networks, vendor networks, or other public networks such as hotels or trade shows where competitors may located. The digital security of laptops in these environments needs to be considered.

## Solutions

One way to protect the physical security of laptops in a hostile environment is by using a security cable. This is a cable that is designed to loop around a large object such as a table or desk and connect to a slot that most laptops have. This does not guarantee that the laptop cannot be stolen, but it will slow down the thief and may cause him or her to look for easier targets.

Because laptops are frequently stolen, securing and backing up the data on the laptop is important. Data encryption programs can be used to secure files or create encrypted volumes on hard drives to keep data secure. These encrypted volumes normally require a private key protected by a password for decrypting the data. Storing all the data in encrypted files or volumes has the added benefit of making backups of user data easy since the user knows the exact location of the sensitive files on the laptop. Some e-mail programs also offer to store local mail in an encrypted format, although not all e-mail data store encryption is well implemented.

The storage of passwords and keys, such as WEP keys, on laptops should be considered. Some wireless cards store WEP keys in the Windows registry in cleartext. If you are relying on WEP for security (which is not recommended), you should consider choosing a card that does not store the WEP keys on the machine, but rather stores them in nonvolatile random access memory (NVRAM) on the Personal Computer Memory Card International Association (PCMCIA) card. Also, if private keys are stored on the machine, such as PGP keys or host keys for Secure Shell (SSH), these should be password-protected and revoked as soon as a laptop is detected to be missing by the system administrator.

Users should be aware that laptops are common targets of theft and should avoid leaving their laptops in a place where they may be stolen. Laptops are vulnerable in the office if left overnight. In many cases, the office may be an uncontrolled environment accessible by many people, including other people from the company, cleaning staff, and visitors. Make sure users know that laptops cost thousands of dollars and that they are often stolen.

Information leakage can also occur when laptop users are in a public environment. Airplanes are a common place for business travelers to do work. Other travelers on the plane could easily "shoulder-surf" the user and read sensitive information directly off the screen.

Laptops that will be operated in a hostile digital environment need to be protected. Protecting a laptop is not substantially different than securing a server. Unnecessary services should be disabled, which may lead to better performance. A host-based intrusion detection system (HIDS) (discussed in Chapter 8) or personal firewall software should be part of a standard laptop configuration. Remember that if you provide a wireless card for your users, they will likely use their computers in a hostile environment, such as an airport or coffee shop. Many laptop users will also likely connect to the Internet unprotected via a dial-up or broadband connection. Therefore, HIDS, personal firewall software, and antivirus software are recommended.

Whenever an attacker can install his or her own software on a laptop, he or she is likely to be able to bypass all security mechanisms. Once the attacker has physical custody of the laptop or an opportunity to install software, it is very difficult to stop him or her. Disabling boot up from a floppy or CD will help prevent an attacker from installing his or her own software or booting to another operating system to access sensitive data. The basic input/output system (BIOS) and hard disk passwords can help prevent a thief from using a stolen laptop or at least accessing the data. A screensaver with a password can also eliminate the window of opportunity that an attacker has to install software and make it more difficult for a thief to compromise a stolen laptop. Make sure blank passwords are not used for any accounts and that unnecessary accounts have been disabled.

These tips cannot prevent a skilled attacker or thief from compromising data on a laptop when he or she has physical custody. Many thieves are not interested in the data that may be contained on a stolen device; however, the previous tips can prevent a thief from accidentally stumbling on any important information.

# Personal Digital Assistants (PDAs)

Many types of PDAs are used in wireless applications. Some are used in a corporate environment. Other specifically designed PDAs are used in medical, industrial, or airport environments. Most special-purpose PDAs run Palm OS or Windows CE and have additional features such as internal wireless cards, barcode scanners, long-life batteries, or magnetic-strip readers. The primary feature of these devices is that they are easy to use. The users of these devices are not always the most technically inclined. Therefore, securing these devices or the applications that they access is a challenge.

### Problems

Many of the security features offered by the manufacturer cannot be relied on because the password protection is poor and many data storage applications are insecure. In addition, adding security features without losing the ease of use is difficult.

Most PDAs have a number of input mechanisms. These include wireless cards, infrared ports, memory devices, serial connections, universal serial bus (USB) connections, or Bluetooth. All of these input mechanisms are attack vectors that can be used to compromise the PDA. In addition, most PDAs have been designed to provide application developers with easy ways to debug applications. These debug interfaces can compromise the device.

PDAs suffer from the same kind of attacks that many Internet applications are vulnerable to—namely, buffer overflows and format string attacks. Because PDA programmers are not used to programming for security, many of these vulnerabilities will probably continue to exist.

Data on a PDA can be easily compromised by an attacker. To make matters worse, memory devices can be copied or backed up without leaving any trace so the user might not be aware that the data on the PDA has been compromised.

## Solutions

One way to secure the data that a PDA accesses is by not storing it on the PDA. This can be accomplished by having the PDA pull information off a secure back-end database or by using a Java or thin client application. Then the data is input from the PDA and displayed on it, but it does not require remote storage on the PDA. The drawback to this is that the application will only be accessible in the wireless coverage area.

As mentioned multiple times in this book, do not rely on client-side security. Client-side security is any mechanism that relies on trusting the client, which may be in malicious hands, to enforce a security mechanism —for example, trusting the client to submit information on login status. Many times this is a hidden field in a web application. The client could lie and say that he or she has logged in when he or she has not. Do not store sensitive encryption keys on a client because a single compromised client could compromise the entire application. Encryption keys should be rotated on a regular basis. If a key is compromised, the window of attack can be reduced.

Many PDAs have password lock features. We discussed that these features cannot be relied upon, but they will slow down an attacker. Sometimes an attacker will only have a limited time with the compromised device. The PDA lockout features will also make it more difficult for a thief to recover an application or data, and the thief can just reset the PDA and erase all the data to be able to use the stolen device. Disable any unnecessary input mechanisms. If your application does not need the infrared port, then disable it. Each mechanism that is unused and disabled reduces the attack vectors against the PDA.

If sensitive data is to be stored on the PDA, then consider using encryption. Historically, the PDA-based encryption mechanisms have been found to be vulnerable to a number of attacks, but they will slow down an attacker and may obscure the data from an attacker who was only after the device. If speed is a problem, consider using Elliptic Curve Cryptography (ECC) for all sensitive data. Even casual PDA users may store sensitive data, such as passwords or credit-card numbers. In addition to encrypting the data, always deploy a power-on and screen-lock password. These deterrents can be very valuable if your PDA falls into the wrong hands.

# Wireless Infrastructure

This section discusses the security issues pertaining to devices used for the infrastructure of wireless networks. This section primarily focuses on wireless networking components, such as access points and bridges, but the principles can be used for a variety of applications.

### Problems

Many wireless infrastructure devices are deployed in hostile environments. These environments include public places such as coffee shops, airports, or outdoors at the corporate campus. These devices are expensive and a target of thieves. Others may want access to these devices to either disable security features like the Extensible Authentication Protocol (EAP) or WEP, or reveal information about the configuration in order to compromise the network.

### Solutions

Management functions can be secured on a wireless infrastructure device by using secure protocols to access it, such as SSH, Secure Sockets Layer (SSL), or Simple Network Management Protocol version 3 (SNMP v3). In addition to using the secure management protocols, if available, insecure protocols such as telnet, cleartext Hypertext Transfer Protocol (HTTP), and SNMP v1 should be disabled. If secure management features are not available, some access points can be administered with a serial port. Inexpensive terminal servers can be used to manage the access points with the added benefit of out-of-band access and can also be used for other networking gear such as routers, modems, and switches that are in the same location. Do not forget to bolt down or lock up equipment in a hostile environment, especially if it is outside. Keeping access points mounted in high places can help prevent theft.

# Handsets

The security considerations for mobile phone handsets should mirror their larger siblings (laptops and PDAs). The problems that the security research community has discovered to date in mobile handsets are similar to those in any other mixture of hardware of software.

## Problems

Mobile handsets are vulnerable to the same types of digital attacks that have been discussed for the other types of wireless devices. These attacks normally take advantage of buffer overflows, format string attacks, or parsing errors, and enable an attacker to run code on the compromised device. An example of this is the short message service (SMS). Recent attacks have shown that the SMS handlers in mobile handsets are vulnerable to attacks resulting in a denial of service (DoS) or execution of commands on the handset. These problems have affected a large number of vendors including Nokia and Siemens, and more open platforms like PDA-based handsets.

In addition, a number of Subscriber Identity Module (SIM) manufacturers have included methods of developing additional proprietary functionality and deploying these applications via a wireless interface usually provides SMS to the relevant subscriber base. Examples of these environments are SimToolkit and MExE. The methods of stopping anyone from sending malicious applications to another user (that is, an application could potentially be sent via the air interface to pack up your phone book and/or SMS inbox and send it back to the attacker) are vulnerable to attack. Certain implementations rely on the Data Encryption Standard (DES); however, the same DES key is used for each SIM. This is a very good example of the potential to introduce and execute malicious code on a mobile platform from a totally wireless attack vector.

## Solutions

Always use a password or the handset-equivalent PIN. SIM PIN can be used to secure phones based on the Global System for Mobile Communications (GSM). To make the best use of this feature, be sure to use all the PINs available. Also, make sure that you note your International Mobile Equipment Identity (IEMI) (the serial number of your phone) and store it in a safe place.

When using your handset to send sensitive information, be sure to encrypt it. When using WAP to send credit-card numbers or other personal details, make sure that you are using Wireless Transport Layer Security (WTLS) (SSL-secured connections). In addition, a large number of attacks against the algorithms used within GSM enable an attacker to clone the SIM of the phone. These attacks normally require physical custody of the phone so be sure to keep your phone secure and notify your mobile operator in the event of loss or theft.

# Conclusion

The security of wireless devices must be seriously considered because it impacts the security of the entire network. Reasonable steps to securing wireless devices can have tremendous payoffs in the overall security of a wireless application. Vendor-provided security mechanisms cannot be relied upon for security, but they do provide a valuable first line of defense against malicious users or thieves. Even simple wireless devices can be hardened against attackers. Disabling unnecessary input mechanisms and functionality along with not relying on client-side security can foil many attacks. Additional details on how the entire application or network can be used to increase the security of your wireless application will be discussed in Chapter 8.

# PART 2

# Wireless Technologies and Applications

# CHAPTER 5

# Introduction to Cellular Networks

Radio spectrum is a finite resource. Unlike wired telephony where each phone has a physical link and a connection to the network, wireless systems have a fixed amount of spectrum available in a given geographic area. This requires wireless networks to share and allocate spectrum within a geographic area so that multiple users can place and receive calls simultaneously.

As the demand for cellular services increases, improved methods for handling wireless spectrum are required. Cellular services have created a virtual cycle. As technology has improved network capacity, more users have signed up for service, creating a demand for an even greater utilization of existing spectrum. When the wireless market matured in the 1980s and 1990s, three different spectrum allocation methods emerged:

- Frequency Division Multiple Access (FDMA)
- Time Division Multiple Access (TDMA)
- Code Division Multiple Access (CDMA)

Each technology is designed to provide access to a given frequency for multiple users (hence multiple access). Each technology uses a different method to divide that frequency into usable chunks (frequency-based division, time-based division, and code-based division). A brief technical review of each method is necessary to understand the pros and cons of each technology and the respective security mechanisms of each as well.

These three technologies all rely on the same fundamental architecture. Each geographic area is divided into cells (usually an area 1 km or less in diameter). Each cell allocates a channel to each individual user and two frequencies are used: one for sending voice and data from the handset to the cell site, and one for receiving voice and data from the cell site. Within each cell there are antennae and a base station that physically connects to other cells in the mobile network and to the wired telephone network. Figure 5-1 provides an overview of a typical cellular network configuration.

# FDMA

FDMA is the oldest frequency allocation method and was first used on the initial analog Advanced Mobile Phone System (AMPS) cellular systems built in the United States in the late 1970s. FDMA is often referred to as

**Figure 5-1**

Typical mobile telephone system

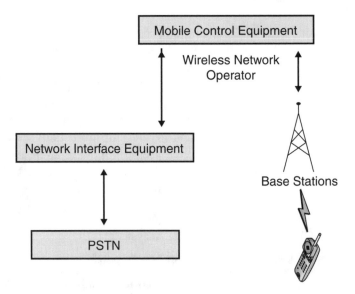

Narrowband Analog Mobile Phone Service (NAMPS). As the term implies, FDMA operates within a narrow frequency range.

FDMA's premise is simple. The available spectrum is divided into channels. Each channel can be used for a single conversation. This method is very similar to standard wired phone systems that allocate a single circuit for each conversation. FDMA also enables conversations to change channels if the transmission weakens. Figure 5-2 provides a simple diagram of FDMA.

FDMA's limitations became apparent as demand increased for AMPS systems. Because FDMA assigns channels even if no conversations are taking place, FDMA does not efficiently use available spectrum. Plus, FDMA is also only capable of voice transmissions; it cannot transmit data.

Owing to these limitations and to meet the growing demand for wireless voice and data, mobile carriers and equipment manufacturers sought better methods for spectrum management. As a result, few remaining FDMA implementations are in use today. For this reason, this chapter will focus on the more widely deployed successors to FDMA, CDMA and TDMA. Figure 5-3 shows the approximate distribution of these bearer technologies.

**Figure 5-2**

The principle of FDMA

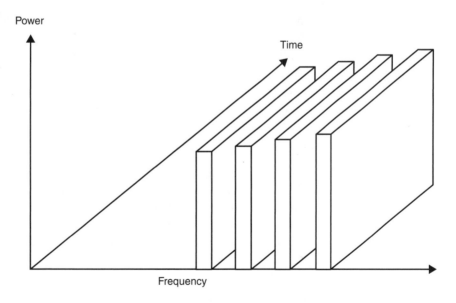

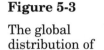

**Figure 5-3**

The global distribution of second-generation (2G) wireless technologies, 2000

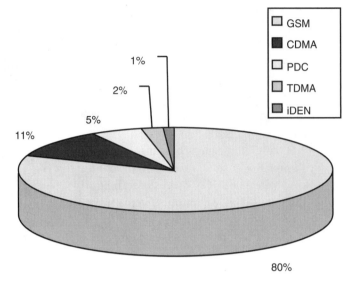

# TDMA

TDMA quickly emerged as a viable replacement to FDMA. Rather than using a single channel for each conversation, TDMA digitizes the voice signal and turns the signal into a series of short packets. TDMA then uses a single-frequency channel for a very short time and migrates to another channel. The voice packets can occupy different time slots in different frequency ranges at the same time, and the receiving end then reorganizes the packets to create the conversation. See Figure 5-4 for details.

TDMA offers the following benefits over FDMA:

- **Digital signal** Because TDMA digitizes the signal, the quality of wireless calls is significantly better than analog-based FDMA signals.

- **Better frequency allocation** TDMA provides significantly more cellular capacity than FDMA. Whereas FDMA requires a single channel for each conversation, TDMA can enable multiple conversations to proceed on a single channel. This enables more simultaneous conversations within a given cell. See Figures 5-5 and 5-6 for more detail.

- **Support for multiple data types** TDMA can easily handle voice, fax, and data transmissions, enabling network operators to offer other nonvoice services like the Simple Messaging Service (SMS) without significant changes to the network infrastructure.

**Figure 5-4**

The principle
of TDMA

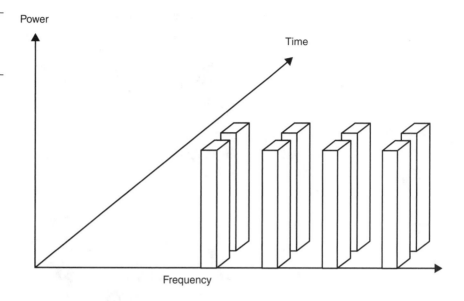

The following example helps demonstrate how TDMA works.

**Figure 5-5**

Four sample
conversations
(from www.iec.org
TDMA tutorial)

| A | Mary had a little lamb |
|---|---|
| B | Hickory Dickory Dock |
| C | Humpty Dumpty sat on a wall |
| D | Jack and Jill went up the hill |

**Figure 5-6**

TDMA
application
of those
conversations
(from www.iec.org
TDMA tutorial)

| RF Channel | Mary had a | Hickory, Dickory | Humpty Dumpty | Jack and Jill |
|---|---|---|---|---|
| Frequency 1 | Slot 1 | Slot 2 | Slot 3 | Slot 4 |

As the figures demonstrate, TDMA could capably divide an existing 30-KHz channel into three time slots that enabled three simultaneous conversations. This meant a tripling of capacity in a given cell. Plus, because TDMA was designed as an improvement to FDMA, the cost to upgrade from a FDMA network to TDMA was insignificant, making it easier for network operators to upgrade FDMA networks and provide better call quality, more capacity, and data services.

TDMA became the dominant wireless network standard in the 1980s and is also referred to by its standard number, IS-54. TDMA received a significant boost when the Global System for Mobile Communications (GSM) member nations selected TDMA as the basis for GSM networks, thereby making TDMA the most widely deployed wireless technology standard in terms of users. Figure 5-7 shows the migration of the TDMA standard over time.

# CDMA

Although CDMA only arrived commercially in the mid-1990s, the underlying concept behind CDMA dates back to the 1940s. In 1940, a Hollywood actress, Hedy Lamarr, and coinventor George Antheil, received a patent

**Figure 5-7**

TDMA standards evolution (from www.iec.org TDMA tutorial)

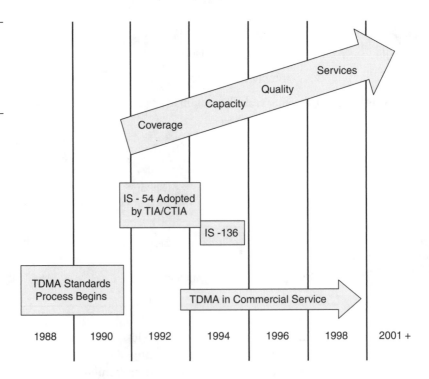

for devising a mechanism called frequency hopping, which enabled torpedoes to be controlled by sending signals over multiple radio frequencies using random patterns. This concept became known as frequency hopping spread spectrum (FHSS) technology. Although Lamarr and Antheil's invention was never widely adopted, it became part of the U.S. government's classified secure communications systems in the 1960s.

## Spread Spectrum Primer

Because CDMA is the only bearer technology that relies on spread spectrum, a brief description on spread spectrum is in order. Although CDMA is not technically a spread spectrum technology, CDMA is almost always used together with spread spectrum. As the title implies, spread spectrum utilizes a wider range of frequency to send a given signal than either TDMA or FDMA.

Utilizing a wider frequency range provides two main benefits. First, by sending a wireless signal over a wider frequency, spread spectrum actually increases signal quality and connections because it reduces the risk of signals not getting through. In narrowband systems, high usage at a given frequency can prevent signals from being placed, as any user who has experienced a dropped cellular call can attest. Second, spread spectrum techniques are more secure than narrowband systems because spreading the signals can decrease the risk of the signal being detected by unauthorized parties. Direct sequence spread spectrum and FHSS technology will be discussed later.

The application of FHSS techniques for wireless networks emerged under the name CDMA in the late 1980s. Pioneered by California-based Qualcomm Corporation, CDMA offered another mechanism for allocating wireless spectrum. CDMA's concept is simple: rather than dividing spectrum by time or frequency, CDMA adds a unique code onto each packet before transmission. The same code is used at the receiving end to enable the conversation to be reconstructed. CDMA thereby enables different conversations to utilize the same frequency band, providing excellent capacity.

## Analogy

Imagine a room with many people talking to each other in pairs. Each person can communicate with his or her pair partner because he or she can hear the other's voice amidst the other conversations in the same room. If each pair speak the same language (a unique code) that is different from all the other languages used in the room, the conversation between any given pair is much easier to understand because the correlation between one conversation and another (interference) is very low.[1]

Following Qualcomm's initial proposal to use CDMA in cellular systems in 1989, the Telecommunications Industry Association (TIA) published a CDMA standard called IS-95 in the summer of 1993. The first commercial CDMA network was launched in Hong Kong in 1995, but it soon migrated to Korea and the United States. By the year 2001, although TDMA was the most widely used technology, CDMA technology was the fastest growing. Figure 5-8 displays the growth of CDMA subscribers.

CDMA offers several benefits over TDMA and FDMA:

- **Stronger security**   Direct spread spectrum technologies like CDMA are more difficult to intercept because they use a greater spectrum range, which means that a much greater range of frequencies must be evaluated. This also makes jamming a CDMA signal much harder than TDMA- or FDMA-based systems.

- **Better frequency allocation**   CDMA increases spectrum capacity eight to ten times more than an equivalent FDMA system, and three to five times more than an equivalent TDMA system.

**Figure 5-8**

CDMA users worldwide, 1996–2000

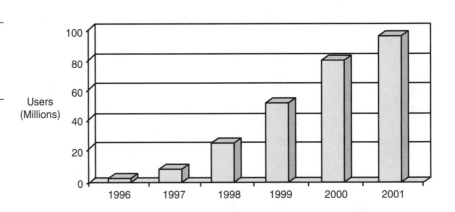

Calmers In-Start Group, 2001

---

[1]Sami Tabbane, *Handbook of Mobile Radio Networks*, Boston: Artech House, pp. 89-90.

▪ **Improved call quality** CDMA offers better and more consistent sound than FDMA systems.

▪ **Simplified system planning** By using the same frequency in every sector of every cell, CDMA networks are easier to plan and design.

Today, an open debate exists about CDMA versus TDMA. A passionate technological dialog has ensued as people debate the pros and cons of these technologies. The next section provides an unbiased view of the two technologies.

# TDMA Versus CDMA

The TDMA advantages are as follows:

▪ **Longer battery life** TDMA requires less transmitter power, which translates into longer battery life for handsets.

▪ **A less expensive infrastructure** TDMA's simplicity requires smaller and less expensive receivers and transmitters, making TDMA networks cheaper to build than CDMA networks.

▪ **Widest deployment** TDMA-based GSM networks are the most widely used wireless network technology, with over 500 million subscribers worldwide. This has led to rapid maturation of the TDMA technology and also makes TDMA attractive to suppliers because of the large market size and global reach.

▪ **International roaming** GSM's global presence enables subscribers to use the same GSM handset around the world.

▪ **Data security** TDMA-based GSM networks adopted the Subscriber Identity Module (SIM) card architecture for mobile handsets. The SIM card is a tamper-resistant smart card that resides on the handset and contains unique information for each subscriber. The security of the SIM card makes it an ideal platform from which mobile commerce services and transactions can be launched because the SIM can provide encryption and digital signatures for transactions.

The TDMA disadvantages are as follows:

■ **Hard roaming handoffs**   TDMA relies on "hard" handoffs when users travel between cell sites. Each user is allocated a time slot, but users traveling from one cell to another are *not* allocated a time slot. If all time slots in a cell are allocated, a new user traveling into that cell could be disconnected.

■ **Distortion**   TDMA signals have a lower signal-to-noise ratio than CDMA, creating the potential for more distorted signals.

The CDMA advantages are as follows:

■ **Bandwidth efficiency**   CDMA offers significantly improved bandwidth allocation, which gives CDMA networks additional capacity over TDMA networks.

■ **Soft roaming handoffs**   CDMA utilizes a technique called "soft" handoffs. When users roam between cells, the handset polls various cells and switches to the cell that offers the best signal and coverage. This theoretically leads to fewer dropped calls than TDMA networks.

■ **Less distortion**   CDMA offers an excellent signal-to-noise ratio, leading to very clear communication quality.

■ **Strong voice security**   CDMA's direct spread frequency technique makes it very secure.

The CDMA disadvantages are as follows:

■ **More expensive**   Owing to CDMA's complexity, CDMA infrastructure and equipment are more expensive than TDMA. This means that CDMA networks are typically more expensive to build than TDMA networks.

■ **No international roaming**   Because of its restricted geographic coverage, CDMA cannot offer international roaming like GSM.

■ **No SIM card**   Although CDMA offers excellent voice security, it does not provide an equivalent to the GSM SIM card. This means that mobile commerce services on CDMA networks have no tamper-resistant vehicle on the handset to store confidential information like private cryptographic keys, credit card numbers, and personal information.

So what do all these issues mean? Although the relative differences between TDMA and CDMA may be subtle, it is important to understand the differences because it can help a user decide which technology and service is most suitable for his or her individual needs. Table 5-1 lists five key issues to consider and which technology is the best fit for those needs.

Ultimately, a lot of decisions will rely on two simple criteria: coverage and economics. Even if you are not traveling globally, the decision should be based on which carrier provides the best price performance for that particular region. For instance, if you are based in Europe, CDMA is not even an alternative; only GSM networks are available. In this scenario, the decision will result from which GSM operator provides the best pricing plans, data services, and customer service.

# PDC

The last bearer technology to review is the Personal Digital Cellular (PDC) system. Although this standard is only deployed in Japan, the tremendous success of Japanese wireless operator NTT DoCoMo means that PDC is still third in the world in terms of subscribers, behind GSM and TDMA. Thus, it is worth a brief review.

PDC's architecture is based on TDMA and operates in the 800-MHz and 1500-MHz bands. PDC further divides available radio spectrum, enabling even greater cellular capacity than traditional TDMA. In the congested and mobile Japanese population, this is a huge benefit. PDC systems can operate in either a full-transmission rate or a half-transmission rate. As might be expected, the half rate enables twice as many as connections in a given frequency, but the tradeoff is slower throughput and a decreased signal-to-noise ratio, leading to a less clear signal. As Table 5-2 illustrates, PDC is more efficient than either traditional TDMA or GSM. The more channels (such as conversations) that can fit into a smaller frequency range, the better.

| | Criteria | Yes | No |
|---|---|---|---|
| **Table 5-1**<br><br>Key Considerations in Selecting a Wireless Voice Platform | Are users traveling globally? | GSM | CDMA |
| | Is voice security a top priority? | CDMA | GSM |
| | Are you planning mobile commerce transactions? | GSM | CDMA |
| | Are users highly mobile within a given area? | CDMA | GSM |
| | Is network congestion an issue? | CDMA | GSM |

**Table 5-2**

Comparison of Spectrum Efficiency (From http://www. mobilecomms-technology.com/ projects/pdc/)

| Technology | Frequency Space | Number of Channels |
|------------|-----------------|--------------------|
| PDC | 25 KHz | 3 |
| TDMA | 30 KHz | 3 |
| GSM | 200 KHz | 8 |

PDC systems also handle data traffic very efficiently. Japanese carrier NTT DoCoMo's extremely popular i-Mode service is based on PDC Packet Data (PDC-P) or PDC. Unlike other wireless data services in GSM that are based on circuit switches, PDC-P is packet-based, making it ideally suited for handling data transmissions. Owing to its packet architecture and efficient spectrum usage, PDC-P enables throughputs approaching 28.8 Kbps, which is considerably higher than the 14.4 Kbps maximum currently offered by GSM.

The advantages to PDC are as follows:

- **Bandwidth efficiency**   PDC offers superior bandwidth allocation over other TDMA technologies and even approaches CDMA's capacity capabilities.

- **Packet data**   PDC-P is a huge benefit because it aligns nicely with the intermittent transfer of data.

- **Easier migration to third-generation (3G) systems**   PDC-P provides a major evolutionary step and clear upgrade to 3G networks. Not surprisingly, NTT DoCoMo is the first world operator to offer 3G services.

PDC's disadvantages are as follows:

- **Limited availability**   PDC is only available in Japan.

- **No global roaming**   As PDC is only available in Japan, PDC phones have no roaming capabilities.

- **No SIM card**   Like CDMA, PDC does not use a tamper-resistant hardware module on the mobile handset.

Ultimately, PDC's importance in the overall wireless market is limited because this standard is gradually being phased out in Japan. As Japan aggressively moves towards 3G networks, the new networks will all be based on new technologies like Wideband CDMA (W-CDMA).

# iDEN: An Emerging Fourth Choice for American Consumers

In addition to plain TDMA (AT&T Wireless), GSM (Voicestream), and CDMA (Verizon and Sprint PCS), American consumers have a fourth wireless network technology alternative: the Integrated Dispatch Enhanced Network (iDEN), which is offered by Nextel. iDEN combines four wireless technologies: dispatch radio, traditional wireless voice, wireless messaging, and wireless data.

Nextel (initially called Fleet Call) traces its origins to another wireless market called Specialized Mobile Radio (SMR). SMR is a legacy wireless technology that was primarily used in the transportation industry (taxi drivers, ambulances, and courier services) for two-way communications. Nextel's vision was to adapt SMR technology to work on existing cellular networks, calling it Enhanced Specialized Mobile Radio (ESMR).

As James Murray explained, Nextel's founder, Morgan O'Brien, had a simple plan.[2] First, Fleet Call would buy up a majority of the SMR spectrum licenses in America's six biggest cities. Then, in each market, Fleet Call would consolidate the spectrum slices from multiple operators into a single large block, allocating the existing dispatch traffic more efficiently to just a couple of channels. This would leave potentially dozens of newly open channels, which could then be used to carry mobile-telephone traffic. The SMR phones wouldn't be as sophisticated as the newer cellular ones, but with cheap spectrum Fleet Call could afford to sell lower-priced service.

Nextel combined the simple functionality of a walkie-talkie with a cellular phone. More importantly, Nextel decided in the late 1980s to select a digital interface instead of analog. Working closely with partner (and eventual equity investor) Motorola, Nextel succeeded in amassing sufficient spectrum to offer a nationwide network. Nextel went live in 1991 and gradually built a nationwide network with over 6 million subscribers in 2001.

Because of the limited SMR spectrum in a given market, the initial SMR systems placed six conversations on a single channel, which severely reduced call quality. By comparison, CDMA and TDMA only allocate two to three conversations per single channel, and Nextel had has to revert to using three conversations per channel.

---

[2]James Murray, *Wireless Nation*, Cambridge, MA: Perseus Publishing, 2001, p. 254.

The iDEN advantage is as follows:

- **Two-way radio feature**   This enables Nextel subscribers to talk to each other by clicking a button, which utilizes the radio dispatch feature on the handset.

iDEN's disadvantages are as follows:

- **Limited geographic availability**   iDEN is only available in North and South America and some portions of Asia. This means that the service cannot offer the same coverage and roaming capabilities as GSM.

- **Single-vendor standard**   As iDEN is only offered by Nextel (and the only handset supplier is Motorola), consumers do not have significant choices for service plans and handsets. Furthermore, the smaller market size has limited competition and is not attractive to other suppliers.

# Security Threats

Now that the basic principles of frequency management in cellular systems have been introduced, a more detailed discussion on the security mechanisms of each system will be presented. Despite the technical differences, the security risks and threats faced by cellular networks are identical.

What are the network operators' primary security goals?

- **Authentication**   Be sure that only valid users are allowed to use the networks.

- **Privacy**   Ensure that conversations cannot be listened to.

- **Data and voice integrity**   Ensure that voice and data traffic cannot be read or compromised while in transit. Also confirm the validity of content and that the content has not been tampered with en route to the recipient. This is a critical requirement for the development of wireless transactions where users might digitally sign an order form on the mobile handset prior to transmission to the content provider.

- **Performance**   Although this is not a security goal per se, the underlying architectures must be highly scaleable and able to perform and process security transactions in a manner that is imperceptible to the user.

What specific security risks and threats must cellular networks contend with?

- **Network and systems availability**   Cellular networks are a vital component of any nation's communications infrastructure. Networks must be capable of withstanding *denial of service* (DoS) attacks or other attempts to bring the network down, either at a networkwide level or within an individual cell.

- **Physical protection**   Given the vast amount of cell sites and equipment that must be deployed remotely in untrusted areas, network operators must ensure that equipment is protected, tamper resistant, and secure. Unlike an enterprise network that can be protected by firewalls and confined within the physical boundaries of a building, mobile base stations must be deployed in a variety of terrains and climates. They must be able to withstand everything from a typhoon to physical intrusion.

- **Fraud**   Network operators must implement measures to prevent cloned or pirated handsets from operating on the network. By the late 1990s, the Cellular Telecommunications Industry of America (CTIA) estimated that cellular fraud cost the industry over $1 billion annually.

Of these three risks, fraud is the most significant and worth a more detailed review.

## Types of Cellular Fraud

There are several forms of cellular fraud. The most obvious is the physical theft of handsets. Although users usually notice the missing handset and quickly notify the network operator to mitigate the risk, it is still a problem and one of the simplest attacks to carry out successfully.

Other possible fraud involves users who sign up for valid service using false identification and billing information. These attacks are increasingly harder to complete successfully as network operators have implemented complex systems meant to track and identify fraudulent activity. In the United States, new subscribers are required to provide valid identification and a Social Security Number. This information is used to perform a credit check on the individual and determine the validity of the information before approving service.

The most costly form of cellular fraud is handset cloning. In this scenario, hackers copy the Electronic Serial Number (ESN) of a valid handset and reprogram another handset with that same serial number. Because the ESN is transmitted during the initiation of each wireless call, hackers with sophisticated eavesdropping equipment can retrieve an ESN, especially if the transmission is not encrypted.

Although billing systems are becoming more sophisticated and can often detect the simultaneous usage of a single serial number, hackers often resell cloned handsets in other geographic regions or countries. Because of the complexity of roaming relationships and potential response latency, it is hard to detect cloned handsets in these environments.

Cloning is usually identified when the valid subscriber receives his or her monthly bill and notices a significant difference in the invoiced amount. Initially, GSM networks were thought to be immune to cloning because of the complexity of cloning SIM cards, but cryptographers were able to crack GSM in the late 1990s.

Cloning is also made easier because the wireless network standards (TIA/EIA IS-95, TIA/EIA IS-136, and so on) are publicly available. Those willing to purchase the specification standards can use these documents to find a network's potential weaknesses.

## Combating Fraud

Network operators have adopted many measures to identify and prevent cellular fraud. Some of these measures include the following:

- **Encryption**   This can reduce fraud because it makes the theft of ESNs much more difficult. GSM networks also only transmit an ESN during the phone's initial use. For all subsequent calls, a temporary ESN is used to minimize fraud.

- **Blacklists**   Operators cooperate to track the ESNs of stolen phones. A central database enables network operators to disable stolen cellular phones on networks around the world.

- **Traffic analysis**   Operators can utilize sophisticated artificial intelligence software to detect suspicious calling patterns, such as a sudden increase in the length of calls or a sudden increase in the number of international calls. Thus, the software can help track possible fraud and, if necessary, disable an individual handset.

■ **Legislation** Many governments have enacted strict legislation that provides stiff penalties and fines for persons directly involved in cellular fraud. In the United States, the Cellular Telephone Protection Act became law in April 1998. This law made it a crime to knowingly possess, use, or traffic in hardware or software knowing it has been configured to alter or modify a cellular phone without authorization.

The growing nature of the mobile market further complicates fraud efforts. Owing to the vast amount of roaming agreements and interconnection agreements between carriers and a corresponding lack of real-time sharing of billing information, it is increasingly difficult for carriers to determine immediately if a roaming user is a valid one.

To fight fraud, the GSM member nations have established a Central Equipment Identity Register (CEIR) in Dublin, Ireland. This large database tracks all GSM handsets in use worldwide and also maintains a list of known pirated or fraudulent handsets. Three categories exist on the CEIR: white list, gray list, and black list.

The white list contains the International Mobile Equipment Identity (IMEI) ranges of all the mobile phones that are approved to operate on the GSM network.

The gray list contains the IMEIs of mobile phones that are *suspected* lost or stolen. Mobile phones on the gray list will still be able to place and receive calls, but network operators will be notified on the usage of all gray list phones.

The black list contains the IMEIs of mobile phones that are *confirmed* lost or stolen. Mobiles in the black category are not allowed to function on any GSM network.

In late 2000, an even simpler method of GSM cloning was discovered. This attack takes advantage of existing legislation in Western Europe that limits the export of strong encryption products to certain nations like Afghanistan, Iraq, and North Korea. Because the default version of the GSM standard does not utilize encryption, computer security experts determined that one could construct a phony base station to jam the signal from the real base station. This phony base station then communicates with the handset and tells the handset to turn off encryption. Through this process, the phony base station could communicate with the handset and retrieve crucial authentication information like the ESN in clear text.[3]

Cloning is also possible on CDMA networks, although it requires some more sophisticated techniques. Successful cloning on CDMA follows the same principles as GSM networks (such as the interception of a subscriber's ESN). However, CDMA networks use an additional mechanism called a base station spreading code, which complicates the retrieval of the ESN. In order to be successful, a CDMA hacker must crack a specific base station in order to obtain the spreading code. Once the spreading code is located, the ESN can be retrieved.

However, as Stuart Jeffery of Synacom points out, obtaining the spreading code is not as complicated as it seems. Because CDMA handsets must know the spreading codes to connect to the network, hackers could disassemble a standard CDMA phone, connect it to a PC, and obtain the spreading codes.

## General Security Principles

To avoid cloning problems and other security weaknesses, wireless network operators and suppliers have adopted numerous security mechanisms. The most basic mechanism is encryption, the process of transforming plain-text voice or data into a format that cannot be understood if intercepted.

Encryption operates on a simple premise. A encryption key is applied to a message that creates an encrypted message. The receiving party applies the same encryption key to decrypt and read the message in plain text. Figure 5-9 illustrates the basic cryptographic principle.

The relative strength of any encryption system is the size of the encryption key. The larger the key, the stronger the system because bigger keys mean that there are theoretically more possible keys to choose from, thereby making the successful discovery of a given key very time consuming.

---

[3]Sarah Robinson, "Cell Phone Flaw Opens Security Hole," *Interactive Week*, September 17, 2000 (http://zdnet.com.com/2100-11-502889.html?legacy=zdnn).

**Figure 5-9**

Basic principle of encryption

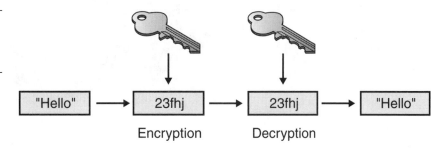

"Hello" → 23fhj → 23fhj → "Hello"

Encryption     Decryption

For instance, if an encryption key were simply a number between 0 and 99, a hacker has only 100 values to search to determine the proper key. A key could be recovered quite quickly by simply applying the 100 values in succession and examining the output. As computers have gotten faster, the capability to search all theoretical possibilities for a given key size (otherwise known as a brute force attempt) has improved significantly.

For example, in the early 1980s, 56-bit keys were the standard, meaning that there were $2^{56}$ possible key combinations. But by the late 1990s, security experts had proven that 56-bit keys could be successfully brute forced. These efforts required massive amounts of parallel computing power (tens of thousands of ordinary PCs simultaneously trying key combinations), but were still able to compromise a 56-bit Data Encryption Standard (DES) key in less than a day. Table 5-3 provides some rough calculations on the relative effort required to complete a brute force attack against given key sizes.

On the wireless side, longer key lengths become problematic because of the limited hardware and processing power on the handsets. For this reason, initial digital networks like GSM have relied on 64-bit keys, even though those have been proven susceptible to recent brute force attacks.

Encryption systems fall into two simple categories: symmetric key systems and asymmetric key systems. Symmetric systems (also known as secret key, single key, or one-key systems) function on a simple premise: the encryption key and the decryption key are the same value, or symmetric. In order to secure encrypted communications, the sender and receiver must possess the same key. The DES algorithm is a well-known example of a symmetric key algorithm.

Within the symmetric systems, the encryption algorithms are either block algorithms or stream algorithms. As the name implies, block algorithms transform blocks of data into an encrypted form. Most block

| Table 5-3 | Key Length | 32 bits | 40 bits | 56 bits | 64 bits | 128 bits |
|---|---|---|---|---|---|---|
| Key Size and Brute Force[4] | Time for years exhaustive search of all keys | 9 hours | 12 days | 2.3 years | 58.3 years | $10.8 \times 10^{38}$ |

[4]Statistics based on current capabilities of $10^9$ (1 billion) calculations per second and are only a benchmark. Additional hardware and expense can further reduce the calculations required.

algorithms process blocks of at least 64 bits in size. Stream algorithms transform individual bits of data into an encrypted form.

In asymmetric systems, different or asymmetric keys are used for encryption and decryption. Asymmetric systems are also known as public/private key systems. In public key systems, the encryption key can be made public, which offers a significant benefit over symmetric systems because it simplifies the key distribution process. The RSA algorithm is a well-known example of an asymmetric algorithm.

The term public in public key cryptography is symbolic in a significant manner. The relative strength of any security system rests on the ability of unaffiliated parties to test and examine the systems for any theoretical weaknesses. Keeping cryptographic algorithms secret from public review only invites suspicion and can lead to weaker cryptographic systems being implemented. This point is relevant in the wireless world as numerous security algorithms have not been subject to global peer review, which opens the door for weaknesses to be exposed on an unprepared public.

# Inside GSM

The GSM network architecture (shown in Figure 5-10) is comprised of eight main components:

- **Handsets with SIM cards**   The SIM card is a microprocessor smart card with about 32K to 64K electrically erasable programmable read-only memory (EEPROM) and is required for GSM networks. SIM cards are available in two sizes: full size (equivalent in size to a credit card) and a smaller version (about the size of a thumbnail). SIM cards securely store various pieces of

**Figure 5-10**

GSM architecture

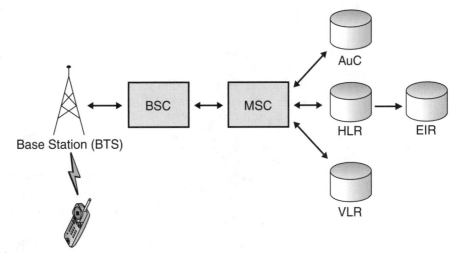

critical information, such as the subscriber's identity as well as the authentication and encryption algorithms responsible for providing legitimate access to the GSM network.

- **Base Transceiver Station (BTS)** The BTS is responsible for providing the wireless connection between the handset and the wireless network itself. There is one base station per cell site.

- **Base Station Controller (BSC)** The BSC manages multiple BTSs. Its main functions are spectrum allocation and management as well as handoffs between different base stations as mobile users move from cell site to cell site. Collectively, the base stations and BSCs compose the *Base Station Subsystem* (BSS).

- **Mobile Switching Center (MSC)** The MSC manages multiple BSCs and provides the physical connection to the wired telephony network. The MSC manages calls between mobiles and the wired network as well as handoffs between different BSCs. The MSC interfaces with four separate databases for maintaining and tracking subscriber information. Those four databases are the Home Location Register (HLR), the Visitor Location Register (VLR), the Equipment Identity Register (EIR), and the Authentication Center (AuC).

- **Authentication Center (AuC)** The AuC authenticates a SIM card.

- **Home Location Register (HLR)** The HLR is a database that stores and tracks all information about valid subscribers on the network where they originate (for example, a British Telecom subscriber's information is stored in British Telecom's HLR). Depending on the number of subscribers, an individual GSM operator may have multiple HLRs. The HLR stores information on the specifics of the user's subscription as well information on individual handsets, such as the International Mobile Subscriber Identity (IMSI) and Mobile Subscriber ISDN (MSISDN). The HLR also tracks where and when a user has roamed outside the home network.

- **Visitor Location Register (VLR)**  The VLR tracks information about roaming subscribers that are currently operating outside the home network (a British Telecom's VLR would track info about a French Telecom GSM subscriber currently in England). The VLR also stores the IMSI and MSISDN of roaming users. Most importantly, the VLR tracks the user and allocates the calls so that when a call is placed to a roaming user, the network knows where to route the call.

- **Operating and Maintenance Center (OMC)**  The OMC is responsible for the overall performance and management of the GSM network. The OMC communicates with the BSS and MSC, and it is usually connected via an X25 network.

## GSM Security

GSM's security architecture is a symmetric key system. GSM utilizes three primary security algorithms. The three algorithms are as follows:

- **A3**  An algorithm used to authenticate a handset to a GSM network.

- **A5/1 or A5/2**  A block cipher algorithm used to encrypt voice and data after a successful authentication. A5/1 is primarily used in Western Europe; A5/2 is utilized in other parts of the world.

- **A8**  A key generation algorithm used to generate symmetric encryption keys.

A3 and A8 are often referred to as COMP128.

It is worth noting that the GSM algorithms were developed by the GSM member nations and were not subject to independent peer review or analysis. As was previously noted, the public academic review of security algorithms is a crucial consideration for the long-term viability of any cryptographic system. Unfortunately, the GSM has chosen a more secretive review process, leading to widespread speculation about the relative strength of the algorithms themselves.

The initial security architecture was developed in the early 1990s. At the time, 64-bit key sizes seemed reasonable, given the current state of personal computing power. Unfortunately, rapid improvements in computing power and analysis now make 64-bit keys increasingly more susceptible to brute force attacks.

The first important step in the GSM architecture is authentication: definitively proving that a user and handset are authorized to use the GSM network. Beacuse the SIM card and mobile network possess the same encryption algorithm and symmetric key, they can establish a trusted connection. In the secure SIM personalization facility, these items are loaded onto the SIM.

The SIM cards for the mobile handsets are personalized by the operator with the necessary cryptographic protocols, keys, and algorithms. The SIM cards are then distributed to retail outlets for distribution to new subscribers. Two kinds of SIM cards are available: Phase 1 and Phase 2. Phase 1 cards only have 3K of memory for storing alphanumeric numbers. Phase 2 cards have 8K of memory and can store alphanumeric numbers and SMS messages.

Upon initial purchase, the SIM card contains the following data:

- **IMSI**   This is the same as an electronic serial number.
- **Individual Subscriber's Authentication Key ($K_i$)**   128 bits in length.
- **A3 and A8 algorithms**
- **User PIN code**
- **Pin Unlocking Key (PUK)**   Only needed if user forgets PIN.

Depending on the network operator's service plan, individual GSM subscribers may also store individual phone numbers and SMS messages on the SIM card. This provides portability in the event that the user changes handsets.

The MSCs possess copies of A3, A5, and A8 algorithms; these are usually stored on a protected hardware device.

## What Is SS7?

A point that is often overlooked in discussions of cellular networks is the physical connection these networks must maintain with the traditional Public Switched Telephone Network (PSTN). People often think of wireless risks as being confined to the handsets and base stations, but the wired network is still a vital component because many wireless calls have to connect to the wired network. Because the cellular authentication process interfaces with the PSTN, a secure interface between wireless and wired networks is essential. This is why the International Telecommunications Union (ITU) created the Common Channel Signaling System No. 7 or SS7 standard.

The SS7 standard defines the procedures and protocol through which networks exchange information. SS7 is basically a digital signaling protocol and network. Information between a wireless network (like authentication information) and the PSTN is handled as an SS7 message. The typical throughput is around 64 Kbps, but most importantly, SS7 communication is handled on dedicated out-of-band channels (not on voice channels).

## GSM Authentication

When a called is placed from a mobile phone, the GSM network's VLR authenticates the individual subscriber's phone. The VLR immediately communicates with the HLR, which in turn retrieves the subscriber's information from the AuC. This information is forwarded to the VLR and the following process commences:

1. The base station generates a 128-bit random value or challenge (called RAND) and transmits it to the phone.

2. The phone encrypts a RAND with A3 and the $K_i$. This calculation results in a 32-bit *signed response* (called an SRES).

3. Simultaneously, the VLR calculates the SRES. This is easy because the VLR possesses the $K_i$, a RAND, and a copy of A3.

4. The phone transmits the SRES to a base station and it is forwarded to a VLR.

5. The VLR checks the SRES value from the phone against the SRES calculated by the VLR.

6. If the SRES values match, the authentication is successful and the subscriber may utilize the network (see Figure 5-11).

7. If the SRES values do *not* match, the connection is terminated and the failure is reported to the handset.

This simple process offers two significant benefits:

■ **The $K_i$ stays local.** Because the authentication key is the most essential authentication component, protecting that key is very important. In this model, the $K_i$ is never transmitted over the air and thus is not susceptible to interception. The $K_i$ is only present in the

**Figure 5-11**

GSM
authentication

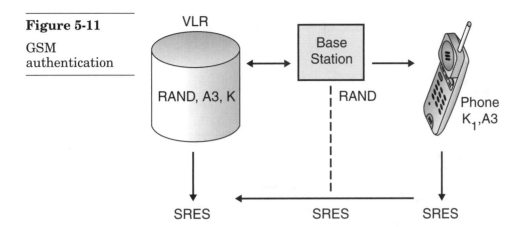

Do SRES calculations match?

SIM card and in the AuC, HLR, and VLR databases. The SIM card is tamper-proof, and network operators restrict physical access to these databases to minimize the risk of compromising a specific subscriber's authentication key.

- **Protection is provided against brute force attacks.** A 128-bit RAND means that there are $2^{128}$ or $3.4 \times 10^{38}$ possible combinations. Even if a hacker knows the A3 algorithm, calculating all the possible SRES values for each given RAND is computationally complex. This makes the probability of determining a valid RAND/SRES pair very remote.

## GSM Confidentiality

After a successful authentication, the GSM network and handset complete a process to establish an encrypted digital link between the handset and the network. Two simple steps must be completed. First, an encryption key must be generated. Second, that key must be used to encrypt the communication. Figure 5-12 outlines the steps.

1. A SIM card takes the previously received 128-bit RAND, combines it with the $K_i$, and uses an A8 algorithm to generate a 64-bit *session key* ($K_c$).

**Figure 5-12**

The GSM
confidentiality
process

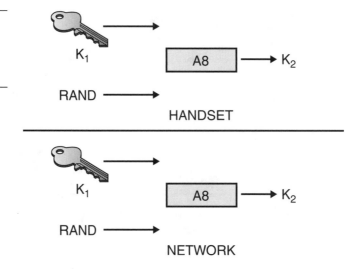

2. The GSM network repeats the same calculation to verify the
   subscriber's identity because the network knows the RAND and has a
   copy of the $K_i$.

3. The $K_c$ is combined with the A5 algorithm to create encrypted voice
   and data communications between the handset and the GSM
   network.

Session keys may also be reused, as this helps improve network performance and reduces the potential for delays resulting from performing
multiple cryptographic operations.

The last step involves subscriber identification. It is essential for the
operator to be able to provide real-time billing information. Subscriber
identification is conducted with two values: the $K_i$ and the IMSI value.

Because the IMSI is a unique value and can be used for illegal cloning
purposes, efforts must be made to minimize the broadcast of the IMSI
over the airwaves. Therefore, the IMSI is only transmitted during the first
time a new handset is actually used. For every subsequent connection, the
networks rely on the Temporary Mobile Subscriber Identity (TMSI).

The TMSI is sent to the mobile station after the authentication and
encryption procedures have taken place. The mobile station responds by
confirming the reception of the TMSI. The TMSI is valid in the location
area in which it was issued. For communications outside the location
area, the Location Area Identification (LAI) is necessary in addition to
the TMSI.

## GSM Algorithm Analysis

The GSM cryptographic algorithms (A3, A5, and A8) were developed privately by the GSM Memorandum of Understanding (MoU) member nations. No global cryptographic review of the protocols or design took place. As mentioned previously, the public review of cryptographic algorithms is essential to the long-term viability of any security architecture.

Unfortunately, GSM members did not follow an open review process. Instead, GSM members created a clandestine committee, the Security Algorithm Group of Experts (SAGE), to develop security algorithms privately. Although SAGE was comprised of leading cryptographers and successfully developed the A3, A5, and A8 algorithms, the closed door review process meant that the GSM members did not benefit from a global analysis of the architecture. Furthermore, efforts to keep the GSM algorithms secret proved impossible. The Internet accelerated interest and debate in the A series of algorithms and during the mid-1990s, information about the algorithms slowly leaked into the public domain. The sudden availability of information about these algorithms, combined with the high profile of the GSM architecture, made these algorithms a tempting target for amateur and professional cryptographers alike. Not surprisingly, the greater scrutiny soon exposed some rather significant weaknesses in the algorithms.

The first published (and provable) attacks occurred in April 1998 when researchers at the University of California, Berkeley, uncovered weaknesses in the A3/A8 algorithms. The specific weaknesses enabled the cloning of GSM phones. Although the initial analysis required physical access to a GSM handset and a SIM card for a period of time to complete a successful cloning exercise, the researchers later noted that over-the-air cloning was increasingly possible as well.[5]

The Berkeley researchers' analysis uncovered several startling facts. First, although A3 claimed to use 64-bit keys, the last 10 bits of the keys had been left blank, resulting in an equivalent key size of only 54 bits. Since 56-bit keys had already proven susceptible to massive parallel-computing-organized brute force attacks, this information now meant that 54-bit A3 keys could be successfully attacked with brute force in a reasonable period of time.

---

[5]http://www.isaac.cs.berkeley.edu/isaac/gsm-faq.html.

The Berkeley team's approach was quite simple. Using a given SIM, the team challenged the SIM with selected queries. The SIM's responses were analyzed and the secret $K_i$ was determined. The attack was conducted with simple hardware, including the GSM phone/SIM combo, a standard smart card reader, and a PC. The process to retrieve the $K_i$ was accomplished in less than eight hours. Once successful, this attack enables the creation of a SIM with the same $K_i$ and the placement of fraudulent calls on the network.

The industry quickly moved to counter these published attacks. The North American GSM Alliance, LLC, consisting of the eight largest GSM network operators in the United States and Canada, responded within a week of the A3/A8 attacks and stressed the following issues:[6]

- There was no risk to subscribers. GSM's design process and proven functionality continues to offer the strongest level of commercial wireless security. Thieves could easily steal GSM phone service simply by stealing wireless handsets, rather than producing counterfeit SIM cards.

- The weakened key size of A3 was not relevant because the GSM deliberately left those bits blank so that operators could localize the A3 implementation to meet their needs. In other words, the algorithm that was broken may not be the same as what is actually deployed, and actual A3 key sizes were likely closer to the original 64 bits.

- This attack did not involve the voice encryption algorithm (A5); thus, GSM conversations were not susceptible to eavesdropping. As long as A3 was safe, there was no risk of over-the-air eavesdropping.

Unfortunately for the industry, weaknesses in the A5 algorithm were uncovered a year later, meaning that the entire basis of the GSM security architecture had been exposed. Cryptographers Alex Biryukov, Adi Shamir, and David Wagner (author of the original A3/A8 analysis) published a paper that described in detail how the A5/1 algorithm could be broken.[7]

---

[6]The following excerpts are taken from "North American GSM Carriers Respond to Recent Publicized Attacks," *Business Wire*, April 20, 1998.

[7]The paper is available at www.cryptome.org/a5.ps.

Some initial setup was required, but once in place, the processing could be completed on an ordinary PC. An industry that a year earlier had proclaimed that eavesdropping was not an issue now found themselves confronting that very issue.

The A5 weaknesses also renewed discussions about the influence of politics in determining cryptography policy. Bruce Schneier pointed out that in the initial GSM design discussions, Western Europe intelligence agencies debated whether GSM encryption should be made deliberately weaker.[8] Germany wanted strong cryptographic protection because of their proximity to the Soviet Union, but they were eventually overruled, leading to the weakened A5 design.

Following these attacks, the GSM members tried to counter the growing concerns about the security weaknesses. However, GSM operators faced a sobering thought. Remedies to this situation were cost prohibitive. Changing any of the security algorithms would require new SIM cards for every subscriber as well as upgrades to the networks to support the new algorithms. As is typical in most information security issues, operators had to weigh the cost of a remedy against the risk of continuing with a system with known weaknesses. Ultimately, operators chose to postpone fixing the current GSM architecture, but decided to design better and more public algorithms in future 3G networks.

The growing awareness about potential chinks in GSM's armor also led to several new encrypted phone products appearing in the marketplace. Although proprietary secure terminals had long been used by military and government agencies, companies began offering secure encrypted handsets that provided another barrier against eavesdropping. In May 2001, a German company began offering its TopSec GSM handset that was based on a Siemens handset, but added a cryptographic chip that was capable of asymmetric and symmetric encryption for voice and data security.[9]

Although the handset's $2,000-plus price tag meant it was not targeted at the mass market, the mere availability of the product demonstrated the

---

[8]Bruce Schneier, *Applied Cryptography*, New York: John Wiley, 1996, p. 389.

[9]Rick Perera, "Encryption Comes Calling on Mobile Phone," *PCWorld*, May 31, 2001 (http://www.pcworld.com/news/article/0,aid,51368,00.asp).

demand for improved security. Plus, the phone (and others like it) suffered from two significant weaknesses:

- In order to enable end-to-end security to function, the receiving party must also possess this phone (or a similarly equipped encrypted ISDN line).

- Certain governments strictly regulate (and in some cases prohibit) usage of encrypted phones for commercial purposes.

These published weaknesses on GSM cryptographic protocols taught the industry several important lessons. First, secretive cryptographic design is a slippery slope. It invites public suspicion and hacker attention, and it becomes increasingly difficult to regulate and control. Second, sound cryptography requires a review process that must be as public as possible. The review process only strengthens security. Although the GSM may have suffered some public embarrassments with these papers, the good news is that the industry has learned from past mistakes. Fortunately, the GSM community has embraced a public review process for future 3G networks.

# Inside CDMA

CDMA networks function on a symmetric key architecture like GSM. The biggest difference is that CDMA networks lack a tamper-resistant SIM card on each handset. Otherwise, the underlying network architecture is fundamentally the same.

Like GSM, authentication is the most important security component of the CDMA network. Without handset authentication, there is no voice or data encryption, and the cloning risks are considerably greater.

CDMA handsets utilize a 64-bit symmetric key (called the A-Key) for authentication. This key is programmed into the handset at the retail outlet and is also saved by the network provider. Software in the handset calculates a simple checksum to verify that the A-Key value has been properly entered.

Owing to the complications of an individual subscriber manually entering an A-Key into a handset, operators have developed devices that can automatically load the A-Key into the handset and transmit the key to the network's database. However, as Stuart Jeffery amazingly pointed out, some network operators have, with the purpose of simplifying subscriber signup, loaded default (all zero) A-Keys into handsets. This is the same thing as having no A-Key at all and opens the door to significant fraud opportunities as cloners can easily detect that default A-Keys are in use and can fully exploit the network. It is for this reason that operators should fully utilize random A-Keys.[10]

Much like the $K_i$ in the GSM world, maximum protection must be applied towards the A-Key. This applies to the handset itself, but also to the network operator. Like the AuC in GSM, CDMA operators restrict physical access to the machines storing the A-Keys.

## Why Not Use Public Keys for Cellular Authentication?

Since all major cellular systems have adopted symmetric key systems for authentication and privacy, people often wonder why asymmetric key systems were never utilized. Asymmetric systems offer several benefits over symmetric key systems, especially in simplifying the key distribution process. However, several factors have influenced the adoption of symmetric systems in initial wireless telephony projects:

- **Hardware limitations**   Asymmetric systems are significantly more computationally complex to process mainly because of the significantly larger key sizes (512, 1,024, or 2,048 bits in length). The computation required for asymmetric systems is easily handled on a PC, but the initial GSM mobile phones contained very slow processors. This meant that public or private key calculations might take several seconds or longer, which was clearly not acceptable to end users. An emerging asymmetric alternative is Elliptic Curve Cryptography (ECC), pioneered by Certicom Corporation. ECC is an asymmetric system whose main benefit is its utilization of 160-bit keys. The underlying math behind ECC is quite complex, but ECC provides equivalent security to RSA with much smaller key sizes, making it ideally suited for today's 2G networks.[11]

---

[10]http://www.cdg.org/library/spectrum/Oct98/fraud_9810.asp.

[11]A good primer to ECC can be found in Carlton Davis' *IPSec: Securing VPNs*, New York: McGraw-Hill, 2000.

■ **Infrastructure requirements** Although handsets have gotten considerably more powerful and capable of processing asymmetric cryptographic systems, the cost of upgrading existing CDMA and GSM networks to support asymmetric systems is prohibitively expensive. Operators are instead looking at introducing asymmetric cryptographic systems into future 3G networks.

One must be careful when comparing symmetric and asymmetric systems. They are not the same and are utilized for different purposes. As Bruce Schneier notes, "Which is better, public key cryptography or symmetric cryptography? This question doesn't make any sense . . . The debate assumes that the two types of cryptography can be compared on equal footing. They can't."[12]

## CDMA Authentication

When a call is placed from the handset, the CDMA network's VLR authenticates an individual subscriber. CDMA networks also utilize an encryption algorithm called Cellular Authentication and Voice Encryption (CAVE).

To minimize the risk of intercepting an individual A-Key in the air, CDMA handsets derive a dynamic value for authentication based on the A-Key. This dynamic value is called the *shared secret data* (SSD) and is calculated using three values:

■ The individual subscriber's A-Key

■ The ESN of the individual's handset

■ A random number

These three values are hashed using the CAVE algorithm. This operation generates two 64-bit values, SSD_A and SSD_B. SSD_A is designated for authentication, while SSD_B is designated for encryption algorithms. SSD_A is equivalent to GSM's SRES, and SSD_B is equivalent to GSM's $K_c$. See Figure 5-13 for details.

When roaming, SSD_A and SSD_B are transmitted to the visiting mobile network unencrypted. This has presented some security challenges because hackers can retrieve SSD values and use them to clone

---

[12]Bruce Schneier, *Applied Cryptography*, New York: John Wiley, 1996, p. 216.

**Figure 5-13**

CDMA
authentication
key operations

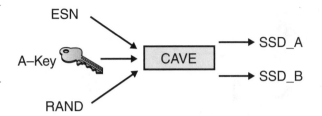

handsets. To combat this, the handset and network utilize a synchronized call counter. This counter is updated on the network and handset with each new call. This helps detect cloned SSDs whose counter values do not match.[13]

The CDMA authentication process is also based on challenge responses and enables the authentication to be conducted by the local MSC or AuC. If an MSC cannot complete CAVE calculations (the physical hardware containing CAVE is not present, for instance), authentication is handled by the AuC (see Figure 5-14). These are the steps in CDMA authentication:

**1.** A mobile phone commences a call.

**2.** The MSC retrieves subscriber information from the HLR.

**3.** The MSC generates a 24-bit random number for unique challenge (RANDU).

**4.** A RANDU is transmitted to the phone.

**5.** The phone receives the RANDU; combines it with SSD_A, ESN, and MIN; and hashes it with CAVE, resulting in an 18-bit value called AUTHU.

**6.** Simultaneously, MSC calculates its own AUTHU based on SSD_A, MIN, ESN, and CAVE.

**7.** AUTHU is transmitted to MSC.

**8.** If the AUTHU values match, the call proceeds.

**9.** If the AUTHU values do *not* match, the call cannot proceed.

---

[13]Sami Tabbane, *Handbook of Mobile Radio Networks*, Boston: Artech House, 2000, p. 197.

**Figure 5-14**

CDMA authentication process (From www.nacn.com/ industry/ industry_ faqitem2_ frame.htm)

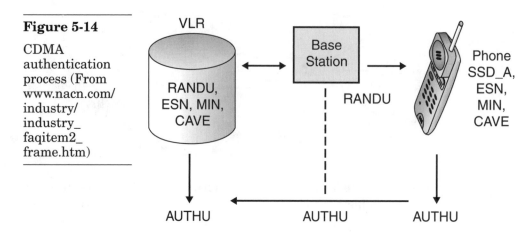

Do AUTHU calculations match?

The CDMA authentication process offers similar benefits to those provided by GSM, such as the following:

- **The A-Key stays local.** The A-Key is never transmitted over the air, and thus is not susceptible to interception. However, since CDMA handsets lack a tamper-resistant storage mechanism like a SIM card to store the A-Key, handsets have to be designed to make the A-Key inaccessible to anyone.

- **Protection is provided against brute force attacks.** A 128-bit RAND means that there are $2^{128}$ or $3.4 \times 10^{38}$ possible combinations. This makes the probability of determining a valid RAND/AUTHU pair very remote.

### CDMA Confidentiality

Voice encryption is implemented in CDMA in a similar fashion to GSM. While conducting the authentication process described earlier, the CDMA handset also completes the following steps:

1. The phone receives a RAND; combines it with SSD_B, ESN, and MIN; and hashes it with CAVE, resulting in an 18-bit value called a Voice Privacy Mask (VPMASK).

**2.** Simultaneously, MSC calculates its own VPMASK using a RAND, SSD_B, ESN, MIN, and CAVE.

**3.** VPMASK is used to create encrypted voice and data communications between the handset and the CDMA network.

A similar process is also used to create a 64-bit data encryption key called the Signaling Message Encryption Key (SMEKEY).

Although the CDMA specification enabled encrypted voice communications, North American CDMA network operators did not always utilize the VPMASK capabilities. Why?

- **Government regulation**   Prior to January 2000, the U.S. government regulations for encryption products were extremely strict. Companies wanting to export encryption products greater than 40-bit key sizes had to request approval from the U.S. Department of Commerce. Encryption products were lumped in the same export control category as nuclear arms and chemical weapons. Although this policy was ultimately relaxed in January 2000, the specter of government regulation over encryption products was a deterrent to companies even developing products with strong encryption capabilities. Qualcomm, considered the father of CDMA technology, endured considerable battles with the U.S. government to try and export CDMA hardware to Southeast Asia and China.

- **Government monitoring**   In the 1990s, the U.S. government consistently pursued policies that sought to maintain government influence over cryptographic systems. For instance, the government aggressively fought (and ultimately lost) a battle over key escrow. This policy would have required makers of cryptography products to maintain a backdoor that government agencies (notably law enforcement) could use to monitor and potentially decipher communications between criminals.

- **The perception of CDMA's superior security**   CDMA's spread spectrum techniques and random codes were widely considered harder to crack than GSM-based TDMA signals. For these reasons, carriers and users often did not perceive the additional need for voice encryption.

This environment meant that encrypted voice remained a delicate issue in Washington, which was reluctant to lose the capability to monitor conversations. Therefore, despite the presence of voice privacy in the CDMA specification, users were usually not able to benefit from it.

### CDMA Algorithms Analysis

Much like the GSM security algorithms, the CDMA algorithms (notably CAVE) were designed privately without widespread public analysis. Surprisingly, CAVE has been able to remain relatively secret, so published attacks against CAVE still have not appeared as of 2001. The lack of published attacks should not be interpreted as a sign of CAVE's strength. Judging from the secretive review process, it is highly probable that CAVE may possess some theoretical weaknesses.

Fortunately, the CDMA community is gradually migrating towards the adoption of publicly referenced security algorithms that will considerably improve the underlying security of CDMA networks. It is also worth noting that future CDMA architectures call for a SIM equivalent. The Removable User Identity Module (R-UIM) will further improve CDMA's security by providing a secure tamper-resistant hardware module on the handset to store cryptographic keys and algorithms. This will place CDMA handset security on par with GSM and enable CDMA operators to offer additional value-adding mobile commerce services.

## Cellular Network and Security—What Next?

The ten-year period from 1991 to 2001 saw dramatic changes in the wireless landscape. The industry moved rapidly from slow, constrained analog networks to high-performing digital networks. These changes, coupled with a global economic boom, led to a robust and fast-growing wireless market.

Unfortunately, as the previous sections demonstrated, cellular network's security architectures were gradually exposed to significant weaknesses as the 1990s drew to a close. Fraud continued to remain a costly problem for the industry, but the cost of fixing the network was actually more expensive, so things remained status quo.

Despite the new security weaknesses in CDMA and GSM, several things occurred to bring optimism into the future outlook for wireless security. First, the highly publicized attacks raised awareness within the industry and galvanized support for building more secure designs into future networks. Second, global restrictions on cryptography (most notably in the United States) were gradually relaxed. This meant that the macro environment surrounding cellular security was considerably more willing to adopt sufficiently secure wireless algorithms and infrastructures.

An important first step in fixing the security problems in GSM occurred with the creation of the Third-Generation Partnership Project (3GPP). This organization contained members from the main telecommunications standards bodies in North America, Europe, Africa, and Asia. The 3GPP was tasked with designing the technical specifications of 3G networks that would be built upon existing GSM networks.

The 3GPP contains numerous committees and working groups tasked with developing 3G standards for everything from radio interfaces to roaming. A technical specifications group (TSG) has been established for security, but even more importantly, this committee's work is publicly available on the Internet, proving to all that the GSM members are not prepared to duplicate the secretive design review process of the past.

The security TSG's mission is straightforward: to enhance the current security provided by GSM networks. Beginning in the late 1990s, the 3GPP team began vigorously evaluating the existing GSM architecture and determining areas of improvement. The goal was not to redesign the entire GSM authentication and confidentiality schema, but rather to improve certain areas where weaknesses had been identified.

The TSG quickly identified the following areas of improvement:[14]

- **Poor algorithms** The TSG openly admitted the published weaknesses of the A5 and COMP128 algorithms, and of the secretive processes that created them. This meant that 3G networks needed better and more public security algorithms.

- **Lack of mutual authentication** The current GSM security scheme authenticated the handset to the network, but not the network to the handset. This led to the published attacks about creating false base stations that could retrieve subscriber's information unknowingly. Related to this was an admission that current GSM security was passive; except for some wireless transactions, users had no notification that security and encryption were actually in use.

- **Inflexible system** Existing GSM security did not easily enable incremental changes to security architectures. Unlike PCs that could

---

[14]From a presentation given by Mike Walker, chairman of the 3GPP Security Group, at Euro-crypt in 2000. The presentation is available at www.esat.kuleuven.ac.be/cosic/eurocrypt2000/mike_walker.pdf.

load patches or security fixes, the GSM infrastructure was not well suited to handle incremental security fixes.

- **Insecurity of backend networks**  GSM networks transferred security-sensitive information such as authentication keys over SS7 links that are susceptible to interception.

The 3GPP group immediately focused on improving the *Authentication and Key Agreement* (AKA) protocol in 3G networks. The AKA contained the following requirements:

- Mutual authentication should be availablef or mobile to network systems and vice versa.

- Larger key sizes. Ciphering keys should be upgraded from the current 64 bits to 128 bits.

- Maintain the uniqueness of ciphering keys (ensure that ciphering keys are not reused).

- Standard algorithms should be used to simplify roaming between different networks. Algorithms also need to be freely exported.

The resulting 3G authentication architecture looks like Figure 5-15. The main difference is that additional security parameters were calculated that can be used for authenticating the network to the user.

The 3GPP also made significant strides in algorithm design and review. Rather than creating something from scratch, the 3GPP selected an exist-

**Figure 5-15**

The 3GPP AKA protocol

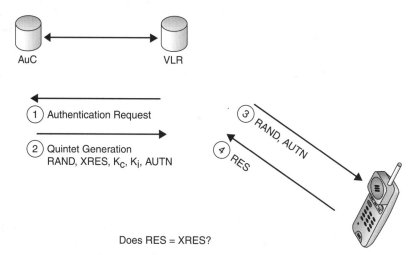

Does RES = XRES?

ing Japanese block cipher called MISTY, modified it, and renamed it Kasumi. This is the basis of 3GPP's replacements for A5/1 and A5/2. The new algorithms are currently called f8 and f9.

More important than the algorithm selection was the process itself. The 3GPP adhered to a rigorous third-party review of Kasumi, f8, and f9, and they published the algorithm specifications. This led to greater confidence in the future 3G security architecture. The mere publication of these specifications before the networks were actually implemented was a major achievement for the GSM community and will only improve the underlying security.

Across the Atlantic, the United States was considering mechanisms to improve security in U.S. cellular networks. Led by the National Institute of Standards and Technology (NIST), similar findings were reached regarding the current 2G digital cellular networks in the United States. Here are the five main shortcomings:[15]

- No mutual authentication

- Poor security algorithms; CAVE not widely studied

- No consistent SIM card mechanism on handsets for key storage

- Voice encryption not always available

- Limited intranetwork compatibility

These findings led the United States to evaluate various alternatives, including two new concepts called enhanced subscriber authentication (ESA) and enhanced subscriber privacy (ESP). Because the future of 3G networks in the United States is unclear, the United States has not advanced as far in new architecture as 3GPP, but they have already identified several likely enhancements, including the following:

- Replacing CAVE with a published algorithm. Likely candidates include the Secure Hash Algorithm (SHA-1). The new algorithm will also increase key size from 56 bits to 128 bits. SHA-1 was originally designed by the United States National Security Agency and is widely reviewed and understood.

- For a new authentication process, NIST is considering adopting 3GPP's AKA scheme, but asymmetric systems are also being considered.

---

[15]Presentation by Doug Rahikaa, "NIST-KMS Key Management Standard User Perspectives/ Requirements: Wireless Applications." February 10, 2000.

▪ Compatibility with other global standards, notably 3GPP's architecture. This is crucial in order to realize the 3G dream of truly global roaming.

Although these new security architectures must still be implemented and deployed in these networks, the new architectures still represent significant steps forward in designing secure cellular telephony networks. The move towards public algorithms and review processes is evidence that the wireless industry understands the importance of security in future 3G networks.

However, one must remember that although the industry is introducing notable improvements into 3G networks, the relatively slow adoption of 3G networks means that legacy 2G networks will still exist alongside new 3G networks. This fact, coupled with the industry's apparent legacy to address security issues in legacy systems, means that users should still remain aware of these security issues and base security policies and infrastructures on these facts.

# The Future

So what does the future of cellular networks hold? Although network operators are migrating towards 3G networks, the competing GSM and CDMA factions are introducing a host of new network standards and technologies. Availability varies by region and technology, but the underlying premise is improved throughput on handsets as well as better spectrum utilization and capacity. Although Chapters 6 and 11 will provide more detail on these emerging new technologies, the basic concepts will be introduced here.

With the wireless market already segregated into three camps (TDMA, GSM, and CDMA), each representative industry player has developed mechanisms to improve throughput. It is worth noting that much of these enhancements are aimed at improving data throughput. The voice issue has already been solved, and each technology does an excellent job of providing high-quality digital cellular voice. Table 5-4 provides a sense of the multiple wireless technology available.

Where the network operators have lagged has been in wireless data. Today, with the exception of Japan, all wireless data are circuit based. This is expensive for carriers and very slow for users. The natural pro-

**Table 5-4**

Bearer
Technologies
(*Network
Computing*,
November, 2000)

| | Service | Data Capability | Availability |
|---|---|---|---|
| GSM | Circuit-switched data | 9.6 Kbps to 14.4 Kbps | Now |
| | HSCSD | 28.8 Kbps to 56 Kbps | Limited rollout in Europe/Middle East/ Africa (EMEA) today |
| | GPRS | IP-based with 28.8 Kbps to 56 Kbps | Now |
| | EDGE | IP up to 384 Kbps | Initial deployments in 2002 |
| | W-CDMA | 384 Kbps to 2 Mbps | Initial deployment in 2002; wider deployment in 2004–05 |
| TDMA | Packet data | Up to 28.8 Kbps | Now in Japan only |
| | EDGE/ EGPRS-136 | IP up to 384 Kbps | Initial deployment in 2002; wider deployment in 2004–05 |
| Wideband TDMA or W-CDMA | | Up to 2 Mbps | Trials were in the fall of 2001; initial deployment in 2002 in Japan |
| CDMA | Circuit-switched data (cdmaOne or IS-95A) | 9.6 Kbps to 14.4 Kbps | Now in United States, South America, and Korea |
| | IS-95B | IP to 64 Kbps | Available in Korea |
| | CDMA2000 1XEV | IP to 144 Kbps | Trials were in 2001; rollout in 2002 |
| | CDMA2000 3X | IP from 384 Kbps to 2 Mbps | Initial deployment in 2002–03 |
| iDEN | Circuit-switched data | 9.6 Kbps to 14.4 Kbps | Now in United States only |

gression for wireless data is to adopt a packet-based architecture (like DoCoMo) and create stronger compatibility with the Internet Protocol (IP). This has appeal to operators and users alike.

Operators like packet-based data because it is less costly to operate (although it does require capital investments to the network) and users like packet data because it is faster to download.

Table 5-4 provides a sense of the myriad choices awaiting wireless users in the coming decade. Users should be less concerned with the acronyms than with the general principle—faster technologies are coming. Wireless operators are hoping that these new networks will drive wireless usage, much like the availability of 56K modems and broadband services helped drive Internet, access revenues in the late 1990s.

The market has emerged into a high-stakes competition between the CDMA and GSM/TDMA camps. CDMA's main argument is that their network progressions require fewer networks (and handset upgrades) than the corresponding upgrades required in the GSM camp. Whatever the differences, it is clear that these technologies will continue to coexist in the marketplace for the foreseeable future.

# CHAPTER 6

# Introduction to Wireless Data Networks

Chapter 5 focused on the underlying technologies for transmitting wireless voice. Although voice remains the dominant application for wireless systems, the demand for wireless data networks has grown exponentially in recent years. The explosion of the Internet has fueled the surge in demand for wireless data. As companies moved existing applications and data to the Web, providing wireless access to that data was a natural next step. In many cases, the wireless revolution was driven by the potential productivity gains offered by real-time access to information and the ability to increase customer satisfaction by providing another mechanism to supply content and services to users.

Wireless data systems predated the Internet explosion in the late 1990s. Basic paging systems had existed since the 1970s and were predominantly used in the medical and public safety communities. These early systems sent a page or beep to a wireless device to notify the user of a new message. The user then called a central number or office to retrieve the information. These systems were simple yet functional. However, like wireless voice networks, the growing demand for pagers exposed the low capacity of these networks, forcing operators and vendors to consider new methods for transmitting wireless data.

The wireless data industry evolved quite differently than the wireless voice market. Most governments and vendors viewed wireless voice as a higher priority than wireless data. As a result, governments played a key role in the development of the standards of wireless voice. In contrast, governments had less involvement with wireless data standards. Wireless data standards tended to be developed by the industry players. Not surprisingly, this led to the creation of multiple competing technologies. Initially, these competing technologies dominated the regions in which the vendors originated, but over time these networks spread to other regions, creating a smorgasbord of alternatives.

Although these competing standards may have caused confusion and prevented the development of a global data network, they still managed to satisfy the demand for wireless data networks. As companies realized the benefits of wireless data, users demanded increased functionality from the existing wireless data networks. There were generally three demands:

- **Faster throughput** Existing wireless data networks remained very slow (less than 19 Kbps). This slow throughput limited wireless data implementations to focusing on very simple tasks that did not consume significant bandwidth. As companies searched to provide more complex applications and services to mobile users, faster download speeds emerged as a top consideration.

- **More global roaming capabilities** The assorted wireless data standards led to regional wireless data networks, but they made global roaming difficult, if not impossible. Like the wireless voice market, users began demanding greater roaming capabilities.

- **Interoperability with the Internet** Since many wireless data networks emerged before the emergence of the Internet, some older standards were not always compatible with the Internet Protocol (IP). As companies extended web applications to wireless environments, interoperability with Internet applications became an essential requirement.

This chapter will progress through various wireless data standards, starting with the oldest and moving forward to the newest standards including the General Packet Radio Service (GPRS). In addition to describing the basic architecture, this chapter discusses the available security mechanisms in detail. Although the Wireless Application Protocol (WAP) is not a wireless standard per se, this chapter discusses it in detail because it has been subjected to more criticism than any other wireless data technology for its security architecture.

Some wireless standards that are gradually phasing out (such as the original paging networks and the Advanced Radio Data Information Service [ARDIS] standard) have been omitted from this chapter. Other wireless data technologies, particularly those on the broadband side, have also been omitted because of the general uncertainty surrounding these technologies. For instance, the Metricom Richochet fixed wireless broadband network emerged as a favorite among traveling executives in the United States in the late 1990s only to have the company file for bankruptcy in early 2001 due to insufficient demand. Metricom's assets have been recently purchased and the future prognosis for the company is unclear.

Wireless data immediately introduces a new series of security concerns and threats. For many companies, the most valuable assets are information and ideas. Companies must confront a crucial dilemma—how to trade off the increased productivity of wireless access to critical corporate information versus the risk of exposing that very information to wireless users.

This is a very difficult question to answer quantitatively, but if companies independently evaluate the information being exposed, they can determine the risk profile for that information, and then determine if the information should be provided for wireless access. In most cases, companies should apply existing security policies for wireless data, but some enterprises are writing entirely new security policies just for wireless.

For instance, if the wireless application is a field service program that tracks the status of repairs in a remote location, the security risks are relatively low. However, if the application involves downloading sales information, pricing, customer information, and so on, appropriate safeguards should be implemented to protect that information, including encryption and authentication. This chapter will provide a fundamental background on the security architecture of wireless data networks. Future chapters will provide some real-world examples on how companies have implemented these standards in a secure fashion.

# Cellular Digital Packet Data (CDPD)

The Cellular Digital Packet Data (CDPD) network standard was developed in the United States in the early 1990s in a collaborative effort between the country's regional phone companies, or Baby Bells (Nynex, U.S. West, Ameritech, Bell South, and Bell Atlantic among others). These operators (or their subsidiaries) were slowly building analog first-generation (1G) cellular networks based on the Advanced Mobile

Phone Service (AMPS) standard and were looking for methods to offer some wireless data services.

As Sami Tabane explains, "The basic idea consists of deploying the CDPD network by using AMPS network software and hardware. The CDPD system transmits data packets on the cellular network's voice channels when they are not used, such as during call setup."[1] By utilizing existing AMPS infrastructure, operators were able offer wireless data services much more quickly and cheaply than any other alternatives.

On a technical level, CDPD has three main advantages:[2]

- **Speed**    CDPD is capable of up to 19.2 Kbps throughput. Although this may still seem slow compared to the wired Internet, this throughput is twice as fast as most other competing alternatives, including circuit-switched data over the Global System for Mobile Communications (GSM).

- **Transmission Control Protocol/Internet Protocol (TCP/IP) based**    Since CDPD networks are packet switched and based on IP, they are compatible with the Internet.

- **Quick call setup**    CDPD does not require any time to establish a call, as opposed to cellular voice systems, which require some time to establish a connection.

## CDPD Architecture

CDPD networks are very similar in design to wireless voice networks. There are the client devices themselves (a PDA, cell phone, or laptop PC with a proper wireless modem), which are collectively referred to as a *mobile end system* (M-ES). Within each specific cell site, a CDPD mobile device connects to a mobile database station (MDBS). The MDBS in turn connects to the mobile data intermediate system (MD-IS), which is responsible for most of the network's administrative functions as well as its roaming users. The CDPD network must also interface with the fixed end system (F-ES). The F-ES is the component that connects the CDPD network to other networks like the Internet. An enterprise and/or the network operator could own the F-ES. See Figure 6-1 for details.

---

[1]Sami Tabane, *Handbook of Mobile Radio Networks*, Artech House: Boston, 2000, 571.
[2]Ibid.

**Figure 6-1**

General CDPD
architecture

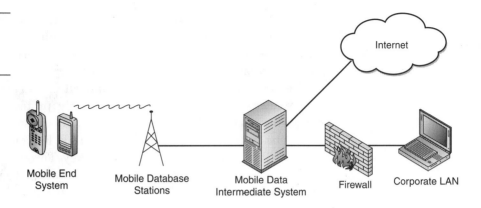

CDPD Security

The security requirements of CDPD are similar to those of a wireless voice network. Data encryption over the air and the ability to prevent fraud and the cloning of CDPD devices are absolutely required. Because of CDPD's slow throughput, security solutions must also provide superior performance.

Because CDPD does not use a tamper-resistant hardware module like the GSM Subscriber Identity Module (SIM) card, the CDPD authentication and encryption process resembles the Code Division Multiple Access (CDMA) architecture. CDPD devices are programmed at the time of manufacture with a unique numeric value called the Network Entity Identifier (NEI). The value is stored in the memory of the CDPD device and is used to authenticate the device on the CDPD network.

However, the CDPD security architecture differs from a voice network in one significant manner. Whereas as a voice network utilizes a challenge response protocol over an unencrypted channel, CDPD establishes an encrypted channel first before progressing with authentication. How do two unknown entities establish an encrypted channel without first authenticating?

This authentication is based on a widely used security protocol called the *Diffie-Hellman key exchange*. Named for two well-known Stanford University cryptographers, Martin Hellman and Whitfield Diffie, this protocol was one of the first public uses of asymmetric cryptography. Diffie-Hellman is not a mechanism that encrypts data, but is a mechanism that enables two unknown parties to exchange private keys that can be used to encrypt data. This makes Diffie-Hellman ideally suited for the CDPD architecture. Because the Diffie-Hellman protocol is used in some WAP implementations, it is worth further review.

Diffie-Hellman's beauty lies in its simplicity. In an asymmetric system, each party has a private and public key. In the protocol, the device sends its public key to the network, and vice versa. Because the keys are public, they can be transmitted over an insecure link. Each party now combines its private key with the received public key. Through this mechanism, each party can generate a secret session key that can be utilized for establishing an encrypted session. Figure 6-2 illustrates the Diffie-Hellman protocol.

There are two issues worth knowing about the Diffie-Hellman protocol. First, Diffie-Hellman does not authenticate the participants; it merely establishes a session key between two parties. For this reason, Diffie-Hellman is susceptible to a so-called man-in-the-middle attack. In this attack, an intermediate party intercepts the device's public key during transmission, replaces it with a different public key, and sends that value

**Figure 6-2**

Diffie-Hellman protocol

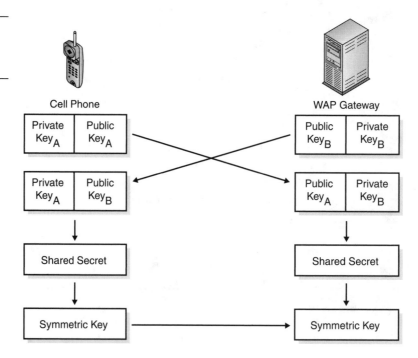

to the intended recipient. The intermediary conducts the same process with the recipient's public key. Through this process, the intermediary can then decrypt and read all traffic. There is protection against man-in-the-middle attacks in the Diffie-Hellman key exchange; however, this protection typically requires the use of a more elaborate public key infrastructure (PKI) architecture.

Getting back to the topic of CDPD, once the Diffie-Hellman protocol has been completed, the M-ES and MD-IS create two ciphering keys. Because Diffie-Hellman has provided each party with the same shared secret, that secret can be utilized to generate a symmetric key. All CDPD encryption utilizes a variable key size stream cipher called *RC4*. This algorithm was developed by RSA Data Security in the 1980s and is part of the CDPD specification. Key sizes in CDPD traditionally range between 40 and 128 bits. The only worthy item to note about RC4 is that although it is trademarked and an RSA Security trade secret, RC4 source code was anonymously posted to the Internet. Although this effort was an anathema to RSA, it benefited RC4 itself since it was available to wider public scrutiny.

To authenticate itself to the CDPD network, the mobile device transmits its NEI along with some additional unique identifiers to the MD-IS. The MD-IS forwards this information to an authentication server (similar to the Authentication Center [AuC] in the wireless voice world) that compares the results. If the results match, the device is authenticated and allowed onto the network.

As an additional level of security, the CDPD devices utilize something called a shared history record (SHR). This is like a call counter and is similar to mechanisms utilized in CDMA. The SHR is a value that is updated and synchronized every time a device connects. This helps prevent against spoofing since the network will reject SHR values that are out of sync.

Given its similarity to existing wireless voice networks, CDPD has similar security vulnerabilities:[3]

■ **No mutual authentication** As in voice networks, the authentication process is one way. The device authenticates to the network, but the network does *not* authenticate to the device. This opens the possibility of someone creating a bogus base station that appears legitimate to the user and retrieving keys and sensitive information.

---

[3]A good review of CDPD security can be found at http://swig.stanford.edu/pub/summaries/wireless/security_cdpd.html.

■ **Local key storage**   Because CDPD devices lack a tamper-resistant module like an SIM card to store the NEI, the possibility always exists that a hacker could retrieve the unique identifiers from the device itself.

The long-term prognosis for CDPD is unclear. AT&T remains the largest CDPD carrier in the United States and their PocketNet service has attracted a considerable user base. PocketNet service is unique in that it is available either with a data-only device or in special dual-mode mobile phones that utilize Time Division Multiple Access (TDMA) for AT&T's wireless voice network and CDPD for wireless data. Given that AT&T is gradually upgrading its existing TDMA network to support GPRS, which will support much higher data rates than CDPD, the use of CDPD will likely be reduced over time in favor of GPRS.

# Mobitex

Mobitex is a wireless data technology developed by Ericsson in the mid-1980s. Currently, over 30 Mobitex networks are in operation around the world in 23 different countries. All Mobitex networks operate in one of four frequency families: 80 MHz, 400 MHz, 800 MHz, or 900 MHz.[4] Mobitex is a packet-based switching technology and is capable of throughput rates of up to 8 Kbps. Mobitex data is transmitted in 512-byte blocks.

Mobitex is an open, nonproprietary system, but the specification is copyrighted and made available under a royalty-free license. The technical details of Mobitex are collectively referred to as the *Mobitex Interface Specification* (MIS).[5]

## Mobitex Architecture

The design of Mobitex networks is similar to traditional cellular voice networks. Each Mobitex hand-held device connects to a base station, which in turn connects to a local switch. The local switch connects to the Mobitex

---

[4]www.mobitex.org

[5]Ibid.

operator's network backbone, but it can also connect to external networks (such as a corporate local area network [LAN] or gateway). In addition to the local switches, Mobitex networks utilize regional switches (which control a set of local switches) as well as a *Network Control Center* (NCC), which handles billing, monitors usage, and oversees network performance. See Figure 6-3 for details on this architecture.

One unique feature of Mobitex is its capability to offer peer-to-peer communication between two Mobitex devices. With peer-to-peer communication, two devices communicate without engaging the entire Mobitex network infrastructure—the base station coordinates all the communication and then ultimately forwards the activity back to the NCC. The main advantage of this approach is that it minimizes the back-haul network traffic. In a cellular voice environment, two cell phones in the same cell area must still communicate all the way back to the Visitor Location Register (VLR). In periods of high usage, this causes congestion and dropped calls. The peer-to-peer capability eliminates this potential issue.

## Mobitex Security Architecture

The Mobitex security architecture is quite similar to other wireless data networks. The main difference is that the Mobitex security specifications

**Figure 6-3**

Typical Mobitex
architecture

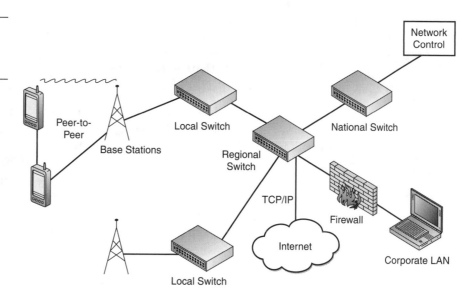

are not widely published and have not been subjected to the same level of scrutiny as other standards. However, the consensus remains that Mobitex is generally secure.

The same general authentication principles that are used in cellular networks are used in Mobitex. Each Mobitex device contains a unique serial number and another value called the *Mobitex Access Number* (MAN). These values are stored locally in the Mobitex hand-held device and are transmitted over the air to the base station where they are forwarded onto the NCC for authentication. The underlying algorithms used for encryption are not disclosed.

Mobitex suffers from the same security weaknesses as CDPD—specifically, the lack of mutual authentication (device to network and network to device) and the local storage of the serial number and MAN pairs.

For people concerned with Mobitex's security model, several security enhancements are available. Because Mobitex is a packet-based network, it is possible to utilize some of the security features available in wired networks to encrypt data at the application layer.

The Palm VII wireless handheld is a good example. This wireless PDA operates on the Mobitex network, but in addition to the traditional Mobitex security measures, each Palm VII completes a Diffie-Hellman exchange with the network. This exchange is then used to create a pair of DES-X keys (a variant of the Data Encryption Standard [DES]) that can be used to establish an encrypted session between the device and the network.

Other software vendors offer similar toolkits or capabilities for organizations to add and enhance existing encryption onto Mobitex networks.

### Mobitex Case Study—Research in Motion's (RIM's) Blackberry

One of the most interesting applications for Mobitex wireless data networks has been the Blackberry wireless e-mail pager offered by Canadian-based Research in Motion (RIM). These interactive two-way pagers were first introduced in North America in the late 1990s and have quickly grown to become a necessary wireless tool for mobile executives. Figure 6-4 displays the growth in RIM users in 2001. Operating on 900 MHz Mobitex networks in North America, these devices can send and receive e-mail messages sent to a normal business user's wired e-mail inbox (see the following illustration of RIM devices). In addition to the models offered by RIM, Compaq and AOL also offer their own branded RIM devices. These devices are displayed in the following illustration.

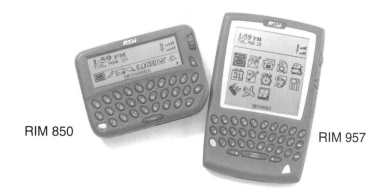

RIM 850    RIM 957

**Figure 6-4**

Blackberry
subscribers
from 2001
through 2002

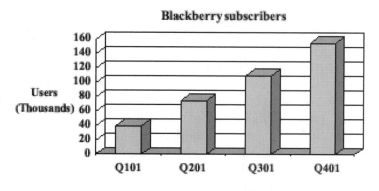

Blackberry subscribers

Users
(Thousands)

Wall St. Journal, Oct. 15, 2001

RIM devices utilize a simple hardware architecture. They utilize a traditional 32-bit Intel 386 processor and contain 2MB of flash memory and
up to 304Kb of static RAM (SRAM). This enables the storage of hundreds
of messages and entries on a single device.

One of the main reasons for RIM's success has been its security model.
RIM's detailed security architecture has enabled RIM to overcome security objections from enterprise customers. In the process, this has helped
RIM devices become some of the first supported wireless data devices in
the enterprise.

RIM's most significant benefit is its tight compatibility with existing
e-mail systems. An RIM device is essentially just an e-mail application
that happens to exist in a wireless form factor. Unlike other wireless
devices that focus on other applications such as addresses, contacts,
memos, and so on, RIM focuses exclusively on corporate e-mail systems

like Microsoft Outlook and Lotus cc:Mail. In the process, RIM pagers essentially function as proxies for a user's PC-based e-mail account. When the RIM device is not connected to a PC, messages sent to the user's e-mail account are automatically forwarded to the user's RIM device. This design, coupled with the increasing importance of e-mail, has helped RIM devices achieve high deployment within the enterprise.

## RIM Security Architecture

RIM's e-mail solution consists of two basic components: the hand-held device and e-mail redirector software. The redirector software is available in two modes: desktop or server.

In the desktop redirector, RIM software is installed on the user's PC. This software communicates with the corporate e-mail server. When the RIM is not connected to the PC (via its docking cradle) and an incoming e-mail message arrives, the RIM PC retrieves, compresses, encrypts, and redirects the message to the user's RIM handheld (see Figure 6-5).

The model enables the end-to-end encryption of e-mail messages from the PC to the handheld. During the installation of the RIM desktop redirector, a unique symmetric Triple DES (TDES) key is created. This key is then transferred to the RIM handheld via the protected serial port link between the PC and the handheld. The desktop redirector encrypts all messages with this symmetric key. Because the handheld has a copy of the symmetric key, it can decrypt the message at the device. This sym-

**Figure 6-5**

RIM desktop redirection

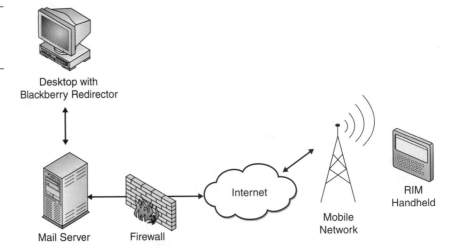

Desktop with
Blackberry Redirector

Mail Server     Firewall     Internet     Mobile Network     RIM Handheld

metric key model also prevents potential attacks against an individual PC (for example, hijacking someone's e-mail account and forwarding messages to another location) because the hacker must have knowledge of the TDES key. The desktop redirector model is illustrated in Figure 6-5.

The desktop redirector model has one distinct disadvantage. It requires that the user's PC be powered on and connected to the network. Because of some of the obvious limitations of this approach, RIM offers a server-based redirection architecture (see Figure 6-6).

In server redirection, the same basic model applies as with the desktop, except that the user's PC does not need to be on or connected to the network for messages to be received on the user's RIM handheld. Instead of the desktop redirecting e-mail to the handheld, the Blackberry Enterprise Server automatically redirects the e-mail to the user's handheld.

The same symmetric key setup in the desktop model applies in server redirection. Users create the TDES symmetric key during initial installation. This key is then shared between the handheld and the Blackberry Enterprise Server to enable end-to-end message encryption.

The Blackberry security model has directly contributed to RIM's success with enterprise customers in North America. Furthermore, RIM has been actively seeking network partners outside of North America to offer Blackberry service in new markets. RIM has partnered with British Telecom who plans to offer Blackberry service in Europe in 2002. RIM is also going to introduce the devices in Hong Kong in 2002. This will provide Blackberry users with some transatlantic roaming capabilities and add to the device's appeal. RIM is also courting additional application developers for the platform and aggressively moving to supporting faster networks like GPRS in future handsets.

**Figure 6-6**

RIM server
redirection

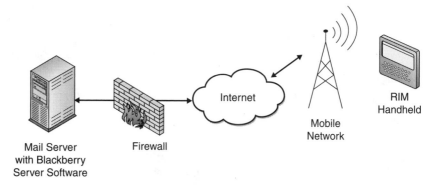

Mail Server
with Blackberry
Server Software

Firewall

Internet

Mobile
Network

RIM
Handheld

This means that Blackberry services will continue in popularity and offer a compelling solution for wireless e-mail and messaging.

## Mobitex Versus CDPD—What Does the Future Hold?

Like CDPD networks, Mobitex networks find themselves competing with faster data alternatives. However, although Mobitex usage will probably wane in the coming years as users migrate to faster services, Mobitex will probably still outlast CDPD for the following reasons:

- **Network infrastructure**   One of CDPD's biggest benefits is that it is designed to operate on the existing AMPS cellular infrastructure, making the network inexpensive to build. By contrast, Mobitex networks require an entirely new infrastructure and hardware, making them more expensive. The initial cost savings are now working against CDPD because the network operators are looking to eliminate AMPS hardware to reduce support costs and migrate toward a 100 percent digital infrastructure. This makes it increasingly difficult for operators to justify the maintenance of the CDPD network. Because Mobitex networks require a greater initial investment, Mobitex network operators have been highly motivated to keep the networks operational.

- **Strong industry association**   CDPD was pioneered by the Baby Bells in the United States. In recent years, there has been considerable consolidation among the Baby Bells—Nynex and Bell Atlantic merged to form Verizon and Ameritech merged with Southwestern Bell among others. This fragmentation has made some carriers deemphasize wireless data services like CDPD. In contrast, the Mobitex Operators Association (MOA) is led by Ericsson with active participants representing the major components of Mobitex. This consistent strong association has helped Mobitex collectively position themselves against new technologies.

- **Greater coverage**   Mobitex has achieved greater critical mass in terms of users and has geographic coverage beyond the United States. This has opened up the possibility of global roaming. This larger market also makes Mobitex attractive to service providers and equipment vendors because they have a large market to service and sell to.

Regardless of the final outcome of these various wireless data technologies, they have all helped to validate the wireless data market. Ironically, the wireless data market, which emerged exclusively to service certain vertical markets like healthcare and law enforcement, will likely evolve back to serving those niche markets again as the mainstream public moves toward faster wireless data network standards.

# General Packet Radio Service (GPRS)

Although second-generation (2G) GSM networks successfully offered high-quality wireless voice services, GSM networks were not optimized for high-speed data. Instead, 2G GSM networks were entirely circuit switched, meaning that wireless data was slow (less than or equal to 14.4 Kbps) and expensive. As operators sought to offer more value-added services like wireless data, they quickly realized that faster throughput was a key requirement. Furthermore, the operators wanted a method that could add high-speed data without requiring massive capital investment or changes to the network.

In the late 1990s, GSM operators developed a new specification for high-speed wireless data called *General Packet Radio Service* (GPRS). As its name implies, GPRS is packet based, as opposed to GSM's circuit-switched architecture. Packet-based switching provides some significant advantages:

■ **Compatibility with the Internet**   Because the Internet is a packet-based network utilizing the IP, GPRS provides an easy connection with Internet-based data. This makes GPRS ideally suited for wireless data and applications.

■ **Always-on connection**   Packet switching does not require that a physical link (such as a circuit) be opened for data transfer. This enables GPRS users to receive information only when they need to, but more importantly, it does not require that a circuit-switched connection be established for every individual call.

■ **Efficient networks**   Packet switching enables data packets to be redirected over the optimal network path and bypass potential network bottlenecks. Furthermore, packet switching means that the radio spectrum is only used during the transmit or receive mode. This enables multiple users to share the same spectrum in a given area. In circuit switching, a dedicated circuit must be opened for each call, preventing multiple users from using the same frequency in a cell site.

## How Does GPRS Achieve Higher Throughput

*The answer is that GPRS can use many time slots in parallel. Chapter 5 described how TDMA allocates a channel into slots for voice transmission. However, in order to maintain intelligible conversations, each voice conversation can only use one channel.*

*Because GPRS is packet based, data can be split into chunks and sent simultaneously on multiple channels to a handset. The handset can then reassemble the data into the appropriate order so that the data can be viewed. Using multiple channels in parallel helps GPRS achieve significantly higher throughput than circuit-switched data.*

One key consideration is that GPRS does *not* increase the capacity of existing cellular networks. GPRS is merely a technology upgrade that enables packet data to be utilized alongside circuit-switched voice traffic within the same radio spectrum. This creates potential problems for the network operators who must efficiently allocate existing spectrum between packet data and circuit-switched voice. Here's another way to look at it. Who has priority—voice or data?

Initial evidence suggests that circuit-switched voice will continue to receive priority on GPRS networks. The reasons for this are simple. First, GPRS-enabled handsets and users will continue to be the minority for the foreseeable future, meaning that operators will focus on satisfying the large majority of voice users first. Second, GPRS-enabled applications are slowly being developed, meaning that operators' revenue streams will continue to be driven by mobile voice. Given the potential customer-service implications of a user not being able to place a call in a given cell because of congestion, operators will continue to give priority to non-GPRS traffic. This does not necessarily mean that GPRS traffic will experience delays or dropped calls. The bursty nature of GPRS means that data can even be sent in heavily congested cells because the phones are continually trying to resend the data. In the circuit-switched world, these retries are equivalent to redialing a phone number, but in the packet data world, the handset handles the retry automatically—the user maintains a passive role.

Of course, there will likely be exceptions to these rules in certain geographic areas and operators are planning GPRS networks with this information in mind. For instance, in cell sites with a high percentage of corporate users, network operators will likely install more Service GPRS Service Nodes (SGSNs) than in sites with more intermittent consumer calling usage because the higher GPRS tariffs will make GPRS the most attractive service to corporate users. This kind of network planning will enable operators to create and develop GPRS networks that are closely compatible with the actual customer mix in a specific cell site.

The first GPRS networks were launched in the spring of 2001 in Europe. Because these networks did not require additional radio spectrum, the cost of building GPRS-capable wireless networks was relatively minor. This contrasted sharply with the emerging third-generation (3G) networks, which required new spectrum and a large infrastructure upgrade. Figure 6-7 provides a sense of the infrastructure requirements for deploying a GPRS network. As another example, in December 2001, AT&T Wireless stated that the network upgrade cost for GPRS was $300 to $400 million, whereas the 3G upgrade cost was at least $1 billion.

The GPRS specifications defined three types of handsets:

- **Class A terminals**   Support GPRS and GSM and the simultaneous operation of both (for example, Class A terminals could receive e-mail while voice calls are in session).

- **Class B terminals**   Support GPRS and GSM, but cannot process both simultaneously.

- **Class C terminals**   Only support GPRS (for example, a hardware card that can plug into a PC or PDA to enable GPRS).

**Figure 6-7**

The upgrade path to 2.5G (GPRS)[6]

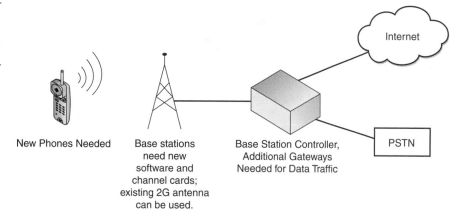

New Phones Needed

Base stations need new software and channel cards; existing 2G antenna can be used.

Base Station Controller, Additional Gateways Needed for Data Traffic

Internet

PSTN

[6]Adapted from *The Net Economy*, June 25, 2001, pp. 50–51.

In Europe, many GSM operators started promoting GPRS to build awareness around the capabilities of these faster networks. Furthermore, because the network upgrade costs were relatively low, the operators could charge relatively modest tariffs for GPRS and still generate a positive return on the investment. In order to utilize GPRS, subscribers only needed to purchase a new GPRS-enabled handset. Monthly fees were usually based on the amount of data sent to an individual's phone.

GPRS subscribers could then utilize significantly higher data throughput for accessing the Internet, and for receiving and sending e-mail. In most cases, subscription fees are based on the amount of data received.

## GPRS Architecture

A typical GPRS network architecture is shown in Figure 6-8. Because of the initial requirement that GPRS networks function on existing GSM networks, the GPRS network architecture utilizes the GSM architecture, which is described in Chapter 5. All of the traditional GSM components are used (base stations, Mobile Switching Centers [MSCs], Home Location Registers [HLRs], and so on), but two new components are added to support GPRS:

**Figure 6-8**

Typical GPRS network architecture

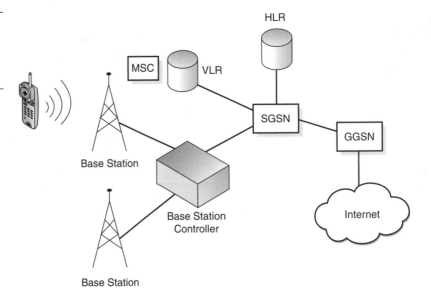

- **SGSN** The SGSN is essentially a data router and controls the delivery of data to users within a given geographic area. An individual SGSN may control and communicate with multiple base station controllers. The SGSN also handles GPRS authentication and encryption.

- ***Gateway GPRS Support Node*** **(GGSN)** The GGSN communicates with multiple SGSNs and serves as the interface (gateway) to external data networks like the Internet. GGSN handles the IP address allocation to mobile stations.

The SGSN and GGSN can also be combined into a single entity called a *GPRS Support Node* (GSN), but that is not a common deployment scenario.

The remaining components of the GSM architecture (the HLR, VLR, and AuC) are still present in GPRS, but in many cases, these components must also provide additional functionality as it relates to a GPRS subscriber. However, GPRS also requires the following new network components (see Figure 6-9):

**Figure 6-9**

Other GPRS components[7]

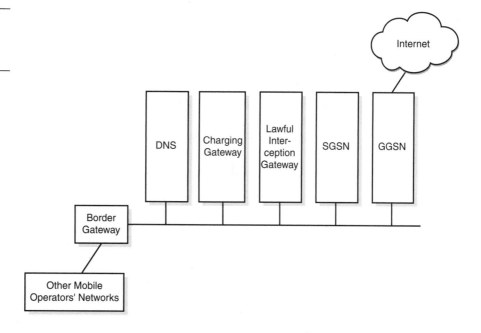

[7]Jussi Rautpalo, "GPRS Security—Secure Remote Connections over GPRS," Helsinki University of Technology, 2000.

- **Charging gateway**  This tracks the individual usage of GPRS data and communicates with an operator's billing system.

- **Border gateway**  This communicates with other operators and enables intranetwork GPRS roaming.

- ***Domain Name Server* (DNS)**  This is same as what is used in the wired Internet. It converts hostnames into a numeric IP address—for example, www.xyz.com could convert into something like 60.16.0.255.

- **Lawful interception gateway**  The lawful interception gateway is a functionality that enables authorities to intercept, or wiretap, GPRS mobile data traffic. Operators in most countries have to provide this functionality in the network before the commercial rollout.

- **Firewall and network management stations**  These are used to protect the GPRS network perimeter.

## GPRS Security Issues

Although GPRS is based on the same fundamental GSM security architecture, GPRS introduces several new security threats that have to be considered and for which appropriate countermeasures must be created. Many of these threats are more of a concern for the network operators since they must implement measures to protect against them.

The single biggest security threat to GPRS is the network's connection to public networks (such as the Internet) means that wireless networks are susceptible to attack from the back end. Previous wireless voice-only networks were closed networks, making access to them considerably harder. This means that operators must take added measures to protect the connection between the GPRS gateway (GGSN) and the Internet.

Another significant development is that GPRS is packet and IP based. This means that GPRS is now susceptible to some of the same security threats facing the wired Internet, including the following:

- ***Denial of service* (DoS)**  This attack consists of sending thousands or millions of simultaneous requests to an individual web server. These requests overwhelm the web server and it crashes, making it unable to provide service to valid users (hence, DoS). In GPRS, it is theoretically possible to launch a DoS attack against the GGSN (thereby stopping all GPRSs for all subscribers) or even against an individual mobile phone to prevent it from operating.

▪ **IP address spoofing**   In this attack, a hacker successfully determines the valid numeric IP address for a given web site. The hacker can then create data packets that appear genuine and send them to unsuspecting users. Because the subscriber cannot tell if the content has been hijacked, hackers can use this attack to retrieve passwords, credit-card numbers, and other sensitive data from users.

## GPRS Security

Because of the new security risks introduced by GPRS, new security mechanisms are required. Furthermore, these enhancements must be implemented using the same security infrastructure, including SIM cards and the associated algorithms. Like the traditional circuit-switched GSM networks, the GPRS security architecture addresses two fundamental security issues—subscriber authentication and data encryption.

Even though GPRS runs on GSM networks, the standard GSM subscriber authentication process, which was described in Chapter 5, is not sufficient for GPRS. A secondary GPRS authentication must take place in order for valid users to have access to utilize GPRS and for operators to be able to bill individual usage.

GPRS subscriber authentication follows the same process as traditional GSM subscriber authentication. The only difference is that the SGSN acts as the VLR. SGSN retrieves the 32-bit random number (RAND), the individual subscriber's secret key ($K_i$), and the signed response (SRES) associated with the specific RAND. The handset and SGSN complete simultaneous calculations to generate the SRES. If the results match, the subscriber is authenticated.

Once a GPRS subscriber has been authenticated, the GPRS network has the option of deciding if data encryption will be used. If it is used, SRES, RAND, and $K_i$ are transmitted from the HLR to the SGSN. The GPRS handset utilizes the same kind of challenge response protocol that was described in Chapter 5 to generate a ciphering key ($K_c$). The ciphering key is then used to establish encrypted data communication between the handset and network. In this architecture, it is extremely important that the proper protection be provided to the SGSNs. Without proper SGSN protection, the entire GPRS system can be compromised.[8]

---

[8]Lauri Pesonen, "GPRS Interception," Helsinki University of Technology, November 21, 1999.

As was indicated in the section "General Packet Radio Service (GPRS)," GPRS packets can be sent in parallel time slots. The GPRS architecture means that GPRS packets are encrypted from the handset to the SGSN. This significantly reduces the risk of eavesdropping GPRS over the air. As added protection, base stations do not have the capability to arrange packets from different time slots into the correct order.[9] This means that even if an intruder compromised a base station, he or she would not be able to decrypt GPRS traffic. Figure 6-10 illustrates the various encryption utilized in a typical GPRS architecture.

The faster throughput and tighter compatibility with the Internet found in GPRS gives users the ability to access traditional wired applications and servers from a mobile handset. Although 2G networks promoted wireless data in 2000 and 2001, the reality is that the slow connection and infrastructure changes meant that wireless data on 2G networks was

**Figure 6-10**

GPRS encryption

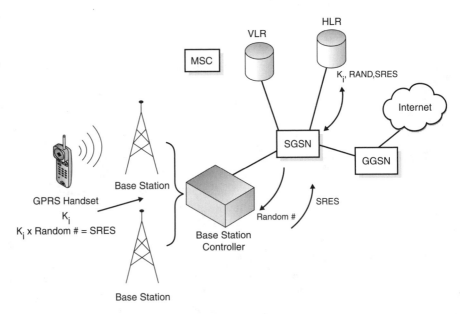

[9]Jussi Rautpalo, "GPRS Security—Secure Remote Connections over GPRS," Helsinki University of Technology, 2000.

never deployed on any wide scale. Therefore, enterprises and users were very interested in adopting GPRS.

The IP-centric architecture of GPRS serves as a double-edged sword. On one hand, it provides seamless compatibility with IP-based networks and applications. On the other hand, IP introduces a whole host of new security threats that enterprises did not have to contend with in 2G networks. Fortunately, the IP architecture of GPRS enables some new security capabilities to be utilized, specifically through the use of virtual private networks (VPNs).

A VPN encrypts data from end point to end point on a public network. VPNs can be configured in multiple ways in the GPRS world (see Figure 6-11).

Ultimately, the preferred approach is a fully encrypted session from the wireless device all the way to the corporate network. Currently, end-to-end VPN connections on GPRS are difficult to achieve.

Everything connected to the Internet must possess a unique numeric identifier. This is called the *IP address*. There are a finite number of IP

**Figure 6-11**

Sample
GPRS VPN
configurations

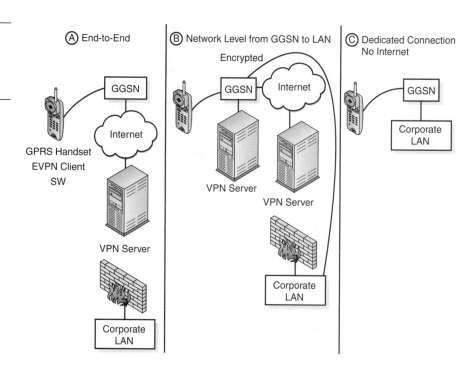

addresses. Due to the tremendous growth of the Internet, these addresses have become increasingly allocated. Because these addresses are in demand, most GPRS operators will not be able to allocate a unique number to each GPRS subscriber. Instead, the operators will likely retain a collection of IP addresses and allocate them on a first-come first-served basis. These addresses will be allocated for each session, meaning that users' IP addresses will likely change each time he or she utilizes GPRS. Because VPNs require an IP address, the dynamic nature of the client IP address complicates VPN configurations.

A solution to fix the IP address situation is underway: IPv6 (the current spec is IPv4). IPv6 will provide a greater number of IP addresses and should deal with the IP addressing problem for decades to come. It will take some time for IPv6 to be completely implemented. Once it is, it is entirely feasible for wireless handsets to have their own static IP address.

In the meantime, immediate VPN solutions for GPRS are available. These do not always provide true end-to-end security, but they provide VPN functionality in several crucial network components.

One alternative that has been identified is to create a VPN between a GGSN and corporate network. VPN servers are installed at the GGSN and the corporate network, enabling data encryption between the GGSN and corporate network.

However, this solution has three drawbacks:[10]

■ **Not end-to-end security**   In this scenario, data is unencrypted between the SGSN and GGSN, meaning that a complete end-to-end encrypted session is not used. It is equally problematic for roaming subscribers. Roaming users would first be directed to a local SGSN, and then directed to the dedicated GGSN on the home network, leaving traffic unencrypted between the SGSN and GGSN.

■ **Added cost**   Both the mobile operator and enterprise have to be equipped with VPN-capable hardware. Plus, this solution requires users to use the operator's GPRS network to create a connection instead of connecting to the corporate VPN gateway directly. This brings added data costs for access.

■ **Trust issues**   This requires an implicit trust between the enterprise and mobile operator.

---

[10]This section is based on Lauri Pesonen in the work cited from http://www.hut.fi/~jrautpal/gprs/gprs_sec.html.

# Introducing the Wireless Application Protocol (WAP)

Although WAP is not a wireless standard like GPRS or CDPD (in fact, it can operate over most network interfaces), WAP is another important component to wireless data services. Even though WAP has been widely criticized in 2000 and 2001 on a variety of fronts (for having a poor user interface, lack of compelling services, and an inadequate security model), it still has considerable support from mainstream industry players and will remain a factor in the wireless world for the foreseeable future.

WAP traces its roots to late 1995 when Unwired Planet was founded to commercialize its vision of accessing the Internet from a wireless handset. Two years later, Unwired Planet joined forces with the wireless leaders Motorola, Ericsson, and Nokia to create the WAP Forum. Membership was open to any participant willing to pay the annual membership fee. By the start of the twenty-first century, the WAP Forum counted over 500 firms among its members, representing a wide host of players in the wireless industry.

The WAP Forum's primary goal was to develop a common architecture for accessing the wireless Internet and collectively promote the benefits of WAP. Although the WAP Forum worked on developing a series of technical specifications starting with WAP v1.0 in early 1998, the WAP Forum is not a standards body; it is an industry association. This means that although the WAP Forum has developed numerous specifications, the WAP architecture is not a technology standard recognized by the main standards bodies, such as the *Internet Engineering Task Force* (IETF).

The WAP Forum's objective to commercialize and popularize the wireless Internet attracted a critical mass of industry players to its membership for a variety of reasons. First, in many regions, the *average revenue per cellular user* (ARPU) was stable or declining. This, combined with some regions reaching high saturation for cellular usage, meant that wireless carriers were anxiously searching for new methods and services to increase ARPU and raise customer retention. For the handset vendors, WAP offered the opportunity to design new data-enabled wireless devices, whereas software developers were eager to create and sell new WAP-specific applications to users and corporations.

The WAP Forum was very successful at promoting the capabilities of the wireless Internet. During the dot-com hype of 1999 and 2000, visions of color-screened cell phones accessing the Internet at high speeds appeared in mainstream technology media. Unfortunately, initial WAP services did not prove especially compelling to users. Connections were slow, the content that was available was a limited subset of the Internet, and service plans and new WAP handsets were expensive. Compounding the problem was the considerable negative attention directed at the WAP security model. Although some of the criticism was exaggerated, the media coverage raised consumer awareness and led users and content providers to reconsider WAP services, particularly those with high security requirements like wireless commerce or financial services.

In order to understand why security became such an issue for WAP services, it is necessary to review the WAP architecture in greater detail.

During the early development of the WAP specification, it became apparent that major changes would be required to enable the wireless Internet. The current 2G wireless networks were capable of data connection speeds of a meager 9.6 Kbps and the wireless handsets contained small monochrome displays with just a numeric keypad.

Partially because of these limitations and in order to simplify the transition from the wired Internet to the wireless world, the WAP specification called for the creation of a *WAP gateway*, which is an additional server that sits between the user and the web server (see Figure 6-12).

**Figure 6-12**

General web and
WAP architecture

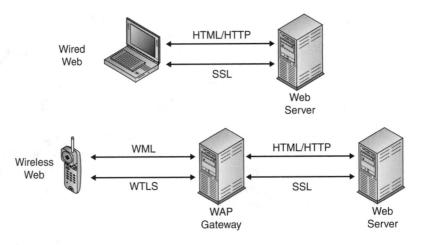

## The WAP Device

The earliest iterations of WAP devices were multipurpose phones. Besides providing traditional voice services, these devices also contained a WAP microbrowser. This browser contained the WAP protocol stack and provided the necessary mechanism to send and retrieve wireless data. Over time, WAP browsers have also been developed for use on PDAs like Palm and PocketPC. These devices can access WAP data through either an external wireless modem or even the PDA's infrared port to a wireless phone.

The WAP stack is identical in concept to the standard TCP/IP stack in standard wired web browsers, but the WAP stack's functionality is vastly different. The differences are primarily due to the major performance characteristics in wired and wireless networks.

For instance, TCP/IP works quite well in the wired world. Individual packets that are lost can be resent and reassembled at the web client without any perceptible effect to the user. However, TCP/IP is not well suited for today's wireless networks because wireless networks are still considerably more prone to dropped packets as a result of signal loss. The performance gap, combined with the overhead associated with communicating about lost packets and the very slow bandwidth of the networks, means that TCP is not well suited for 2G circuit-switched networks. These same differences can also be attributed to the rest of the WAP stack, as seen in Figure 6-13.

**Figure 6-13**

Wired web protocol versus wireless web protocol

| | Wired Web Protocol | | Wireless Web Protocol |
|---|---|---|---|
| Content | HTML JavaScript | | WML WMLScript |
| Session | HTTP | | Wireless Session Layer (WSP) |
| Security | TLS/SSL | | WTLS |
| Transport | TCP/IP | | Wireless Transport Layer (WDP) |

WAP is responsible for sending requests for web pages from the WAP gateway and interpreting the responses so that they can be viewed on the handset.

The WAP microbrowser presents content in Wireless Markup Language (WML), which is closely related to Hypertext Markup Language (HTML). In addition, WAP microbrowsers can also execute scripts via the WMLScript programming language, which is similar to the JavaScript found in wired browsers. Because of the performance limitations of WAP devices, WMLScript is usually executed on the WAP gateway on behalf of the user and the results are compressed and transmitted to the user.

## The WAP Gateway

As the name implies, the WAP gateway serves as the central interface to the Internet. All requests and data from the wireless devices must pass through the WAP gateway before proceeding onto the Internet. In the initial WAP rollouts, the WAP gateway was always managed and maintained by the network operator. Depending on the subscriber base, an operator might utilize multiple WAP gateways for load balancing. The WAP gateway serves several key functions:

- **Protocol converter**  Converts WAP protocols (such as the Wireless Data Protocol [WDP] and Wireless Transport Layer Security [WTLS]) to wired protocols (like TCP and TLS).

- **Content converter**  Translates HTML web pages into WML compatible content.

- **Performance optimization and overhead reduction**  Given the low bandwidth and throughput of the phone, the WAP gateway's routines are designed to compress data as much as possible and minimize the number of roundtrips that must take place between the client and the gateway. For example, the WAP transaction layer (WTP) is similar to the wired HTTP protocol, but although HTTP utilizes several hundred bytes in its overhead (for error correction and so on), WTP's overhead is considerably smaller.

When a WAP gateway receives a request for content from a WAP device, the WAP gateway will translate that request into HTTP and retrieve the content from the original web server. Although the WAP gateway is capable of converting HTML to WML dynamically, in most WAP implementations, the content provider creates a subset of data in the WML format. Given WML's interoperability with HTML, this is not an enormous task, but it does point out that some effort must be expended to enable existing web content for wireless devices.

## WAP Security Model

As Figure 6-13 indicates, the WAP security layer is different from the wired world. Rather than relying on the ubiquitous Secure Sockets Layer/Transport Layer Security (SSL/TLS) protocol, the WAP specification adopted WTLS. This protocol was designed to provide authentication, data encryption, and privacy for WAP users. WTLS was included in the WAP 1.1 specification.

As we have seen with other components of the WAP model, traditional SSL is not suitable for wireless networks primarily for performance reasons. SSL works fine in a PC world where the client PC has significant processing power, ample battery supply, and a relatively fast connection to the web server. A WAP device has none of these features, which explains the reason for developing WTLS.

The WAP specification also created a WMLScript function called SignText that provides capabilities for providing digital signatures on WAP devices. Although SignText-compliant products are just being introduced into the market, the SignText capability will add significant value to existing WAP environments by providing a level of nonrepudiation that can be used for security-sensitive transactions.

The WAP specification introduces three different classes of authentication:

- Class 1 authentication is anonymous. Neither client nor gateway can authenticate each other.

- Class 2 authentication is server authentication only. This is equivalent to shopping over a SSL link from a wired browser. The SSL protocol authenticates the server (so that the user knows it really is the corporation's web site).

- Class 3 authentication is both client and server authentication. This requires the use of a PKI.

Although Class 3-capable devices introduce the possibility of a true wireless public key infrastructure (WPKI), they also introduce a whole host of unresolved business issues. Specifically, in Class 3 devices, the critical issue is how the user's public/private key is going to be managed, installed, supported, and so on. Although the likely client location for key storage is the SIM card, operators faced the subtle fact that new WAP subscribers were mostly existing subscribers who brought their existing SIM cards with them, making it difficult to upgrade their SIM cards.

This led to the WAP Forum's development of the Wireless Identity Module (WIM). Just as the SIM card contained the necessary information for authenticating and processing voice calls, the WIM concept was driven by the need to have an equivalent mechanism for storing keys and information specifically related to WAP services. Although the WAP Forum did not specify a preferred WIM architecture, two possibilities emerged:

- **Integrated SIM/WIM card** In this scenario, the WIM card is just a virtual card. It uses some of the unallocated memory on the subscriber's SIM card to store information.

- **Dual-slot phones** Handsets contain a separate slot for a WIM card. This opens several new possibilities—most notably that it takes the WIM personalization out of the operator's exclusive realm and enables content providers to issue their own WIM cards to users. This is especially of interest to banks that prefer to maintain and manage their own security infrastructure. The dual-slot architecture does have some user interface issues, particularly for users who may have to juggle multiple WIM cards (like they already do with credit cards).

Due to the global economic slowdown in 2001, handset vendors' plans for Class 3 phones were scaled back or postponed, so the final WIM architecture is still unclear. Nonetheless, this issue will likely be a key trend to follow in the years ahead as the banks and network operators compete to build trust relationships with their subscribers.

At the time of this writing, Class 1 WAP devices were widely available. Each handset vendor had one to two Class 2 compatible devices, but Class 3 devices were just becoming available. Initial WAP usage focused almost exclusively on Class 1 and 2 authentication.

Although this provided server authentication, many WAP services continued to rely on Class 1 authentication. Furthermore, the WAP specification was designed so that the web server had no knowledge of whether the WAP client or WAP gateway connection was encrypted or not. So although the content provider could release sensitive data via SSL to the gateway, the provider had no knowledge of whether the information was being sent in the clear to the device.

Again, the WTLS protocol specified a process to minimize the amount of communication required between the client and server. The Class 2 authentication process completes itself in four steps:

1. The WAP device sends a request to the WAP gateway.
2. The gateway responds and sends a copy of its certificate (containing the gateway's public key) to the WAP device.
3. The WAP device retrieves the certificate and public key, generates a unique random value, and encrypts it with the gateway's public key.
4. The WAP gateway receives the encrypted value and decrypts it with its corresponding private key.

This process is simple, but it enables the creation of an encrypted pipe with minimal roundtrips between the user and the gateway. Unfortunately, the WTLS protocol only encrypts data from the WAP device to the WAP gateway. From the WAP gateway to the content web server, information is transmitted over standard SSL. Because the data must be converted from WTLS to SSL, there is a brief millisecond in time when data is unencrypted on the gateway (see Figure 6-14).

This brief millisecond soon became known as the *WAP Gap*. Even though the practical risks of this gap were extremely minor, the press and analysts used the gap to proclaim that WAP was insecure. Information security vendors were quick to enter the fray, promoting various *end-to-end security solutions* that mitigated the WAP Gap risk, even if such solutions did little to address the issue.

Even if the WAP Gap was not a practical weakness, the maelstrom of negative publicity quickly dampened consumers' interest in WAP services.

**Figure 6-14**

WAP security architecture

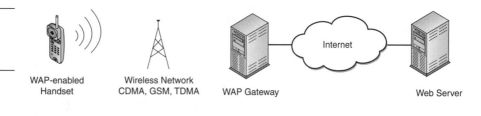

WAP-enabled Handset     Wireless Network CDMA, GSM, TDMA     WAP Gateway     Internet     Web Server

WTLS     SSL

Security-sensitive applications like wireless banking were especially hard hit. On a positive front, this publicity made security a top priority for WAP Forum members who immediately set out to address these issues in future versions of the WAP specification.

### Key Points about the WAP Gap and WTLS

The practicality of taking advantage of the WAP Gap was very low. Hackers would require physical access to the WAP gateway and would have to sift through vast amounts of data as well as know the exact moment in time when a connection was made to retrieve the data in the clear.

WAP gateways are almost always deployed in very secure environments. Because the WAP gateway must also track usage information for billing purposes and interface with the wireless voice billing systems and the HLR, the gateway is usually located in a secure building with limited administrative access and firewall protection.

For those concerned with the WAP Gap, enterprises and content providers have the option of hosting the WAP gateway themselves behind their firewall. Although this requires the enterprise to purchase, deploy, and maintain its own WAP gateway, it is still a feasible alternative to the WAP Gap issue. In fact, many banks and financial service vendors adopted this approach in 2000 in order to offer secure wireless banking.

WTLS was never meant to serve a static standard. Given the current limitations of circuit-switched networks, WTLS was the best alternative. In fact, the WAP Forum is already migrating to a TLS-centric design in WAP v2.0. Although this specification will not be supported in products until 2002 and 2003, the SSL/TLS specification will eliminate the WAP Gap entirely. This new specification will dovetail with the arrival of faster handsets and networks that will enable cryptographic functions to be completed directly on the device.

# Conclusion

In the last 15 years, we have seen an explosion in wireless data networks, applications, and users. Amazingly, the past growth is nothing compared to what many analysts are predicting for the future. Although the recent global recession has dampened some of the original forecasts, most surveys still predict a massive increase in wireless data users. The Ovum

Group has even forecast that more people will connect to the Internet via a wireless device than a wired device by 2005. This is especially true in regions and countries where incomes and infrastructure will not support a large home-PC-based Internet market.

However, although people are generally optimistic about the future of wireless data, considerable disagreement remains over the future of the various wireless data network technologies. Generally speaking, the technologies will converge over time to those standards that best offer two capabilities—speed and packet switching. The other wireless data standards will be forced to adapt to avoid being eliminated. This will likely entail developing and marketing solutions to certain vertical industries and geographic markets.

Much like the wired Internet, users will continue to demand more bandwidth, which bodes well for standards like GPRS. In addition, operators will use these initial higher-speed networks to test the market and plan implementations for future 3G networks.

Despite its initial stumbling, WAP will continue to endure. It still enjoys strong support from its members, is consistently adopting the specification to address potential limitations, and will only benefit from the higher-speed networks being built.

Remember that the wireless data market is still a relatively young market. Although networks and standards emerged in the early 1990s, wireless data did not experience anywhere near the stratospheric growth rate of wireless voice. Consequently, wireless data took longer to achieve critical mass and longer for compelling applications and services to be built for those networks. As a result, users can expect to see further innovation in the wireless data market in the years to come.

# CHAPTER 7

# Wireless Standards and Technologies

With a plethora of wireless technologies and options becoming available in today's developing wireless arena, the possibilities run the gamut from short-distance infrared to long-haul satellite. How do you make heads or tails of all of these new technologies? Which technologies will be successful? Which ones will be shelved? This chapter will try to provide a basic understanding about the available and up-and-coming options. Of course, because wireless technologies are still in their infancy with regards to wired networking, rapid developments continue to happen and do not stop for the publication of books. However, this chapter will discuss the current and future wireless technologies at the time of this writing. We will start by examining the underlying technologies. Then we'll look at how these fit in with current and future standards.

## Current and Future Technologies

Currently, wireless technologies use either radio or light waves to move information from one point to another. Most of us have been wireless users for years with our mobile/cordless phones and television remote controls. However, wireless technologies continue to evolve. For example, mobile phones, the veterans of the wireless world, are beginning to delve into the world of data transmission. Let's look at the basics of how these technologies work.

## Infrared

Infrared radiation (IR) involves electromagnetic waves in the spectrum just below visible light. Being close to visible light lends infrared a number of the same properties that visible light has. For example, like light waves, infrared travels in straight lines and bounces off objects, but it cannot penetrate physical or opaque objects. Data can be transmitted over infrared in much the same way that light is used to transmit data in fiber optics—by pulsing it (turning it on or off). This is the same type of technology used in many remote control units for TVs, VCRs, and so on.

## Radio

*Radio* is the use of electromagnetic waves that are emitted when an alternating current is input to an antenna. This can be used to transmit data invisibly through the air to devices such as radios, televisions, and mobile phones. Radio is the most widely used technology for wireless communications. As with anything good, only a limited amount of usable radio frequencies is available, and radio is used in an almost endless number of ways in today's world. Most of the usable radio spectrum has already been allocated for specific uses by different regulatory bodies, for example, the Federal Communications Commission (FCC) in the United States, the Radio Equipment Inspection and Certification Institute in Japan, and the Conference of European Postal and Telecommunications (CEPT) in Europe.

Many of the frequencies in the radio spectrum require a license. Some frequencies allocated in the radio spectrum have been made available for use without a license. One of these groups of unlicensed frequencies is known as the industrial, scientific, and medical (ISM) band because it is allocated for use by the industrial, scientific, and medical fields. If certain implementation requirements are followed, such as transmission power restrictions and the use of transmission technologies that will not interfere with existing radio devices in this band, this spectrum can be used for other purposes without the need to obtain a license or register with one of the previously mentioned regulatory bodies. In the United States, the ISM band also includes some of the 900 MHz range, but the 2.4 GHz range typically has the most unlicensed usage. See Table 7-1 for international details.

Due to the limited amount of bandwidth and the primary usage of the ISM band for the industrial, scientific, and medical fields, an additional set of frequencies has been allocated in many countries specifically for wireless local area network (LAN) use. This band is in the 5 GHz range and is referred to in the United States as the Unlicensed National Information Infrastructure (UNII) band, which spans from 5.15 to 5.35 GHz and 5.725 to 5.825 GHz. However, it may be some time before this band becomes widely used for LANs due to backwards compatibility issues with existing wireless LAN technologies that use the 2.4 GHz range.

Even with the specific allocation of radio frequencies for wireless LAN use, radio frequency availability is still limited. Therefore, a number of interesting ways to fit more data into the existing available frequencies have come into use. Some of these include the use of spread spectrum techniques and Orthogonal Frequency Division Multiplexing (OFDM).

## Spread Spectrum

Spread spectrum refers to the method of dividing data and sending it over a "spread" or wideband of different frequencies. Spread spectrum signals use multiple frequencies (wideband) and appear to be radio noise to narrowband devices. This kind of noise can be easily filtered out, which is what enables the coexistence of narrowband devices. Some common spread spectrum methods are frequency hopping spread spectrum (FHSS) and direct sequence spread spectrum (DSSS).

| Table 7-1 | Region | Allocated Spectrum |
|-----------|--------|--------------------|
| International Details | United States | 2.4–2.4835 GHz |
| | Europe | 2.4–2.4835 GHz |
| | Japan | 2.471–2.497 GHz |
| | France | 2.4465–2.4835 GHz |
| | Spain | 2.445–2.475 GHz |

In FHSS systems, the transmitter and the receiver hop from one frequency to another in prearranged synchronized patterns. The hops occur frequently with very little time being spent on any one frequency. This reduces the possibility of interference with other devices and enables several overlapping FHSS systems to be operational at the same time.

DSSS pushes data through a binary encoding process that spreads the data by combining it with a multibit pattern or *pseudo-noise code*. The resulting data is now somewhat hidden and inflated. For example, if the bit pattern is 11 bits long (which is typical for most DSSS wireless applications), then 1 bit of data would now be 11 bits long. This data is modulated and then sent out over multiple frequencies (which typically consist of about 22 MHz of bandwidth) at the same time. Since the original data bit was encoded into 11 bits, the data is more resilient to air loss because the data has a tremendous amount of redundancy.

## OFDM

OFDM is a multicarrier modulation method that divides a communications channel into a number of equally spaced frequency bands. Each band is then used to transmit a portion of the user information. Each band is independent of, or orthogonal, to every other band. This multicarrier approach also reduces multipath problems where the reflected radio signals bounce back from different sources with slightly different timing. At the same time, it increases the performance and data throughput.

# Current and Future Standards

Standard-setting bodies are beneficial for a number of reasons. Primarily, they provide a basis for interoperability between vendors' products. They are also forums for discussing all the important issues related to a particular technology. Of course, if no one buys into the standard, the standard is effectively no good. So, for this reason, many standards are consensus based. A number of standard-setting organizations exist, but the two that are having the most impact on wireless technologies are the Institute of Electrical and Electronics Engineers (IEEE) and the European Telecommunications Standards Institute (ETSI).

# IEEE 802

The IEEE (www.ieee.org) develops standards in a wide range of electrical/electronic fields. The 802 Local and Metropolitan Area Networks Standards Committee (LMSC) of the IEEE Computer Society defines specifications related to LANs (www.ieee802.org).

# 802.11

In 1990, the LMSC formed the 802.11 workgroup to begin developing a wireless LAN standard (grouper.ieee.org/groups/802/11/). Seven years later, the first IEEE wireless standard was completed, which provided a mandatory 1 Mbps and an optional 2 Mbps data transfer rate using the 2.4 GHz ISM radio band. Of course, the decision to use that particular radio band was not arbitrary but based on the face that it was available for unlicensed use in most countries around the world. This is partly why this standard has been so successful.

The 802.11 standard defines the interface between wireless clients and their network access points. Specifically, this includes the Physical (PHY) and the Media Access Control (MAC) layers. It also defines the security mechanism Wired Equivalent Privacy (WEP) (described in Chapter 3) and an outline of how roaming between access points should work.

The PHY layer defines the wireless transmission. Three different types of transmissions are defined in the 802.11 standard—diffuse infrared, DSSS radio, and FHSS radio. The most commonly used transmission today is DSSS radio transmission. Notably, DSSS is the technology specified in the newer 802.11 standards. The PHY layers all support a mandatory 1 Mbps data rate with an optional 2 Mbps rate as specified in the original specification.

As the name indicates, the MAC layer controls access to the physical media, which, in the case of 802.11, is either radio transmission or infrared light. Due to the nature of the PHY layer and the devices that normally use wireless, the 802.11 MAC layer performs some extra functions (such as error recovery, roaming functionality, and power conservation) that are not normally provided by a MAC used in wired networks. This serves to hide the physical characteristics of the wireless medium from the higher networking layers. The MAC has two main standards of operation: a distributed mode (carrier sense multiple access with collision avoidance [CSMA/CA]) and a coordinated mode. The distributed mode uses basically the same methods that wired Ethernet networks use (carrier sense multiple access with collision detection [CSMA/CD]) to share the same wire. The coordinated mode uses a centrally coordinated polling mechanism to provide support for applications that require support for real-time traffic.

The 802.11 specification also specifies the optional use of encryption for security by means of the WEP feature. Since wired networks have a measure of physical security that is unavailable for wireless networks, encryption is used to provide an equivalent privacy similar to a physical boundary (like a wall). Some key failures of WEP that have been widely discussed include the lack of key management, the use of a static shared key, and the implementation flaws of the RC4 algorithm. These issues have been addressed somewhat by various proprietary solutions. However, the IEEE is trying to address these security issues via the task group 802.11i, which is discussed in the section "802.11i."

# The ABCs of 802.11

If you've been following the 802.11 standards, you've probably seen all the letters that crop up behind 802.11. For example, you may have seen 802.11b, 802.11a, and 802.11i. What do these letters behind the 802.11 standard mean?

Well, these are actually different 802.11 task groups (subgroups) that have been formed and given specific areas of wireless networking to investigate and standardize. Some involve higher-speed technologies, whereas others involve specific areas that need an implementation solution such as security. Some of these have completed their tasks, but many of these are currently in progress. At some point, these should become new wireless technology standards. For more details on the tasks of the working groups, please see their web site at www.ieee802.org/11/.

The letter indicates the order of the task group's creation/proposal—for example, 802.11a was proposed before 802.11b and so on. This may be somewhat confusing because 802.11a seems to be newer than 802.11b. What happened? Very simply, the task assigned to the 802.11a task group involved a more complex modulation technology (OFDM) than that used in 802.11b Complimentary Code Keying (CCK) DSSS; hence, 802.11b was finished sooner than 802.11a. The following sections will examine the different task groups in greater detail.

## Tough Choice: 802.11a, 802.11b, or 802.11g?

So which one should you choose? As we mentioned earlier, it's difficult to say which one is going to win the majority vote over time. However, if you need faster data rates right now, 802.11a is the only high-speed 802.11 solution with shipping products. As a result, many are questioning the viability of 802.11g because it is currently a draft standard and not expected to be fully approved until late 2002 or early 2003 with vendor products perhaps by early 2003. As an interesting side note though, Intersil has already released a chip set to support the 802.11g draft standard. Only time will tell. With many technologies, the lack of reverse compatibility with old standards prevents the adoption of new technology. However, one compelling reason to go with 802.11a is if you have problems with radio frequency interference from wireless phones, microwaves, or Bluetooth devices because this standard operates outside the range of these devices.

## 802.11b

The most widely recognized 802.11 standard currently is the *b* standard, so it will be discussed first. In September 1999, 802.11 High Rate, or 802.11b, was approved as a standard for a high-speed extension to 802.11, providing data transfer rates of up to 11 Mbps while still using the 2.4 GHz radio band.

Data rates mentioned in this chapter refer to the physical interface data rate. Data throughput rates are usually much less than the physical interface data rate due to the MAC overhead, errors, and collisions. See Table 7-2, which shows the 802.11 interface comparisons for throughput rates. This extension uses CCK with DSSS, and because it uses the 2.4 GHz range, it is fully backwards compatible with DSSS implementations of 802.11.

| Standard | Capacity | | Interface | Frequency | No. of Channels in the Approved Frequencies | | | Shipping |
| --- | --- | --- | --- | --- | --- | --- | --- | --- |
| | PHYS | Real Throughput | | | U.S. | Asia | Europe | |
| 802.11 | 2 Mbps | N/A | IR with PPM | | | | | No |
| | 2 Mbps | 1.6 Mbps | 2- or 4-level GFSK over FHSS | 2.4 GHz | 79 | 23 | 79 | Yes |
| | 2 Mbps | 1.6 Mbps | DBPSK /DQPSK over DSSS | 2.4 GHz | 3 | 3 | 4 | Yes |
| 802.11b | 11 Mbps | 6 Mbps | CCK over DSSS | 2.4 GHz | 3 | 3 | 4 | Yes |
| 802.11a | 54 Mbps | 31 Mbps | OFDM | 5 GHz | 12 | 4 | 0 | Yes |
| 802.11g | 54 Mbps | 12 Mbps | CCK over OFDM, CCK over OFDM PCB-22 | 2.4 GHz | 3 | 3 | 4 | Fourth quarter 2002 to second quarter 2003 |

**Table 7-2**  802.11 Interface Comparisons

To make it easier to refer to and more memorable, the interoperability organization called the Wireless Ethernet Compatibility Alliance (WECA) has also given this standard the moniker *WiFi*. With this moniker, you have the assurance that any WiFi device has been tested for interoperability with other 802.11 devices. This standard has become very popular and makes a wireless LAN an increasingly more viable option both technically and financially.

## 802.11a

802.11a is another high-speed interface definition. However, it uses a completely different radio band—the 5 GHz band. Designed to pump through 54 Mbps, it also uses the new modulation scheme of OFDM. For additional information, see www.ofdm-forum.com. WECA refers to 802.11a as *WiFi5*.

A current disadvantage of 802.11a is that the portion of the 5 GHz band defined and approved for unlicensed use in the United States is different from that allocated in other countries. As a result, interoperability with products from other countries will become somewhat of an issue. An 802.11 task group has been assigned to allocate or unify this radio band in other countries.

802.11a is not backwards compatible with the 802.11b or 802.11 standards because it uses a completely different radio band (2.4 GHz for 802.11b versus 5 GHz for 802.11a). This could eliminate current investments in 802.11/802.11b wireless infrastructures that organizations may already have, or it may be a barrier to the adoption of 802.11a. Some manufacturers are trying to address this issue by manufacturing devices that work with both 802.11a and 802.11b such as Proxim's Harmony Fast-Wireless access point product. Synad is another company that has announced the development of an 802.11a/b chipset.

However, the use of the 5 GHz range in the long run should provide cleaner transmissions without interference from other devices that use the 2.4 GHz band such as cordless phones, microwave ovens, and baby monitors. The Bluetooth standard also uses the 2.4 GHz band.

The spectrum available in the 5 GHz range is also much larger than that in the ISM band, allowing for up to 11 distinct channels compared with 3 channels (with the use of some overlapping in 802.11 and 802.11b) for the 2.4 GHz band. Companies such as Atheros (www.atheros.com) are taking advantage of this by combining multiple 802.11a channels to increase the data rates.

# 802.11g

The next working group of note is 802.11g. Interestingly, 802.11g is another high-speed extension (currently a draft standard) that is similar in nature to 802.11b. 802.11g uses a Texas Instruments (TI) technology to get data rates up to 22 Mbps or OFDM with DSSS (the same technology in 802.11a) for data rates up to 54 Mbps. A major reason for the 802.11g standard is that it provides a higher data rate while maintaining backwards compatibility and interoperability with current 802.11b DSSS-based products.

802.11g has a couple of drawbacks. The biggest issues deal with radio frequency interference from other devices that use the same 2.4 GHz radio band such as wireless phones, microwaves, and Bluetooth devices. This may make 802.11g only an interim solution on the way to some standard that uses the 5 GHz band.

This task group has also had some delays due to vendor politics between TI and Intersil. Intersil is currently the largest 802.11b chipset maker, and they proposed the use of OFDM for 802.11g. Around that time, TI, who would like to become a chipset provider, proposed the use of its technology. In the current draft, the standard specifies the use of both of these technologies. Intersil released the first chip set designed to support the IEEE 802.11g draft standard in January 2002.

# 802.11j

This task group was proposed by the joint IEEE, ETSI, and Multimedia Mobile Access Communication (MMAC) 5 GHz Globalization and Harmonization Study Group (5GSG) and was to be tasked with making 802.11a and the high-performance radio LAN (HiperLAN) standards interoperable. HiperLAN is a European wireless LAN standard and is discussed later in the section "HiperLAN/2." The idea was to create a single global standard for wireless LAN in the 5 GHz band, rather than multiple standards. After some work was accomplished in unifying the usage of this band across the United States, Europe, and Japan, this group was discontinued.

## 802.11h and 5GPP

802.11h is a feature enhancement for the 5 GHz PHY (802.11a) and adds Transmit Power Control (TPC), which limits the PC card from emitting more radio signal than is needed, and Dynamic Frequency Selection (DFS), which lets the device listen to what is happening in the airspace before picking a channel. TPC and DFS are European requirements. So 802.11h is essentially an adaptation of 802.11a in order to meet the European implementation requests for the 5 GHz band. When 802.11h matures, it will eventually replace 802.11a as WiFi5, according to WECA.

## 802.11e

This task group is assigned to add multimedia and quality of service (QoS) capabilities to the 802.11 MAC layer. Because this is a MAC layer modification, the benefits derived here will benefit 802.11a, 802.11b, and 802.11g devices. QoS refers to the ability to implement guarantees of specified data transmission rates and error percentages. The work from this group will also have an impact on the 802.15 and 802.16 standards. Having a QoS standard for wireless devices may pave the way for the adoption of 802.11 protocols for multimedia and voice over IP (VoIP) devices.

## 802.11i

The 802.11 standard has a number of serious security issues. Because of this, the 802.11 task group *i* was formed to look at ways to the current security vulnerabilities. Currently, they have developed a trio of improvements known collectively as the Temporal Key Integrity Protocol (TKIP). The basic improvements recommended in the current proposal are the mandatory use of 128-bit temporal keys, fast packet keying, and key management. 802.1x will likely be used to solve authentication and key distribution problems.

## 802.11f

We mentioned earlier that the 802.11 standard defines some additional MAC functionality including roaming. Roaming is required when a wireless client is moving between access points or distribution systems. Although the 802.11 standard defines the basic message formats for inter-access point communication, not much else is specified. Because of this, Aironet, Lucent Technologies, and Digital Ocean teamed up in 1996 and began developing the Interaccess Point Protocol (IAPP). IAPP has been further developed by the 802.11f task group and is currently awaiting approval. It specifies the information that needs to be exchanged between access points in order to support a distribution system and roaming (basically a wireless backbone) for wireless clients. Table 7-3 provides a summary of the discussed 802.11 task groups.

# IEEE 802.15

802.15 is an 802 work group tasked with creating wireless personal area network (WPAN) standards. WPANs allow for wireless connectivity between fixed, portable, and moving devices within or entering a Personal Operating Space (POS). A POS is defined as a space roughly 10 meters around a person. 802.15 networks are different from 802.11 networks because they require much less range and are more concerned with reducing power consumption, size, and cost. There are four sub task groups to 802.15 (http://ieee.802.org/15). Currently, these are referred to by number rather than alphabetical notation.

**TG1** This task group created a WPAN standard based on the Bluetooth 1.x specification with a 1 Mbps data rate (700 Kbps actual throughput). Just as with the 802.11 specification, 802.15 defines both the PHY and the MAC layers. This standard was scheduled for approval in December 2001, but was not approved by the time of this writing. Some of the devices that could be networked using this standard include computers, personal digital assistants (PDAs), printers, headsets, pagers, and cellular phones.

**TG2** TG2's objective is to provide interoperability between the 802.15 and 802.11 standards. In order to accomplish this, the group is developing a recommended practice guide for the IEEE 802.15 WPAN operation and suggested modifications to the 802.15 and 802.11 standards. These suggestions should enable 802.15 and 802.11 devices that use the same 2.4 GHz range to successfully coexist with each other.

| 802.11 Task Group | Purpose | Band | Status | Notes |
|---|---|---|---|---|
| **Table 7-3** 802.11 Standards | | | | |
| 802.11 | Wireless LAN. | 2.4 GHz | Approved—1997<br><br>Updated—1999 | Defines the PHY and MAC for wireless LANs. IR, FHSS, and DSSS are defined PHY. Data rates up to 2 Mbps. |
| 802.11a | Develop a PHY in the 5 GHz band. | 5 GHz | Approved—1999 | Defines a high-speed PHY using the 5 GHz band. Uses OFDM. Data rates up to 54 Mbps. |
| 802.11b | Develop a faster PHY (than 802.11) in the 2.4 GHz band. | 2.4 GHz | Approved—1999 | Defines a high-speed PHY using the 2.4 GHz band. Uses CCK with DSSS. Data rates up to 11 Mbps. |
| 802.11c | Develop MAC bridging functionality for 802.11. | N/A | Folded into 802.1D standard for MAC bridging | |
| 802.11d | Determine the requirements necessary for 802.11 to operate in other regulatory domains (countries). | N/A | Ongoing* | |
| 802.11e | Provide QoS and classes of service. | N/A | Ongoing* | Uses distributed coordination function (DCF) and point coordination function (PCF). |

*continues*

| Table 7-3 (cont.) | 802.11 Task Group | Purpose | Band | Status | Notes |
|---|---|---|---|---|---|
| 802.11 Standards | 802.11f | Multivendor access point inter-operability by use of an IAPP. | N/A | Ongoing* | This involves recommended practices above the MAC layer. |
| | 802.11g | Develop a faster PHY (than 802.11b) in the 2.4 GHz band. | 2.4 GHz | Draft standard 2001 | 22 Mbps is possible by using PCBB-22. Alternatively, OFDM can be used for up to 54 Mbps. |
| | 802.11h | Enhance the MAC and the 802.11a PHY with spectrum and power management in the 5 GHz band. | 5 GHz | Ongoing* | Objective is to obtain European regulatory approval. |
| | 802.11i | Security enhance-ments to WEP. | N/A | Ongoing* | Uses TKIP. |
| | 802.11j | Make 802.11a and HiperLAN interoperable. | 5 GHz | Discontinued | |

*As of the time of the writing (February 2002)

**TG3** This group aims at achieving higher data rates of 20 Mbps or more in WPANs. Low cost and low power operation are also targeted goals. The draft standard for this was completed in November 2001.

**TG4** This group is working on lowering power consumption by 802.15 devices in order to achieve battery lifetimes of months or years. The focus for this group is low data rate (the maximum data rate of 200 Kbps) applications such as sensors, interactive toys, smart badges, remote controls, and home automation.

# IEEE 802.16

802.16 is another IEEE 802 task group (WirelessMan.org), but this task group is assigned to create a wireless metropolitan area network (WirelessMAN), which is also known as *broadband wireless access*. There are three sub task groups for 802.16, which are discussed in the following sections.

**TG1** TG1 defines a wireless interface (PHY) that operates in the 10 to 66 GHz range with data rates of 2 to 155 Mbps. The standard uses Demand Assignment Multiple Access with Time Division Multiple Access (DAMA-TDMA). DAMA provides dynamic capacity assignment. This work has been completed, and the 802.16 standard was approved in December 2001.

**TG2** This group aimed to provide recommended practices for the coexistence of broadband wireless access systems. This was completed, and the report "IEEE Recommended Practice for Local and Metropolitan Area Networks—Coexistence of Fixed Broadband Wireless Access Systems" was published in September 2001.

**TG3** This group is working on extending the 802.16 standard to include operation in the 2 to 11 GHz range and expects to be finished by the summer of 2003. The new standard is referred to as 802.16a. With 802.16a, the usable range will be from 2 to 66 GHz.

# IEEE 802.1x

802.1x is an approved standard (June 2001) that provides network port authentication. Basically, the standard defines an authentication framework using a variety of existing protocols (such as the Extensible Authentication Protocol [EAP] or Remote Access Dial-In User Service [RADIUS]) for all 802-based LANs—both wired and wireless. This technology is already available in Windows XP and with Cisco's LEAP and provides the framework for overcoming many of the security shortcomings of current wireless technologies.

Some key aspects of this standard include the mandatory use of 128-bit keys for RC4 data encryption, encryption key rotation, and the blocking of any network activity until after successful user authentication. Also, with 802.1x, there is no need to have static WEP keys distributed to the stations.

# ETSI

ETSI (www.etsi.org) is the European counterpart to IEEE.

## HiperLAN/1

In 1991, ETSI formed the Subtechnical Committee RES10 to develop a HiperLAN. The resulting standard was the HiperLAN/1 standard (approved in 1996) and defines the PHY and MAC specifications for wireless high-speed communications. HiperLAN/1 uses gaussian minimum shift keying (GMSK) and specifies data rates of up to 20 Mbps between portable devices.

One advantage of HiperLAN/1 is that it works in a dedicated bandwidth (5.1 to 5.3 GHz, which is allocated only in Europe) so it doesn't have to use spread spectrum technologies in order to coexist with other radio usage as is the case in the 2.4 GHz ISM range. Also, the protocol uses a variant of CSMA/CA and includes optional encryption and power savings.

Another nice feature of HiperLAN/1 is ad-hoc routing. For example, if your destination is out of reach, intermediate nodes will automatically forward it through the best route within the HiperLAN/1 network (the routes are automatically recalculated regularly). HiperLAN/1 is also totally ad hoc, requiring no configuration and no central controller. Interestingly, very few HiperLAN/1 products are commercially available.

### HiperLAN/2

In 1997, ETSI formed the Broadband Radio Area Network (BRAN) group to work on HiperLAN/2, which was approved in February 2000. Hiper-LAN/2 is a redesign of HiperLAN/1 and was the first standard to use OFDM.

HiperLAN/2 and IEEE 802.11a are similar in their use of the 5 GHz band and OFDM to attain data rates as high as 54 Mbps. However, a key difference between the two standards is in the MAC portion of the systems. HiperLAN/2 uses Time Division Multiplexing (TDM), whereas 802.11a/g use CSMA/CD. Because of this, HiperLAN/2 can provide QoS, while IEEE 802.11a does not currently include it. HiperLAN/2 is regarded as wireless Asynchronous Transfer Mode (ATM).

A major drawback of HiperLAN/2 is that it currently has no shipping products, and none are expected until in 2003. It is possible that a joint standard may exist between ETSI and IEEE because a joint project, referred to as the *5 GHz Unified Protocol* (5-UP) project, is currently being worked on. The objective of the project is to provide a single universal standard in the 5 GHz range for wireless LANs.

## Bluetooth

Bluetooth (named after the Viking king of Denmark known for his skill in getting people to talk to one another) is a low-cost, short-range wireless specification for connecting devices. It was originally developed by Ericsson and was intended as a way to replace the cabling between cellular phones and laptops with a small, low-powered, and low-cost radio solution.

The Bluetooth Special Interest Group (SIG) was formed in order to make the technology an open, interoperable standard. The first release of the Bluetooth specification was in July 1999. The SIG is now driving the development of the standard (www.bluetooth.com).

The Bluetooth standard uses low-powered radio in the 2.4 GHz range and avoids interference from other radio signals by the use of very fast frequency hopping (1,600 times a second) between 79 frequencies at 1 MHz intervals. A range of 10 meters and an optional 100 meters are defined in the specification. IEEE is in the process of developing a standard that incorporates Bluetooth technology (refer to the section "IEEE 802.15").

Because Bluetooth uses the same band as the 802.11, 802.11b, and 802.11g standards (the 2.4 GHz range), there have been concerns about the coexistence of these devices in the same physical area. However, a number of studies have shown that it is possible for these to operate together. 802.15 TG2 is actually tasked with suggestions to improve interoperability between Bluetooth devices and other 802.11 standards that use the 2.4 GHz band.

## HomeRF

HomeRF (www.homerf.org) is a label for a group of manufacturers that came together in 1998 to develop a standard for wireless connectivity between personal computers and electronic devices. The standard that resulted is the Shared Wireless Access Protocol (SWAP), which allows for voice and data transmission with data rates of up to 1.6 Mbps.

Targeting the home market, the premise behind HomeRF was that 802.11 devices would be too costly and complicated for home/consumer markets. The popularity of 802.11 devices has quickly dispelled this notion and somewhat displaced HomeRF's market share. In order to try and recover, HomeRF is working on SWAP 2.0, which will use wideband frequency hopping (WBFH) to increase the data rate of the standard. It is also trying to differentiate HomeRF from the other wireless standards by promoting it as a standard for wireless communication between not just data but also voice and multimedia devices.

## Ultrawideband Radio (UWB)

In February 2002, the FCC approved the use of ultrawideband (UWB) radio in the 3.1 through 10.6 GHz band, opening the way for the use of radio impulse technology in wireless LANs.

Instead of traditional sine waves, UWB radio broadcasts digital pulses that are timed very precisely on a signal across a very wide spectrum at the same time. The transmitter and receiver must be coordinated to send and receive pulses with an accuracy of trillionths of a second. This actually sidesteps the multipath issues typically associated with radio signals. With the current power restrictions mandated by the FCC, UWB signals appear as radio noise to other frequency users. This is why UWB has been approved for use in the 3.1 to 10.6 GHz range. UWB also has a low power consumption, making this a very desirable technology for many portable wireless applications.

# Conclusion

Having standards is wonderful for interoperability and decreased cost. Wireless standards are rapidly advancing—even for the computer industry. As with all new technologies and standards, there will be winners and losers. I still have a Beta Max in the garage. No one can predict which standards will be the winners, but I would predict that the winning standards will address cost and reverse compatibility issues.

# PART 3

# Wireless Deployment Strategies

# CHAPTER 8

# Implementing Wireless LANs: Security Considerations

In the previous chapters, we discussed the possible threats to systems and the technologies that can be used to counter those threats. To properly understand and counter the risks, the functional goals of the wireless network must be fully understood. We will explore the security considerations that should be applied to different layers of the wireless network—namely, the physical, network, and application layers. The physical section will cover radio frequency (RF) coverage, equipment placement, and building construction. The network section will cover the general network architecture, wireless local area network (LAN) medium access protections, and mobility and virtual private network (VPN) considerations. The application section will cover application communications tunneling encryption.

## Common Wireless Network Applications

In order to reduce risk, you must understand the avenues of attack. In Chapter 2, we illuminated the major threats. In this section, we examine the various common network configurations where wireless Ethernet is deployed. Many companies use wireless Ethernet as a drop-in replacement for Ethernet when mobility is needed or when wiring is difficult or impossible. Some historic buildings are very limited in wiring possibilities so wireless Ethernet is the only option for network connectivity. Another common way to bridge networks over short distances between buildings is to use a wireless bridge and directional antennae.

Wireless Internet service providers (ISPs) generally provide last-mile wireless access to fixed-point locations to either a home or business. This configuration is called *point-to-multipoint*, where the customers connect to the ISP upstream access point via a client adapter at the customer premises. Because the network is not designed with mobility in mind, it operates similarly to point-to-point configuration, differing only in that multiple clients can connect to one access point.

The last two scenarios involve client roaming between access points. Roaming occurs because the wireless user moves out of range from the access point that was providing network services. As the client moves out of range, the link deteriorates and is eventually lost because no other access point is in the vicinity. When the existing link begins to deteriorate, the client may also search for another access point to roam to. The roaming process drops the existing Transmission Control Protocol (TCP) connection and requires a new network connection upon association with the new access point. This leaves the wireless network designer with the problem of maintaining the TCP state during network disassociation and reassociation.

Networks that permit roaming are often large and cover vast distances. When designed poorly, they can be a network administrator's nightmare. However, if designed with security and performance in mind, the administrator will be rewarded with a high-performance, dynamic wireless environment that can also facilitate wireless network incident response.

## Physical Security Considerations

Good security engineering examines the problem from all angles, and when building a wireless network, you must begin at the physical layer. Control over the wireless coverage will reward the administrator with fewer headaches down the road. Understanding the boundaries of your network makes network incident response a less daunting task and can actually lead to better network performance. Key points on infrastructure

## Site Surveys

Site survey software is commonly bundled with your network card configuration utility. Simple site surveys do not require the purchase of commercial sniffer software, but for advanced site troubleshooting, commercial software is highly recommended.

placement also assist the designer and implementer in successfully deploying a wireless network that eliminates areas without coverage and focuses radio signals into needed areas.

### Site Survey

A site survey is used to determine the physical environment in which a wireless LAN is installed. The site survey has two components: the physical walkthrough and the signal strength and access point placement evaluation. Having a site plan for the building or area that will be surveyed is recommended, but it is not always needed. During the physical walkthrough, the engineer takes note of the surrounding areas and the obstacles that need to be overcome. For example, dense vegetation, out buildings, large metal objects, large open distances, and building construction must all be noted. The buildings must be carefully evaluated. Outer- and inner-wall construction, window treatments, and window glass material must all be identified and considered when determining the placement of the access point and antenna.

The second component of the site survey is performed with access points and a roaming wireless client. An access point is installed in a potential service location and the wireless client is walked around while the user monitors the signal strength. Network coverage is evaluated and fine-tuned for optimal performance and security. A proper design for directional antennae occurs in this phase. After the general coverage is determined, the overall signal strength of the access point can be adjusted to contain wireless network exposure inside a controllable range.

### Equipment Placement

You should follow several guidelines when deploying equipment in the field:

- Ensure that the access point is installed out of the normal reach of employees. Where possible, conceal the access point from sight.

- If the access point is installed outdoors, make sure the equipment is properly secured, discouraging tampering.

- When appropriate, sector network areas with directional antennae. This places RF where you intend it to be. It also quantifies areas where users are when connected to that cell. This is very useful when tracking down problems or running through incidence-response procedures.

- Name the access points so that they can be tracked down easily during frantic troubleshooting events.

Once the access points are in the best possible configuration, you should perform a perimeter sweep to ensure that excess radiation isn't bleeding into unintended areas. Most access points designed for corporate and enterprise use have an adjustable power output and can be trimmed down to remove excess bleeding.

### RF Containment

The objective of RF containment is to attenuate or limit the scope of your network within the known boundaries. This is very important in large networks where roaming is necessary, but it also deprives would-be attackers from detecting the network or certain portions of the network, which lowers your drive-by profile. When combined with directional antennae, it also normally has a performance benefit.

In addition to attenuating the transmit power on the access point, you can also perform the following physical tasks to limit the amount of RF bleed out of buildings and rooms. When designing a new facility, specific rooms can be designed to prevent the leakage of excessive RF energy by installing metallic film or foil under the drywall. Metallic paint can also be applied to walls to add a layer of attenuation. Metallic window blinds provide better attenuation over cloth or plastic blinds. These simple details may result in the difference between a wireless perimeter extending tens of feet from the intended area to hundreds of feet.

# Network Security Considerations

The needs of the enterprise drive the majority of the network architecture, and security and performance must be considered from the onset of the project. In the following sections, we will discuss the major wireless network scenarios, provide best practices, and share some thoughts on how you would build a network to meet your goals in a secure manner.

The general consensus is to treat all wireless networks as untrusted anonymous hosts just like the traffic originating on the Internet. Access is granted once the host successfully presents the qualifying credentials to an authentication server and all communications travel over an encrypted tunnel between the two systems. This still holds true to a point, but when possible, you should segment the networks in order to minimize physical-layer denial of service (DoS) attacks to shield critical networks from the external threats. As stated before, segmenting can also significantly assist in incident-response activities.

Segmenting off administrative communications channels is difficult with access points because the administrative interfaces are often limited to the Ethernet port. Some access points have out-of-band management through a serial port, but that can also be difficult to manage in large distributed networks; however, it is the only secure method. Most access points do not allow you to push configurations across many access points through the serial interface, but you can usually do it over the Ethernet or wireless interface. If possible, configuration capabilities over the wireless interface should be disabled to prevent attackers from tampering with the configuration. Management of the access point should be considered when choosing a brand of access point. Telnet, cleartext Hypertext Transfer Protocol (HTTP), and unencrypted Simple Network Management Protocol (SNMP) should be avoided. Instead, try using Secure Shell (SSH) or Secure Sockets Layer (SSL) for managing network devices. Some terminal servers with SSH capabilities can be configured to access the serial port on access points.

## Physical and Data Link Layer Security Controls

We will continue to follow the International Organization for Standardization (ISO) model as set forth in the earlier chapters by looking at the physical and data link layers. The 802.11 wireless Ethernet standard has minimal and flawed authentication and packet encryption methods defined within. However, as mentioned previously, when used in conjunction with

Wired Equivalent Privacy (WEP), 802.1x augments and corrects some of the standards pitfalls. A high-level overview is shown in Figure 8-1.

Using 802.1x with dynamic WEP keys eliminates most of the attacks against WEP, as defined in 802.11-1999 and 802.11b, as long as keys are rotated frequently. Shared authentication should never be used; always use an open system because the shared authentication scheme leaks WEP key information to attackers through known plaintext methods. One of the downfalls of 802.1x is that it requires more back-end equipment and a Remote Access Dial-In User Service (RADIUS) server with 802.1x capabilities. This additional management overhead should be considered.

Recently, many vendors have implemented WEP *key hashing*. Key hashing is the process of hashing the initialization vector (IV) and shared key before generating the RC4 stream. This is a highly effective way to prevent someone from recovering the WEP key by using passive attacks. At the time of this writing, all key-hashing features of wireless devices are vendor proprietary and not interoperable.

Another common 802.11-based security mechanism is the use of Media Access Control (MAC) access control lists. A MAC access control list is a list of physical addresses that are allowed to access the wireless network. This security mechanism is found in almost all access points. It enables the network administrator to enter lists of valid MAC addresses into an access control list, limiting network access. With some access points, the

**Figure 8-1**

High-level 802.1x diagram

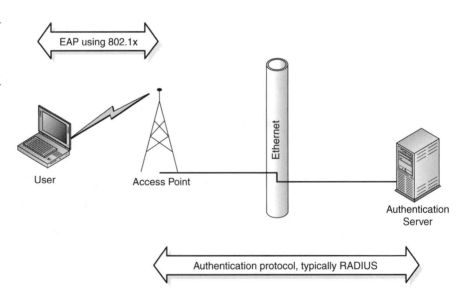

list can then be pushed out to all participating access points. The downfall of this practice is that the MAC addresses of all wireless clients and access points are sent in the clear, even when WEP is enabled.

Changing the MAC address of a network card is a trivial task. Many times it is a configuration option in the driver. An eavesdropper can easily compile a listing of valid MACs, detect when one disassociates, and attach to the network with that valid MAC address. Even with their limitations, MAC access controls are still useful in some circumstances. They can be powerful tools in preventing roaming clients from accidentally attaching to an open wireless network. However, the administrative overhead needs to be considered because keeping track of valid MACs and updating all access points with the valid address can be a time-consuming task.

## VPN Tunneling

As alluded to in the previous chapters, VPN tunneling works extremely well in many environments, as shown in Figure 8-2. It is a proven technology and many companies are already equipped with a VPN gateway. Sometimes adding access to the VPN from the wireless network can be as simple as adding a network card to the VPN gateway or changing some firewall rules. When roaming is required, network designers need to take network subnetting into consideration. The IP address must remain the same for it to work seamlessly. In many cases, the VPN tunnel will drop when roaming and will reset TCP connections. This may require the user to reenter authentication credentials.

**Figure 8-2**

VPN architecture

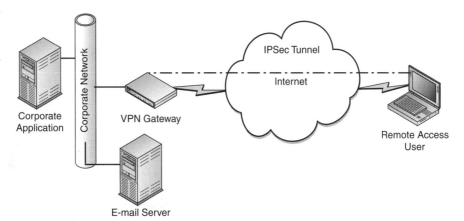

MobileIP may be used for roaming. MobileIP may prevent the VPN connection from getting torn down when traversing between access points. MobileIP can also be used across different wireless network types. You can use MobileIP on cellular telephone data services, eliminating the enterprise's requirement of a separate infrastructure to support mobile telephony applications.

## Intrusion Detection Systems (IDSs)

Your network will never be 100 percent secure. Not all attacks can be stopped and excessive security measures can sometimes be prohibitive to business. In other words, attempting to prevent all possible attacks is not only an exercise in futility, but it may not be worth the effort. Many people who want to secure their houses install alarms instead of bars on the windows to notify the police in the event of a break-in. The equivalent to home alarms in the digital arena is intrusion detection systems (IDSs). IDSs take many forms, but they normally break down into two categories: host based and network based.

A host-based IDS (HIDS) is normally a piece of software that monitors the system for suspicious activity. This involves monitoring system files for changes or the installation of new software, drivers, or kernel modifications. Sometimes an HIDS also monitors the network connections, looking for suspicious connections and new programs, listening for incoming connections, and initiating new outgoing connections. Some personal firewall software has an HIDS component.

A network-based IDS (NIDS) is based on a modified packet sniffer. It is installed on a network and has the capability to examine network traffic, as shown in Figure 8-3. The NIDS either monitors for suspicious activity by comparing network traffic to signatures of known attacks or monitors for anomalies. Anomaly IDS systems have a learning mode in which they build rules based on the normal network traffic patterns. Then they monitor traffic with the created rules and alert any suspicious activity. Some systems are a hybrid of the two technologies. Many commercial IDS systems and some open-source systems are available.

One of the benefits of using NIDS over HIDS is that a single NIDS sensor can monitor a network containing many hosts, thus simplifying the installation and configuration of the IDS. Some HIDS can dramatically decrease the performance of the host operating system. Be sure to fully test the impact of different IDSs on your applications before deploying them to the entire network. Various forms of IDSs are included in the designs discussed in the following sections.

**Figure 8-3**

IDS architecture

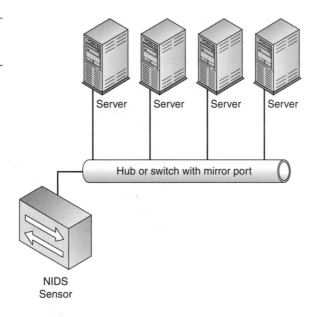

Due to the administrative overhead of monitoring IDS sensors and keeping IDS signatures up-to-date, many companies choose to outsource this service. An outsourced IDS service provides or sells sensors to be placed on the network and monitors them from the Internet or a dedicated telco link. The monitoring service is responsible for updating changes and alerting administrators of any suspicious activity. These services are expensive and are not for every enterprise. You should evaluate your in-house security and monitoring expertise before deciding to use an outsourced IDS provider.

Some people feel that an IDS can also involve reviewing logs for suspicious events. Regularly reviewing and archiving logs should be the standard practice on any network. Many intrusion-related events do not produce suspicious-looking logs during the event so the effectiveness of these systems as IDSs is limited.

Additional IDS resources include

www.snort.org

www.sourcefire.com

www.nfr.com

www.enterasys.com/ids/

www.counterpane.com

## Application Security Considerations

Wireless networks are often set up to offer a specific application. This may include roaming agents in airports, inventory tracking in warehouses, e-mail, or service of the "killer app" to end users. Many times these applications have already been hardened to work on a hostile network: the Internet. In these cases, wireless security precautions, such as WEP and IP Security (IPSec) may not be needed. Instead, SSL/Transport Layer Security (SSL/TLS) and SSH may be good ways to secure an existing application.

# Enterprise Campus Designs

The following section deals with the security needs of the enterprise campus. Many applications are available for wireless networking on a campus. In some cases, these designs can be combined into a hybrid design to solve multiple business problems. Key design concepts are highlighted as best practices. Use these best practices when evaluating your current design or when creating a hybrid design for your application.

## Enterprise Design 1

One of the most difficult challenges that wireless network designers face is the need to support many different platforms, operating systems, and hardware vendors with a single infrastructure. The following design was used in a campus that needed to support a large population of engineers and salespeople. Many of the engineers used different operating systems such as Windows, Linux, Berkeley Software Distribution (BSD), which is a Unix-like operating system, and Solaris. To make matters worse, many of the engineers used their personal laptops, which had a wide variety of wireless network cards. Due to the highly sensitive nature of the data being transmitted on the network and the network resources, security was a key concern. Because the users were not very technical, ease of use also played an important role.

The solution to the problem proved to be easier than first anticipated. The company already had an infrastructure for providing access from a hostile network (the Internet) with the corporate VPN. The network designers remembered the pain and agony that it took to meet the engineers' functional requirements with the VPN and did not want a repeat with the wireless network. The decision was made to build a completely separate wireless network that would not have Internet connectivity and the internal network would only be accessible through the corporate VPN.

The corporate VPN consisted of an IPSec appliance and an SSH gateway that was configured for port forwarding. Token-based one-time passwords (OTPs) were used on the IPSec appliance and the SSH gateway. The corporate VPN already had a requirement for using a company-approved secure build or utilizing a personal firewall with a company-standard rule set.

The installation proved to be easy. Additional network cards were added to the IPSec appliance and the SSH gateway for connectivity to the wireless network, as shown in Figure 8-4. Only a few more machines were needed to make the network fully functional. A server was added to provide Dynamic Host Configuration Protocol (DHCP) and Domain Name Server (DNS) services to the wireless users because the VPN and SSH clients were configured to connect to a hostname, not an IP address. Another server was added to the wireless segment as an NIDS and a syslog server to capture logs from the access points and DHCP server. Finally, a terminal server was installed to manage the access points and Ethernet switches because the only network-based management options offered by the vendor were cleartext (telnet and HTTP).

The best practices include the following:

- Segment the hostile wireless network from the rest of the internal network.

- Disable the management of access points with the wireless interface.

- Harden the DHCP/DNS server.

## Enterprise Design 2

Another option for implementing a secure wireless network is to use 802.1x. At the time of this writing, 802.1x is still in draft form and vendor interoperability is limited at best. However, 802.1x is a valid option for adding security to a wireless network. It is a new technology and still has not had the time in the market or been under public scrutiny to show what implementation-specific caveats and details need to be addressed.

**Figure 8-4**

Enterprise
design 1

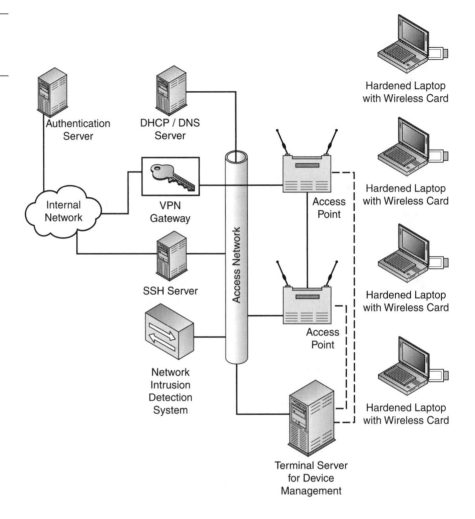

However, 802.1x shows great promise and should be considered in a wireless network designer's toolkit.

This design does not suffer from the limitations of the previous design. In this case, the users were exclusively using Windows and all hardware was provided by the company, so using a vendor-specific implementation was not a problem. The vendor chosen was one that the network designers were very comfortable with: Cisco.

The 802.1x implementation used the existing corporate directory services. However, a new RADIUS server was necessary for the vendor's

802.1x implementation of EAP over RADIUS, and additional features were required. 802.1x not only provided authentication services, but it was also used for dynamically creating WEP keys. RADIUS session timeouts of three hours were used to force the changing of WEP keys on a frequent basis. The implementation also used the key-hashing features mentioned earlier in this chapter. The architecture is shown in Figure 8-5.

The best practices include the following:

- Use 802.1x for authentication and encryption.
- Change keys frequently; three-hour timeouts are used.
- Use key-hashing features.
- Advanced proprietary integrity checking features are used.

**Figure 8-5**

Enterprise design 2

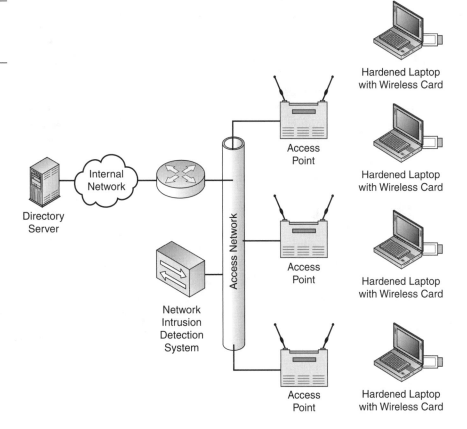

- The wireless network is kept segmented from the rest of the network to enable future network changes.

- NIDS is used on the wireless network.

## Enterprise Guest Network

Another application for a wireless network at an enterprise campus is for a guest network. A similar configuration can also be used at universities or training centers. At one corporation, contractors and vendors frequently needed access to the Internet. The information security team did not want people attaching to the network who had not signed the acceptable use policy so a guest network was set up. This was a separate network set up to protect the enterprise's intellectual property.

The first implementation of this guest network was adding data connections in strategic locations, such as conference rooms and visitor cubicles. After one visitor infected machines on the internal (nonguest) network with a virus by accidentally plugging into the wrong jack in a conference room, the network architects began searching for another solution. The decision was made to set up a wireless network that would be used by guests needing Internet access.

A process was followed to set up the guest network during its initial implementation without wireless, but the design evolved into a wireless network. Functional requirements were presented to the network architects. The guests needed the applications of web surfing and VPN access. The security group was concerned that an open network may give free Internet access to malicious attackers. After considering the functional requirements and the concerns of the security group, a design was proposed and approved.

The network was set up with a web proxy that required a username, password, and a packet filter that allowed VPN connections, as shown in Figure 8-6. The access points that were used offered DHCP services so a DHCP server was not needed. The proxy server was used to capture logs from the access points and provided DNS services. An NIDS was also added to the network. The help desk has a supply of wireless cards that can be checked out for guests and visitors. When a wireless card is checked out, a username and password are created on the proxy server and an instruction sheet with configuration instructions is provided. Each username and password expires after one week.

**Figure 8-6**

Enterprise guest
network

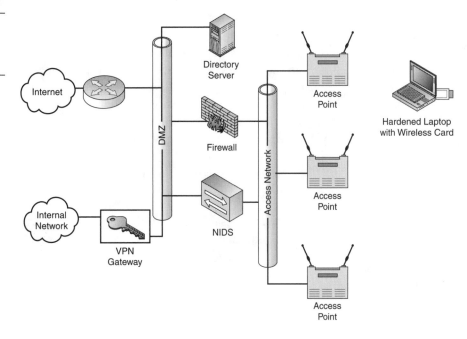

The best practices include the following:

- The guest network is segmented and firewalled from the rest of the network.
- NIDS is installed on the hostile guest network.
- Users must agree to an acceptable use policy in order to use the network.
- Network uses 802.11 standards to give the maximum hardware support.
- Corporate laptops are hardened before using the wireless network.

## Enterprise Point-to-Point Configuration

The cost savings of replacing a traditional telco point-to-point connection with a wireless link can be tremendous; wireless links can also be set up much faster than traditional telco links. Existing wireless networking technologies can be used to create these point-to-point links. In many cases, ranges can be extended by using directional antennae and amplifiers. The security benefit of using a directional antenna is that it makes the link much more difficult to sniff or jam. This link is trivial to secure because both ends of the link are static and known.

In this commonly found scenario, you can easily use traditional IPSec-based VPN-tunneling software or appliances to protect all traffic flowing between one end of the bridge to the other, as shown in Figure 8-7. These VPNs can be set up using VPN appliances, routers, or software-based VPNs.

The best practices include the following:

- Use directional antennae to eliminate signal loss and boost power.
- Configure access points to only connect to the other end of the connection; many times this is accomplished with entering a MAC address.
- Use WEP.
- Use IPSec tunnel mode.
- Use a strong form of encryption, such as Advanced Encryption Standard (AES) or Triple Data Encryption Standard (TDES).
- Rekey the VPN frequently.

**Figure 8-7**

Point-to-point connection

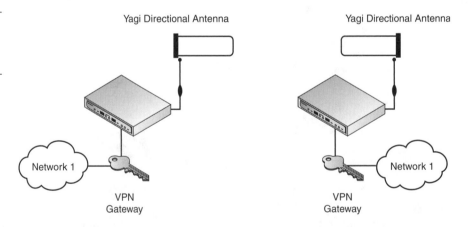

# Wireless ISP Design

Metropolitan area networks (MANs) have seen a rebirth from almost certain doom with the adoption of wireless network technologies. Many regional and specialty ISPs are starting to offer wireless Internet access. This Internet access can be limited to a small area or can be offered in coffee shops, hotels, or airports. In order to prevent customer support calls and improve the customer experience, the network needs to be open. In this scenario, you don't know who is going to join the network. Therefore, network resources need to be well protected.

In order to meet customer requirements, an open design is required. The network administrators chose to implement a separate back-end network for management. During implementation, careful consideration was given to finding a vendor that had features for securing managing network devices, such as access points and routers. Unfortunately, no vendor was offering this during the buildout of the network so a separate management network was necessary. The management network had the added benefit of giving the network designers a lot of flexibility to roll out new applications. See Figure 8-8 for details.

The network was set up with a dynamic firewall that would open up holes for Internet access after users authenticated to the billing server. This was an off-the-shelf product that had some security holes, but building a custom solution would be cost-prohibitive. A VPN was used to access the management network for the network operation and management functions.

# Retail and Manufacturing Designs

Wireless networking has proven to be a killer app for many network retail and manufacturing companies. The return on investment (ROI) for wireless applications has proven to be significant. Unlike the corporate campus, the common workstations for a retail or manufacturing wireless application are personal digital assistants (PDAs), bar-code scanners, and other thin clients. The following network designs were used in these environments.

**Figure 8-8**

Point-to-multipoint configuration

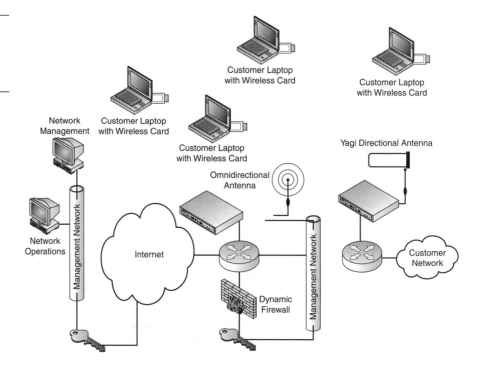

## Kiosk/Roaming Agent Design

Wireless applications can dramatically increase customer satisfaction. Customer-service applications are often wired to a desk or service point that may not be in the most convenient place for the customer, or a new application may need to be rapidly deployed into an existing store, or kiosk, and wiring constraints may prevent the adoption of the application.

This wireless design is for an application that has a very large user population that does not have much technical expertise, so the equipment and user experience needed to be simple. PDAs with bar-code scanners were chosen as the equipment for this application. The PDA had all the necessary functionality, but needed the capability to add a small printer. A quick proof-of-concept application was created using a wide-open wireless network and a modified web browser. All the functionality was there, but the security concerns needed to be addressed.

The application designers tried using off-the-shelf software modified for the particular environment, but after initial testing, the decision was made to customize an application. The application programmers were able to port the minibrowser application to IPSec using a cryptographic toolkit from a commercial vendor. The toolkit was designed to handle all the sophisticated cryptographic functions without the programmer needing to learn how to write IPSec software. Due to the highly public environment of the application, the designers chose to harden the application and use WEP and MAC access controls. A pair of VPN gateways and servers providing DHCP, DNS, and logging were set up for the entire network, serving hundreds of stores, as shown in Figure 8-9. An IDS system was also set up for network monitoring and detecting suspicious activity.

The best practices include the following:

- All traffic is authenticated and encrypted.
- An IDS system is used for watching the network.

**Figure 8-9**

Kiosk/roaming agent diagram

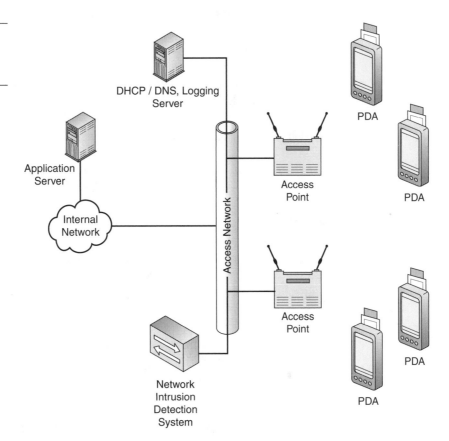

- Standard-based 802.11 security features are used, but are not relied on.
- A hardened server provides network services (DHCP and DNS).

## Warehouse Design

The early adopters of wireless technology included the manufacturing and warehousing industries. Wireless was adopted mainly for the mobility that it provides and to prevent significant wiring changes that are frequently needed in a warehouse. Internet and e-mail are not common applications in the industry. The most common are inventory tracking and shipping applications. Many times these run off a PDA or connect to a thin client or terminal. Many of these early implementations used telnet or a simple browser for user input in conjunction with a bar-code scanner or magnetic-strip reader. WEP was used to secure these applications because cleartext protocols were being used. After the shortfalls of WEP were publicized, a network redesign was needed.

Once the wireless network was installed, there was no going back, but security was still needed. The network was redesigned to keep the functionality and ease of use while adding security. If a malicious attacker were to attack the network, downtime could be very expensive. Troubleshooting wireless networks is also expensive because in many cases the staff is not immediately available and often must travel to the site. Many warehouses and manufacturing companies lose money if products cannot be delivered on time. During the network redesign, using a technology that uses licensed frequencies was considered, but it was cost-prohibitive and not available in all locations.

The existing network was used with a few modifications. Shared key authentication was replaced with an open system. WEP keys were rotated on a monthly basis. MACs were utilized when the feature was not previously enabled. Then an IDS was added to the network. SSH was used to replace the telnet application and port forwarding to the e-mail server that was added for the program. The network was also designed to allow the addition of thin clients using an encrypted protocol. The network is illustrated in Figure 8-10.

The best practices include the following:

- Use encrypted protocols.
- Use a firewall or packet filter to limit network exposure.

**Figure 8-10**

Warehouse design

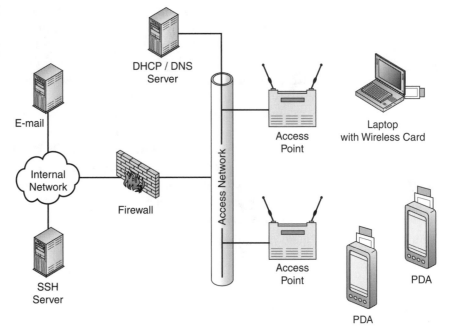

- Monitor for potential failure conditions or attacks.
- Regularly change WEP keys.
- Use MAC access controls.

# Small Office/Home Office Design (SOHO)

One of the biggest challenges in securing a Small Office/Home Office (SOHO) wireless network is deciding how much security to use. You would not buy a million-dollar safe to protect a thousand-dollar diamond. To make matters more difficult, SOHO configurations are often implemented with inexpensive hardware that does not offer many security features. However, achieving adequate security for your SOHO is still possible. The decision about security should be made before purchasing hardware to ensure that the hardware has the necessary features.

The primary question that needs to be answered is how will adding wireless to your SOHO change the current threats? Some SOHO networks are connected directly to the Internet through a broadband connection. If this is the case, then adding a wireless connection to the network does not significantly change the threat to the already Internet-connected machine. However, a new threat to the network bandwidth is being introduced. A malicious user could attach to the wireless connection for free Internet access.

To make matters worse, this malicious user may attack other sites or use your Internet connectivity to introduce a new virus on the Internet with your connection. Therefore, steps must be taken to secure the wireless connection. Very destructive viruses, such as the Melissa virus, have been introduced to the Internet using stolen Internet access accounts. Although the authorities were eventually able to track down the writer, the person with the stolen AOL account went through much heartache. Tracking down a wireless user who attached to someone's unprotected access point could be very difficult, if not impossible, and may leave the negligent owner liable. By the way, make sure that your desktop computer has a virus-scanning program and it is kept up-to-date. For more information on virus protection, please see www.mcafee.com.

Now let's take a step back and examine the threats toward the SOHO machines. As stated before, many times these machines are directly connected to the Internet. In some cases, these may be protected by a firewall or router, which provide a level of protection. In either case, if you add a wireless connection to a SOHO network, the machines on the network must be hardened. Hardening hosts may involve many different processes, but this normally involves disabling unnecessary services, using strong passwords, deleting unused accounts, or adding firewall software.

Reasonable steps should be taken to secure a SOHO wireless network. Use the security features of the access point, which may include WEP and MAC access controls. Consider purchasing a high-end access point with advanced security features. Cisco produces access points with very advanced security features (such as LEAP, an 802.1x implementation) that cost just a little bit more than most access points and will give you much better performance and radio coverage. It is money well spent. The components of a typical installation are shown in Figure 8-11.

The best practices include the following:

- Access point—use WEP and MAC access controls. This will significantly increase the level of complexity of an attack.

**Figure 8-11**

SOHO design

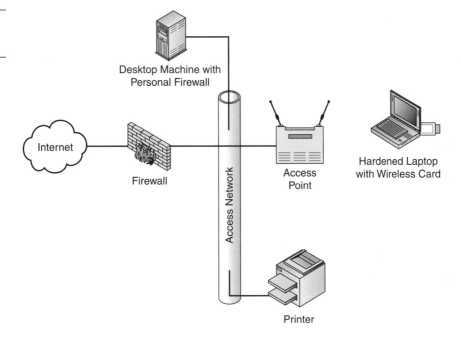

- Network hosts—add personal firewall software to machines and add strong passwords to the printer and router.
- Turn off the equipment when it is not in use.

# Conclusion

The security needed for wireless networks is dependent on the application. Only after careful consideration of the value of the network resources and the data transmitted on that network can appropriate security mechanisms be implemented. In most cases, security mechanisms add additional cost and overhead. The costs of all security mechanisms need to be calculated in advance to figure out what is appropriate for your application. By using the designs and best practices contained in this chapter, you can implement a secure wireless network.

# CHAPTER 9

# Enabling Secure Wireless Access to Data

Although first-generation (1G) and second-generation (2G) wireless networks were primarily designed and used for voice traffic, interest in accessing data on these networks increased dramatically in the late 1990s. Because these networks were also capable of handling data, network operators viewed wireless data as an important new potential revenue stream. Consequently, network operators quickly launched wireless data services and actively promoted these capabilities through advertisements.

Initially, most wireless data services were based on simple informational queries such as stock quotes, weather, traffic, and travel schedules. Operators chose these services for several reasons (both business and technical):

- **Consumer demand**  These initial wireless data services were targeted at the so-called power users—those with a high monthly usage. This particular demographic tended to have ample airtime and have the least price sensitivity for mobile services so an incremental $5 or $10 per month was not a barrier to usage. Travel-oriented services such as traffic, weather, and airline information, were attractive because the data's value was directly related to timeliness and convenience.

- **Bandwidth** These initial data services did not require significant bandwidth. For instance, a query for a stock price might entail transmitting only four characters or less (for the ticker symbol) from the handset. Similar queries like weather and travel information did not require significant amounts of data to be transmitted either to or from the mobile device. This meant that these services could be applied to current 2G networks without having a significant effect on the end user's experience.

- **Low security** Due to the growing public concern over the Wireless Application Protocol (WAP) security architecture, operators focused on delivering content and services where security was not a high priority. This removed the security issue as an obstacle to using the service.

- **Informational versus transactional** Related to the security issue cited previously, the initial wireless data services were deliberately aimed at serving up information and not requiring any kind of transactional processes to be invoked on the wireless device. For instance, digital signatures were usually not utilized in these initial rollouts, not because of a lack of customer demand, but because the current data services did not require signatures.

Unfortunately, a consumer's initial experience with these 2G data services was generally unsatisfactory. Although many consumers took advantage of promotions and cut-rate pricing to try wireless data, few users evolved into frequent users. In North America, the slow throughput of the networks and erratic coverage led many users to stop using wireless data altogether. In regions such as Europe, demand in wireless data increased, but the long-term experience was similar to that in North America—a large consistent user base did not develop. The only exception was short message service (SMS), which grew dramatically and proved to be a lucrative new revenue stream for operators.

The continued frustration with wireless data was a main driver behind operators' aggressive attempts to upgrade the wireless networks to provide faster throughput. This was especially true in regions like Europe where mobile voice had penetrated a vast majority of the population, meaning that future mobile voice revenue was directly correlated with the ability to get the few remaining users to sign up for service. Thus, wireless data became an important strategic thrust for these operators. However, deploying these networks took time and money; therefore, coverage was often restricted to a few select metropolitan areas.

Rather than waiting for the faster networks to be completed, network operators began marketing and selling wireless data capabilities to the corporate user. Unlike the ever-fickle consumer, the corporate users' needs were well understood, and they were not particularly concerned about incremental fees.

For a corporation, the primary need was access to corporation information and applications from a wireless device. In fact, the marketing mantra, "Access to any application from any device on any network," soon became ubiquitous in the wireless sector. Any vendor who did not include this phrase in their marketing materials of 2000 was deemed a nonplayer.

Corporations were attracted to wireless data for five key reasons:

- **Improved productivity**   Providing employees with real-time access to corporate information would allow for quicker distribution of information and enable employees to obtain important business information faster than before.

- **Alignment with the growing mobility of customers and employees**   As companies expanded, employees increasingly found themselves out of the physical office for a large portion of time. This often meant that the trusty PC or laptop was not always powered on and connected to the network. Therefore, companies needed to consider alternative methods to disseminate information to a geographically disperse work force and customer base.

- **Quantifiable return on investment (ROI)**   As the economy tightened during 2000, corporate IT departments focused exclusively on pilots and projects that could generate a positive ROI. In most cases, wireless projects made the cut because expenses and the potential upside were generally well known and easy to calculate.

- **Improved customer service**   Wireless data services enabled mobile users to get immediate reports on customer relationships or issues and respond to those issues in a very fast manner, thereby improving customer satisfaction.

- **Competitive advantage**   As more companies adopted wireless technologies to maintain contact with customers, partners, suppliers, and employees, many companies realized that wireless connectivity was a necessity.

Within a few months, an entire industry sprouted up that was dedicated to providing wireless applications and services to the corporate segment. This industry consisted of two segments:

- **Wireless pure plays**   In the go-go days of 1999 and 2000, numerous startups were funded to create new wireless applications to sell to corporations. Many of the wireless pure plays were located in wireless hot spots like the Silicon Valley, Stockholm, Sweden, and Helsinki, Finland. The thinking behind many of these companies was that modifying existing legacy corporate applications for wireless environments was too cumbersome. It was simpler and easier to build wireless applications from the ground up and optimize them for the low-bandwidth, minimal processing capabilities of the wireless devices.

- **Traditional software vendors**   Eager to jump onto the wireless bandwagon, traditional software vendors quickly offered up wireless versions of their existing products. Some of the largest software vendors even formed separate wholly owned subsidiaries to focus exclusively on the wireless market. Examples included OracleMobile, iAnywhere (a subsidiary of database vendor Sybase), and Wireless Knowledge (a joint venture between Microsoft and Qualcomm).

Despite the dot-com implosion in 2000, the wireless sector continued to attract optimism and funding, which was reflective of the ongoing belief in wireless' value to the enterprise.

Unfortunately, enterprises soon learned that behind all the glossy marketing brochures and presentations was a large complex corporate IT infrastructure that had not always been designed with wireless in mind. Products required customization and professional services and countless hours of testing. Wireless access was not as simple as promised.

The IT organization faced critical pressure (especially from senior management) to deliver a wireless strategy. Some companies went as far as appointing a Chief Wireless Officer (CWO). As companies began talking to vendors and determining their needs, they realized that executing a wireless strategy offered two distinct and radically different options:

- *Build it yourself.* Instead of trying to patch together old legacy applications to work in a wireless environment, enterprise IT departments could build an entirely new infrastructure exclusively for wireless.

■ *Reconfigure existing networks to become wireless aware.* This approach enabled enterprises to realize the full capabilities of their existing network and applications.

Table 9-1 lists some key issues to consider between the two options.

The most immediate benefit of option 1 is the time to market. Instead of trying to connect multiple different systems and relying on middleware to connect everything, this approach enables the creation of a *greenfield* wireless environment that does not interfere with existing applications. In highly competitive markets where time to market is of significant value, this option makes sense. It is also viable for enterprises whose wireless projects involve entirely new applications and services. For instance, a company may have decided to offer a new customer relationship management (CRM) application for the first time. In this case, option 1 works because the company does not have an existing CRM application that needs to be modified.

However, the most significant drawback to option 1 is the potential higher administrative and infrastructure costs of managing a separate wireless system. In addition, enterprises must also allocate an appropriate amount to end-user training. If a wireless project involves an application that users are already familiar with, there are obviously fewer training requirements.

Option 2 may be a more painful alternative in the short term, especially for older legacy applications that are not easily adaptable to wireless environments. Nonetheless, this option is still viable for companies that believe that wireless will not introduce any new applications but will extend the capabilities of existing applications instead.

As of the spring of 2002, market data on the percentage of companies selecting option 1 over option 2 was elusive. There are companies adopting each approach and even some that are adopting both approaches

| **Table 9-1** | | **Option 1** | **Option 2** |
|---|---|---|---|
| **Building Stand-alone Wireless Infrastructure Versus Adapting Existing Wired Infrastructure** | Ease of getting to market | Low | High |
| | Customization and system integration efforts | Low | High |
| | End-user training requirements | High | Medium |
| | Administrative overhead | High | Medium |
| | Infrastructure requirements | High | Medium |

simultaneously! Regardless of which approach is currently in favor, the last 18 months have taught enterprises several key things:

■ *Wireless data takes time and effort.* Companies that were wooed to adopt wireless projects in 2000 and 2001 often set unrealistic expectations for the actual delivery of production-ready systems. This means that any successful wireless project should set reasonable expectations and delivery dates up front—and be willing to modify during the project's duration.

■ *Focus on a manageable amount of data and applications.* This is related to the previous conclusion. Many enterprises thought they could wirelessly enable every application. The difficulties of this have companies asking, "Do we even need every application wirelessly enabled?" Focusing on the most crucial applications first (such as CRM) helps keep a project's scope in check and avoids committing to more than can be delivered.

■ *Manage expectations.* Although much of the wireless hype of 2000 has subsided, there continues to be tremendous enthusiasm about wireless technology and its potential benefits. Organizations seeking success with wireless deployments need to manage expectations with senior management as well as with the end users to minimize disappointment or confusion.

# Planning for Wireless Data—Important First Steps

Once your organization has decided to offer wireless data, five key questions should be answered. The answers to these questions will affect the wireless architecture and the necessary security measures required for that architecture:

■ *What is your organization's current wireless usage?* This should involve a thorough inventory of wireless usage in your organization. Invariably, this exercise will turn up interesting information, such as a group of users who may be experimenting with wireless data (and potentially violating current security policy in the process).

■ *Are you using multiple carriers for wireless voice services?* Companies with national operations often utilize multiple carriers due to the different regional network footprints of the various carriers. This can prove to be a potential problem on two fronts. First, it reduces the ability to obtain maximum volume pricing. Secondly, it requires any potential wireless application to be compatible with (and tested against) the various bearer protocols (such as Global System for Mobile Communications [GSM], Code Division Multiple Access [CDMA], and Time Division Multiple Access [TDMA]). It could also complicate efforts to enable intraemployee data communication because SMS systems are not always compatible between different operators.

- *What departments, user groups, and geographic regions are currently wirelessly enabled?* This is related to the wireless inventory discussed previously, but many companies have very specific mobile phone eligibility policies, meaning that only certain departments use mobile phones. Because the initial wireless data project will likely involve the user group already most familiar with cell phones, it is necessary to understand this user base's familiarity with the current wireless technologies.

- *What are your top three goals for adding wireless data?* This question seems obvious, but surprisingly, many companies, when pushed, cannot provide a sufficient answer. Some of this is due to the lingering effects of the wireless hype of 2000, which created the sensation that every company should have a wireless strategy, regardless of industry size or need. Companies are now demanding more quantifiable and practical results from new technology projects. This requires the IT organization to think carefully about the expectations for wireless data. Is it real-time access to data? Improved communications?

- *Lastly, how do you plan to measure success?* This is directly related to the previous point. Many IT projects commence with a general consensus about the need and potential benefits, but little attention is devoted to measuring the project's results and thereby gauging success. With wireless projects, the success metrics should be clearly identified before the project initiation date. Define the problem, understand the solution, and estimate the potential benefits of the solution. For example, if the issue is a mobile worker's inability to get access to corporate e-mail when traveling, then the wireless solution is a messaging application and a potential metric might be faster turnaround time on messages. Defining the metrics and tracking those metrics during the pilot allows the collection of sufficient data that can be used to determine whether to advance the pilot project into production.

The answers to these questions provide an organization with an excellent handle on the business drivers as well as the individual preferences of users. The next step is creating a reasonable pilot project. Wireless pilots benefit from the "geek gadget factor"—there is usually no shortage of willing participants! In choosing pilot candidates, select as diverse a group as possible. Although this increases the project's complexity, restricting a wireless pilot to an individual department in a single location does not allow all critical obstacles to be identified.

Consider the geographic location factor. Any wireless pilot should utilize multiple locations, mainly to verify network system coverage in different areas. A worst-case example would be launching a wireless project into production solely based on feedback from a pilot in Boston only to find out that the Chicago group cannot receive consistent coverage in their region.

## Potential Wireless Application Scenarios

Once the necessary feedback for potential wireless pilots has been obtained, the next step is determining the actual pilot architecture. Fortunately (or unfortunately), the wireless world is full of choices, meaning that there are often multiple configuration options for a single application. Although there is seldom a perfect architecture, this section highlights the predominant architectures that can be utilized for enabling wireless data.

### Informational Query Wireless Architecture

This architecture is designed for simple data requests and is the typical WAP architecture. It is common for more consumer-type usage, such as retrieving weather, traffic information, sports scores, and stock quotes. Nonetheless, depending on your industry, this approach could serve you well. A potential example might be a mortgage banking business that needs to have daily updates on the latest mortgage rates. Although this information is proprietary, it has a short shelf life (less than 24 hours), meaning that the productivity benefits may outweigh the risks. Figure 9-1 demonstrates a sample wireless architecture for an information query architecture.

**Figure 9-1**

Informational
wireless
architecture

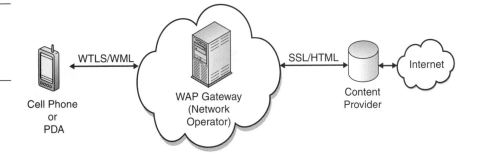

This architecture is predicated on the presence of a WAP gateway on the network operator's presence. The good news is that this removes the need for the enterprise to buy, install, configure, and support their own WAP gateway. The downside is that the enterprise has to rely on a third party (the network operator) to maintain security and network performance. Although service level agreements (SLAs) and security audits can mitigate this potential risk, the biggest downside to this approach is the security mechanism. Although the session from the WAP gateway to corporate application can be protected via Transport Layer Security/Secure Sockets Layer (TLS/SSL), Wireless Transport Layer Security (WTLS) must be utilized from the gateway to the wireless device. Furthermore, the corporate application has no method of determining if WTLS was actually used by the client device so data could actually be sent unencrypted from the gateway to the client device.

Because of these security issues, this architecture should be considered carefully, but it may still be appropriate for applications with reduced security requirements.

## Transactional Wireless Architecture

This architecture addresses the main security weaknesses identified in the previous architecture. Instead of interfacing with the network operator's WAP gateway, the company installs a WAP gateway inside the corporate firewall. This means that the WTLS can be utilized from the handset through the firewall. Any decryption or conversion to TLS/SSL occurs within the safer confines of the corporate network. In this scenario, the WAP gateway can be either a dedicated machine, or it can be located on the same machine as a web server. Figure 9-2 demonstrates a sample wireless architecture for a transactional architecture.

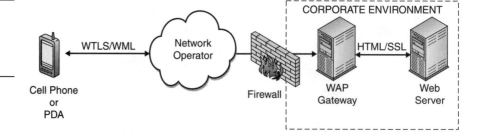

**Figure 9-2**

Transactional
wireless
architecture

The obvious downside to this approach is that it requires the purchase, installation, and support of a WAP gateway. However, judging from the initial wireless data experiences of 2000 and 2001, many companies are willing to absorb this cost. Many of the major banks in North America and Europe that offered wireless banking services have adopted this exact architecture. Although future versions of the WAP specification will address this encryption problem by utilizing TLS/SSL directly from the handset to the application, this architecture will remain viable for the next few years.

Table 9-2 summarizes some of the key differences between hosting your own WAP gateway versus relying on a network operator.

Although the two previous architectures are often thought of from a pure consumer perspective, these architectures are still applicable for a corporate user and even for a proprietary application. In fact, the largest cost of each approach is not the WAP gateway but rather the cost of modifying the target application to become wireless aware. Many people have become swept up in the publicity storm surrounding the WAP Gap and have paid less attention to whether the actual application can even handle wireless communication.

**Table 9-2**

Comparison of
Two WAP
Architectures

| | Operator WAP Gateway | Corporate-hosted WAP Gateway |
|---|---|---|
| Infrastructure costs | Low | High |
| Overall security model | Medium | High |
| Encryption through firewall | No | Yes |
| Administrative costs | Low | High |

## Wireless Messaging

The most popular wireless application is wireless messaging. In a survey of North American mobile professionals conducted in the spring of 2002, Cahner's InStat Group found that over 70 percent of the respondents listed e-mail as the most crucial application for wireless access. Not surprisingly, providing wireless access to corporate e-mail is high on corporations' wish lists.

Mobile e-mail is also very industry specific. A January 2002 survey by ResearchPortal.com examined how users in various industries retrieve e-mail. The results are printed in Table 9-3.

The obvious conclusion from this table is that cell phone-based e-mail continues to be the minority, reflecting some of the ongoing user interface issues with cell phones.

Like most other wireless technologies, enterprises discovered that wireless e-mail was available in a multitude of choices. In North America, enterprises could opt for a stand-alone messaging service like that offered by Research in Motion (RIM), or they could utilize a wireless middleware product that provided wireless access to an existing corporate e-mail account from a wireless phone.

Although exact figures on the usage between a stand-alone solution versus the proxy approach are not generally available, the initial data suggests that stand-alone solutions have been more widely adopted. RIM has been the demonstrated leader in this category with over 250,000

| **Table 9-3** E-mail Activity by Device (ResearchPortal. com, January 2002) | **Industry** | **Data Device (Personal Digital Assistant [PDA])** | **Voice Device (Cell Phone)** | **Desktop PC** | **Notebook PC** |
|---|---|---|---|---|---|
| | Finance | 22% | 4% | 28% | 46% |
| | IT | 18% | 6% | 27% | 49% |
| | Utilities | 11% | 3% | 8% | 78% |
| | Construction | 10% | 3% | 18% | 69% |
| | Manufacturing | 9% | 2% | 20% | 69% |
| | Healthcare | 7% | 3% | 28% | 62% |
| | Transportation | 7% | 3% | 19% | 71% |

users nationwide, but Motorola and Palm also offer interactive messaging devices.

The success of the stand-alone solutions is not by accident. These stand-alone solutions have been optimized for e-mail, meaning that the devices offer better ergonomics and user interfaces than multipurpose devices.

Nonetheless, these stand-alone solutions create other problems. For one, they may require end users to carry another device in addition to their cell phone. This creates potential headaches for the end users and does not fully utilize the large installed base of wireless phones in use within the enterprise. Secondly, most wireless data networks do not have as large of a network footprint as the cellular networks, meaning that potential disruptions in service (and therefore the ability to send/receive e-mail) are going to be higher in a stand-alone solution than in a proxy approach.

Table 9-4 summarizes some of the key differences between the two approaches.

These criteria are not all-inclusive but merely highlight some of the key issues to consider as part of any wireless project. Ultimately, the decision about which application to pilot will be driven by a host of factors, including the economy, market, and geography. However, answering these questions early in the process will help you determine which wireless solution is best suited for your business.

Figures 9-3 and 9-4 display the various configurations for wireless messaging. The proxy method generally requires less capital investment, mainly because users can utilize existing cell phones, thereby saving the cost of purchasing an additional device. However, the configuration of the

**Table 9-4**

Stand-alone
E-mail Versus
E-mail Proxy

| | Stand-alone Solution | Wireless E-mail Proxy |
| --- | --- | --- |
| Voice and data on a single device | No | Yes |
| Integration with the existing e-mail system | Yes | Yes |
| Synchronization with the e-mail account | Yes | Not always |
| Network coverage | Good | Excellent |
| Acquisition costs | High | Low |

**Figure 9-3**

Wireless e-mail
proxy
architecture

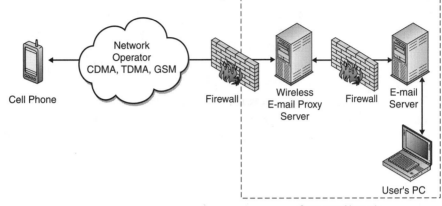

**Figure 9-4**

Stand-alone
wireless e-mail
architecture

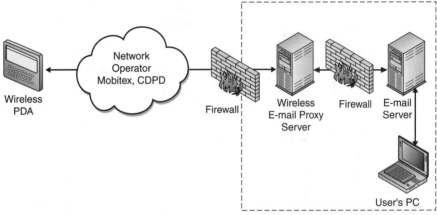

proxy requires some effort, and it can be complicated if an enterprise has
not standardized on a single e-mail platform because each platform will
need customization. The biggest downside of this approach is that it does
not always offer real-time synchronization with the user's inbox because
these phones do not always connect with a desktop. This is mainly an
issue for end users who have to reconcile the inbox on their PC manually.

The stand-alone process was described in detail in Chapter 6 and basically involves new client devices and software components on the server
and the desktop.

During the pilot process, organizations should also start defining the parameters of a wireless policy. Although it may seem premature to expend energy when the pilot's success is unclear, doing so will help the organization be better prepared if and when the pilot goes into production. This is particularly true in wireless projects. Given the "wow" factor that often accompanies wireless projects, organizations may find that the pilot generates such positive comments that the production plan is accelerated as users demand the capabilities. This is akin to letting the genie out of the bottle in way that makes it very difficult to stop the groundswell of popular support. This is why planning ahead pays dividends in the long run.

# Wireless Policies

An often overlooked issue that has significant security ramifications involves wireless policies. Many large companies have implemented elaborate IT processes and procedures, but in the rush to wireless, many companies have neglected to create adequate wireless policies to reflect the increasing threats posed by wireless voice and data. Put simply, companies need to create wireless policies and enforce them rigorously. Failure to do this could leave a company's IT infrastructure at risk. The information security industry has also created confusion by focusing only on individual security threats such as viruses or denial or service (DoS) without considering these threats within the larger context. Figure 9-5 summarizes the holistic process that needs to be followed for an effective wireless policy.

Defining the risk is always a difficult proposition, but rather than attempting to quantify the total risk, it is more important to think in relative terms. For instance, what industry are you in? How competitive is

**Figure 9-5**

Define the risk and develop and enforce policies.

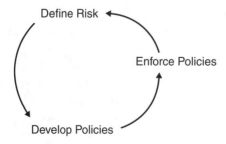

your industry? Are you already a target for wired hacking? Answering questions like this can help determine your relative level of risk tolerance and therefore help you build a wireless policy that is highly correlated with your risk profile. The risk question also must weigh the potential economic benefits of a wireless solution against the potential increased exposure. Judging from the large amount of wireless projects across industries, it is clear that the benefits exceed the potential increased exposure.

A wireless policy should comprise of two key components. The policy does not need to be an encyclopedia of regulations, but it should map out the key issues in a manner that end users can easily understand.

IT administrators should use the wireless device's limited computing powers to the organization's advantage. For example, a company should not become too concerned about a rogue employee downloading vast amounts of data (such as financial data or customer lists) to a mobile device for the simple reason that these devices are not capable of storing vast amounts of data. Although mobile device capabilities will increase in the future, PCs will still dwarf these devices in terms of the capabilities they can bring and the damage they can cause to an organization.

## Wireless Logistics Policies

The first level of the wireless policy should cover basic logistical processes such as the following:

■ *What criteria are used to define which end users are authorized to utilize cell phones?* This is an obvious question, yet many companies have very nebulous definitions around this. (Is it based on the title, department, or amount of travel time per quarter?) The more nebulous this definition, the more problems it will cause, particularly on the economic side as significant numbers of marginal users are given cell phones.

■ *Are there any specific restrictions on usage of cell phones?* This component has a practical and security aspect. For instance, can users place international calls from a cell phone? Should calls on a toll-free line be made from a landline instead of a wireless phone? These questions may seem mundane, but the economic implications can be huge. Consider a user who calls the company's toll-free line from a cell phone. In this scenario, the company is paying for wireless airtime and the cost of the toll-free line. The security aspect on cell phone is the most overlooked component of an IT security policy. Specifically, this means you will allow your users to place cell phone calls in public settings (for example, from airplanes, hotels, conferences, and so on). Eavesdropping on an airplane or in an airport waiting area is an obvious threat, and your competitor could be on the same flight as you. Do you want to take the chance? Obviously, this aspect needs to be weighed against the productivity benefits of using cell phones in the first place, but restrictions on usage in very public places is worth considering.

■ *What happens when cell phone users leave the company, either involuntarily or voluntarily?* Because of the small size of wireless devices, they are often not turned over at the termination of employment, exposing the company to potential billing charges.

■ *Is your organization supporting wireless voice, wireless data, or both?* Can end users carry multiple devices? Previously, companies could dictate what non-PC hardware end users could carry. The tremendous growth of PDAs and other devices has made it very difficult for companies to enforce this.

■ *What training and end-user education will be provided?* Again, this is an overlooked area. People mistakenly assume that people can use a phone, yet they miss a more subtle point in that these training sessions are the very medium in which end users are educated on wireless processes. Many companies have had an IT employee drop off a new wireless device on an employee desk with nary a brief primer. This nonchalance can breed problems, especially when users start loading applications and other data onto these devices.

■ *Lastly, what are the punishments for abuse or violation of the wireless policy?* Will cell phone privileges be revoked? Is the termination of employment a possibility, depending on the severity? By simply defining the penalties, users will be more aware of the rules and thus less likely to break them.

## Wireless Security Policies

The second component of a wireless policy should encompass the following security issues:

■ *Develop procedures for lost or stolen wireless devices.* Who do users contact if a device is lost or stolen? The network operator? The IT help desk? There are benefits of using either, but the main goal is to prevent fraudulent usage and assist in provisioning a new cell phone to the end user.

- *Apply local device protection*. Many devices and PDAs offer password-locking features, but these are often not utilized. Despite the known weaknesses of passwords, passwords are still better than no protection at all. Local device protection is more important for wireless data devices because these devices can store sensitive data, whereas the typical cell phone can only store basic contact information. Fortunately, devices are becoming more capable of local security. Whenever available, this capability should be utilized. In addition, it should be enforced in the same manner as the general IT password policy regarding the frequency of changes, the reuse of the same terms, the use of alphanumeric characters, and so on.

- *Minimize usage of unauthorized wireless devices*. Also known as the *Palm Pilot Phenomenon*, this issue arose from the rapid popularity of Palm handhelds among corporate users. Even though the devices were not supported by their employer, many users purchased PDAs themselves, connected them to the employer's PC, and synchronized potential confidential corporate data onto these devices. Unfortunately, this rule is hard to enforce or track, especially if your employer is a multinational corporation with thousands of employees. However, this issue exposes the need to maintain appropriate synchronization and data transfer rules for those devices that are supported within the organization and the need to spell out the punishment for users caught synchronizing or storing confidential data on these devices.

- *Define data encryption procedures*. As Chapter 6 demonstrated, the current wireless data networks provide reasonable data encryption, but emerging virtual private network (VPN) products for handhelds, such as Certicom's movianVPN, are now available for mobile devices, providing enterprises with additional mechanisms for protecting data as it is sent over the wireless interface. The second (and often overlooked) component of data encryption is protecting the data at rest. This means encrypting data on the server and also securing it on the mobile device. Unfortunately, due to the limited computing capabilities of mobile devices, there are still only a few data encryption products for wireless devices.

- *Define data storage procedures*. This is closely related to the encryption procedures. What (if any data) can be stored on the mobile device? Companies should be careful about allowing large amounts of data to be stored on the device. For one, it affects network performance. Secondly, given the known security issues on the device, it exposes sensitive data if the device is lost or stolen. For these reasons, enterprises should minimize the amount of data that can be stored on the device.

▪ *Define authentication procedures.* An easy method to define wireless authentication procedures is to just adopt the same procedures enforced for wired PC users. If remote users over dial up have to utilize two-factor authentication and a VPN, the same rule should apply. In other words, treat your wireless users just as you do your remote users. Unfortunately, this is harder to implement in practice mainly because of the immaturity of the technology. Although a multitude of VPN and authentication products is available for wired access, vendors have been slow to port these solutions to mobile devices, which may force enterprises to take a step backward and utilize passwords.

▪ *Define synchronization procedures.* Companies that confronted the Palm Pilot Phenomenon mentioned previously soon realized that they were often powerless to prevent usage of these devices (this especially true if the entire senior management team carries one). Because they could not stem the proliferation of devices, the IT organization instituted policies around what data and applications could be synchronized. These policies vary, based on the synchronization architecture utilized. Figures 9-6, 9-7, and 9-8 outline the three basic synchronization architectures.

**Figure 9-6**

PDA-to-PC desktop synchronization

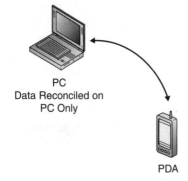

PC
Data Reconciled on
PC Only

PDA

**Figure 9-7**

PDA-to-PC-
to-server
synchronization

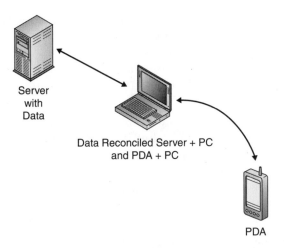

**Figure 9-8**

PDA-to-server
synchronization

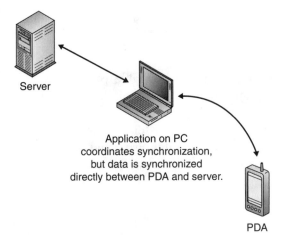

The PDA-to-PC desktop synchronization is the most common scenario. An individual user has a PDA that he or she connects to his or her PC and then synchronizes with local applications on the PC, such as the calendar, address list, and so on. In this scenario, the IT organization may not even have knowledge of the usage, and the user is free to store and synchronize any and all information he or she chooses.

In PDA-to-PC-to-server synchronization, data is retrieved from a central application or data source, reconciled with the client PC, and then synchronized on the PDA. This approach generally requires some level of support and knowledge from the IT organization and can be a useful mechanism to utilize the PDA for something beyond a basic calendar and contact management machine.

PDA-to-server synchronization is the most advanced scenario and essentially renders the client PC a mere pass-through for data from a server. The immediate benefit is much tighter control over data and better methods to ensure that each device is as up-to-date as possible. The most obvious downside is that it could involve some custom application development (although the PC is a pass-through, an executable application must still run on the client PC to establish the connection between the PDA and server. AvantGo's web-clipping software for Palm and PocketPC handhelds is an example of this kind of synchronization, which is also known as a conduit application (for example, the PC is a conduit for information from the web server).

# Conclusion

The wireless world is a veritable cornucopia of different technologies, standards, and architectures. This book is not intended to espouse one particular method or network technology over another but aims to highlight the most salient points for a given technology. Understanding these points will hopefully enable organizations to make well-informed decisions and ultimately create a wireless infrastructure that maps well into the future.

There is no doubt that wireless data offers tremendous opportunities for enterprises and consumers. Although the technology downturn of 2001 may have eliminated many marginal wireless players, the good news is that the best-positioned companies and technologies are surviving, meaning that ample choices still exist for wireless data.

This chapter was not meant to provide a comprehensive overview of every possible wireless configuration available to an enterprise but rather to outline the available architectures and highlight other issues that should be considered as part of a wireless data project. Ultimately, the policy and intangible issues are more important than the architecture because it is through careful execution of these issues that a wireless project will be successful, regardless of the underlying architecture.

A few final points are worth noting:

- *Things change*. Just like any technology, wireless technologies continue to evolve. This requires you to keep track of the market and technologies. It does not necessarily mean that a current wireless architecture has to be completely future-proof, but your organization should be aware of new developments and be posed to take advantage of them. An easy example is faster networks. When these come online, what does it mean for your wireless project? Do you just need new devices? Will your application still function?

- *Create metrics*. The dot-com era is over, and business fundamentals are back in vogue. Therefore, any project (whether it is hiring someone or a new technology) needs to provide clear benefit and value to the corporation and end user. Although wireless may still be a very hot area, today's cost-cutting obsession means that projects must be backed up with solid measurements.

- *Security is cheap*. Although the Gartner Group estimated that smart phones, PDAs, and other mobile appliances could cost more than $2,500 a year to support at a standard comparable to a PC, implementing adequate security is just a small fraction of that total cost. Put in this perspective—security is a worthwhile investment.

Now that we have described the basics of enabling wireless data access, the next chapter provides some examples of real wireless applications, the underlying architectures, and the relative business benefit.

# CHAPTER 10

# Real Examples from the Wireless World

Many technology books and articles focus heavily on an underlying technology but are deficient on discussing actual implementations that organizations can use as a reference point for their own usage. This lack of publicly available implementations is particularly pronounced with information security products because companies are often reluctant to disclose actual security product usage in fear that doing so will provide potential hackers with a blueprint that can be used to penetrate the corporate network.

In reality, this so-called *security by obscurity* approach hurts information security vendors and the customers they serve. The lack of public announcements about product usage makes it very difficult for vendors and the market to ascertain trends and needs. This issue becomes particularly exacerbated with cross-product interoperability. If vendors do not know the most common customer configurations, it makes it difficult to prioritize which products need to be interoperable. Taken to the extreme, it leads to generic marketing statements like "interoperates with all major firewalls," leading prospective customers to believe that interoperability is available out of the box. In reality, customers usually painfully discover that interoperability is not as straightforward as the brochures proclaim.

On the customer side, this obscurity is equally problematic. Many companies are afraid that announcing security product usage is an admission of weakness about the underlying company's security infrastructure. In fact, these authors believe the opposite. Public admission of security product usage demonstrate a company's commitment to protecting their information and networks. This should be reassuring to shareholders, employees, and the industry because it demonstrates a company's willingness to protect its interests and brand, which will hopefully lead to increased valuations.

The wireless hype cycle of 1999 and 2000 turned many of these preconceived beliefs upside down. Companies and vendors went out of their way to announce wireless projects and strategies. Some of this was driven by the mentality at that time that any forward-thinking company *must* have a wireless strategy. Wireless vendors were happy to oblige and add to the hype by churning daily announcements about new applications, devices, and customer deployments.

Initially, the wireless hype cycle was concentrated heavily on generic consumer applications being provided by the network operators like directions, travel information, and weather. However, as customers started demanding wireless access to more security-sensitive data like wireless banking, security emerged as a key feature. Unlike wired projects where specific security product usage was often secret, the increased awareness of wireless security issues forced companies to confront wireless security head-on and actually announce what products were being used. This was especially true following the tragic events of September 11, 2001, which further raised concerns about information security and withstanding hostile attacks. Going public with actual security product deployment had two immediate benefits:

- *Address the myth that wireless security was an oxymoron.* The ongoing dialogue about the WAP Gap had created the impression that wireless networks were completely insecure. This perception led many users to forego wireless data altogether and forced some enterprises and content providers to reconsider wireless strategies. In announcing actual wireless deployments, vendors and customers allayed the wireless security concerns and started to convince people that wireless access to data could be implemented in a secure fashion.

- *Security became an enabling feature.* For one of the first times in the information security industry, strong security was actually an enabler to increased revenues from wireless projects. This was a dramatic step forward. Previously, information security products and staffs were treated as a cost center or as an insurance policy. In the wireless world, security products became an essential requirement. Those companies that took security seriously were more likely to experience stronger customer retention and incremental revenues than those who did not.

The premium placed on security in wireless environments created a self-perpetuating product cycle, as shown in Figure 10-1. Customers evaluating wireless services increasingly demanded strong security functionality. The companies servicing those end users discovered that without sufficient security capabilities, end users would migrate to a competitor, leading the companies to demand greater security features in the suppliers' products. This cycle will only assist in the continued evolution of the wireless security industry. Users will get increasingly savvy and aware of security issues and demand additional functionality into the future, ultimately leading to better products.

One final note about the awareness of wireless security issues. In the wired world, security exploits have tended to be targeted at specific vendors or products. Microsoft has often been a frequent target of criticism about insecure products and architectures. The large installed base of Windows-based PCs and applications has made them a tempting target for hackers. Plus, the large installed base has also helped accelerate the diffusion of security weaknesses across networks. The ILOVEYOU virus of 2000 demonstrated how quickly viruses could spread within PCs running Microsoft programs.

**Figure 10-1**

Wireless security product feedback cycle

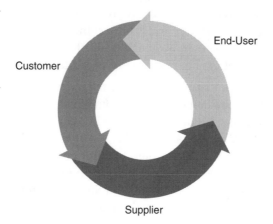

Unfortunately, the high-profile incidents have sometimes created the perception that Microsoft's products are inherently insecure. Although Microsoft has made significant strides in improving security of their products, people do not always proactively install necessary security patches, meaning that previously known weaknesses continue to be exploited. Plus, the continued growth of PCs running Windows applications means that Microsoft continues to be a high-profile hacking target. However, Microsoft is not alone. Large software companies like Oracle and mainstream content providers like eBay have also been subjected to potentially embarrassing security breaches. Like Microsoft, these breaches do not necessarily mean that an entire application or web site is insecure but merely highlight the complex interdependencies in today's IT environments that increase the likelihood of weaknesses being discovered.

In contrast to the wired world, security weaknesses in the wireless world are generally directed as the industry and not at an individual vendor or content provider. There are several reasons for this:

- **Lack of an equivalent Windows standard**   The wireless world lacks a single dominant operating system or hardware configuration. There are multiple operating systems and hardware configurations. This requires hackers to specialize on specific applications or devices. The multiple operating systems also significantly complicate the distribution of viruses that require a homogeneous environment to spread and inflict the most damage.

- **Immature code base**   Related to the previous point, the multiple wireless operating systems are considerably less mature than their Windows counterparts. This means that the wired products have been deployed for a significantly greater time period—thereby increasing the likelihood of discovering vulnerabilities. The wired code bases are also increasingly complex with multiple interdependencies, which complicates efforts to track every possible weakness.

- **Different hacking culture**   Much of the wireless hacking activity has been focused on criminal activity, namely the cloning of phones and Subscriber Identity Module (SIM) cards to enable free wireless voice calls. Although some of these efforts have been led by academics and respected cryptographers to point out flaws in current cellular systems, hackers have been far more interested in exploiting these systems for commercial gain than for pure notoriety or publicity. This contrasts sharply with the wired world, where an increasing number of hacks and exploits are being discovered by hackers mainly to point out weaknesses in software products and to force the vendors to fix them. This different hacking culture has resulted in fewer academic-type analyses than the wired world.

- **Dearth of shipping products**   Despite the hype surrounding wireless, new wireless product releases have been few and far between. Some can be attributed to economic reasons (global 2000 to 2001 slowdown delayed product introductions), and some can be blamed on technical issues (product release cycles for new wireless products tend to be longer), but the net result is that besides new cellular handsets, there is not a high volume of new applications being released into the wireless market. This will change with 2.5 and third generation (3G) networks, but the reduction in products has made it difficult for the creation of one high-visibility vendor.

- **Poor security standards**   Wireless security weaknesses have been directed at the industry rather than individual firms because many of the wireless standards and protocols have inherent weaknesses in them. This means that anyone adhering to the specification risks being labeled insecure. Two perfect examples are Wireless Application Protocol (WAP) and 802.11. Both were conceived with good intentions, and vendors aggressively developed products that conformed to the specification. Companies that did not follow the specs risked being labeled proprietary. Unfortunately, the vast majority chose to be standards compliant, leaving them exposed to criticism about the product's general lack of security when, in fact, the standard itself was the culprit. To paraphrase the late U.S. President John F. Kennedy, "A falling standard sinks all vendors."

Despite the differences between the wireless and wired worlds, the design and implementation of secure wireless solutions has progressed, and there are now multiple production-level examples worldwide. The breadth of eligible wireless case studies is also indicative of a company's willingness to forge ahead with wireless projects even in the face of potential security limitations. This reflects that growing realization that wireless technologies are becoming a key component of any company's IT arsenal. In avoiding wireless projects because of security concerns, companies risk losing revenue and customers to competitors who proceed with wireless projects. For these reasons, many companies are proceeding with wireless projects, using a best practices and common sense approach to minimizing security risk whenever possible.

# Introduction to the Case Studies

Owing to the wireless hype of 1999 to 2000, there are ample eligible wireless data success stories. Some successes are often cynically referred to as *marketicture* in reference to the lack of substance behind the press releases. For this chapter, case studies were selected on a variety of criteria, of which commercial success was but one. The fact remains that the largest revenue-generating wireless data services are few and far between (NTT DoCoMo excepted). The goal here is to present solutions across a variety of industries and geographies that demonstrate solid wireless security architectures on today's second-generation (2G) networks.

These case studies focus on applications where security was a key consideration. There are numerous wireless deployments in production for which security requirements are secondary. Examples include generic field service-type applications where workers use wireless devices to transmit trouble tickets and other information about problems with field equipment. For instance, many of the major beverage producers equip the delivery trucks with wireless devices to update information about malfunctioning soda machines. The electric utility also employs similar applications. Given that the relative value of the underlying data is quite low, security is not a significant requirement for these implementations, so this chapter will not focus on such implementations. If the reader is looking for case studies in this category, the mainstream IT press (*Information Week*, *PC Week*, and so on) invariably cover deployments of this type on a frequent basis.

## NOTE:

*Each case study was based on information available from publicly available sources. Actual company names and specific product usage was deliberately omitted.*

# Case Study 1

Organization: Internet banking subsidiary of large European bank

User base: Consumers

Geographic location: One single European country

Application: Wireless Internet brokerage

Business requirement: Extend existing wired Internet brokerage service to wireless environments without sacrificing security.

Wireless solution: WAP-compliant solution running on Global System for Mobile Communications (GSM) network utilizing WAP-compliant handset and Java application on Palm personal digital assistant (PDA).

Background: This organization, one of the world's largest financial institutions, successfully entered the online brokerage world in the late 1990s with a web-based Internet stock brokerage service. This enabled users to conduct stock brokerage transactions through a browser. The wired system implemented several security safeguards including firewalls, Secure Sockets Layer (SSL) encryption, and usage of a hand-held hardware token for 2 factor user authentication.

As wireless applications began to take off in Europe in 1998 to 1999, the division looked to extend the same capabilities to wireless devices. Although wireless extensions to existing consumer banking applications were not viewed as a major revenue source, it was viewed as an important feature for product differentiation and to improve customer retention.

This new service needed to utilize the same ironclad security as utilized in the wired application. Unfortunately, the limitations of the WAP architecture meant that an end-to-end SSL solution was not feasible. However, the organization developed a solution that maintained end-to-end security.

Rather than relying on native WAP technology, the organization developed a Java application that could operate on the Palm PDA platform. By doing so, the application was written to support native SSL. For the wireless connection, users launched the application on the Palm device and utilized the Palm's infrared connection to interface with the wireless phone and make the connection to the banking server. In this model, the

**Figure 10-2**

Wireless Internet
banking solution

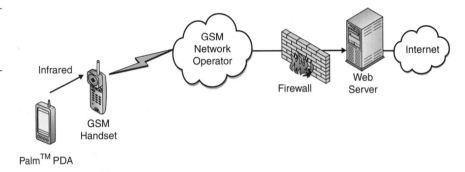

WAP terminal merely serves as the access mechanism to the wireless network. See Figure 10-2 for a generic architecture.

This solution was soon duplicated by other providers in multiple verticals as a simple workaround to the WAP Gap security issue. By doing so, the WAP gateway issue is eliminated, and native SSL can be utilized from the client device all the way to destination application. Furthermore, this approach provides another benefit in that the user interface is presented on the considerably larger Palm screen as opposed to the small mobile phone screen. The Palm's stylus input also makes for simpler data entry.

The only significant downside to this approach is that it requires multiple devices. However, the organization correctly forecasted that early adopters of wireless data services were likely to be technical savvy users and increasingly likely to carry a Palm device. This multidevice capability also opened some interesting promotional aspects as the bank could have conceivably given away a free Palm PDA (preloaded with the wireless application) to the best customers, thereby increasing customer loyalty and retention.

Ultimately, this service will need to be modified to eliminate the need for a separate PDA, but this wouldn't likely happen until WAP 2.0-compliant handsets with complete SSL capabilities become available. In the meantime, it offers a unique workaround to some of the security issues with current WAP architectures.

## Case Study 2

Organization: Multinational manufacturing firm.

User base: Employees.

Geographic location:  North American initially, followed by Europe.

Application:  Wireless e-mail for mobile executives.

Business requirement:  Enable wireless access to existing e-mail infrastructure.

Solution:  WAP-compliant handsets connect to existing Microsoft e-mail accounts via middleware. The solution used on both GSM and Time Division Multiple Access (TDMA) networks.

Background:  This organization faced an increasingly common enterprise IT problem—how does one improve end-user access to critical corporate information without sacrificing security? In addition, as end users became increasingly mobile, the average user might not access the corporate network until the end of the business day, which affected response times (reducing customer satisfaction) and often hampered decision making (increasing organizational inefficiency).

Much like airline pioneer Southwest Airlines discovered that planes do not make money when sitting on the ground, employees do not generate revenue or increase shareholder value when tethered to a PC synchronizing e-mail for three hours a day. It was for these reasons that wireless e-mail emerged as the dominant initial wireless application for most enterprises.

This organization also had three other requirements that are commonly shared by other companies

- **Compatibility with existing e-mail infrastructure**   The last thing the company wanted was to create separate wireless e-mail accounts for users. Thus, the wireless solution had to interface with the existing e-mail system, in this case, Microsoft Outlook.

- **Network independence**   The company's diverse geographic operations meant that their users were dispersed among the major network operators, so both Code Division Multiple Access (CDMA), TDMA, and GSM users needed to be supported.

- **Consistency with existing security policy**   Given the rapid deployment plans, the IT department did not have time to create entirely new security policies just for the wireless application. This meant that the application had to conform to existing wired security policies pertaining to encryption, authentication, and any other relevant rules.

The organization considered the Blackberry e-mail pagers, but the incremental hardware cost was significant, and the company had already deployed WAP-enabled mobile phones to a large majority of their employees.

The organization's ultimate implementation relied on using a wireless e-mail middleware server that could communicate with their existing Microsoft Exchange server. The organization also created a separate Demilitarized Zone (DMZ) to host the middleware server. Figure 10-3 displays the architecture in greater detail.

Creating the DMZ is an important consideration because it isolates the corporate network from potential wireless attacks. A key component here is proper configuration of the firewalls. Only those most crucial ports (such as ports 80 and 443) should be enabled.

## What Are Ports?

*Many information security discussions often talk about opening ports on a firewall. Although the principle of opening holes in a firewall may seem counterproductive, restricting access based on certain ports is an adequate defense mechanism. So what are ports? A port is basically a fixed numeric value contained within a packet of data that tells a given packet where to go. Put another way, a port informs the recipient where to listen for an incoming transmission. Many port numbers are often fixed; for instance, all web traffic generally travels on port 80. In addition, a California-based organization called Internet Assigned Numbers Authority (IANA) is responsible for managing and allocating ports to vendors. In the security spectrum, ports 80 and 443 are most relevant because port 80 is for all web traffic, and port 443 is utilized for the SSL protocol. Because only data corresponding to these port numbers will be allowed through, opening a port on a firewall does not pose a grave security risk.*

**Figure 10-3**

Corporate wireless e-mail solution

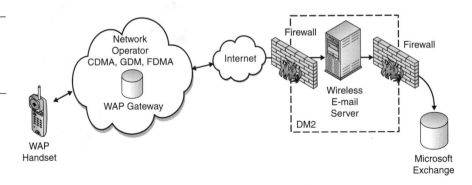

**Figure 10-4**

Data traffic flow
for Case Study 2

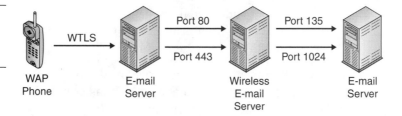

Figure 10-4 illustrates the data ports that are utilized for this connection. A key element in this case study is that it relies on existing WAP technology. The company was well versed in the WAP Gap issue, but timeliness was essential, so the company moved ahead with the wireless project and sought to minimize the WAP Gap issue. By utilizing the DMZ and enforcing secondary authentication, the company mitigated the potential WAP issue. Also, this solution enabled the organization to utilize its installed base of WAP terminals and keep their current e-mail accounts. Although this project was still in early deployment at press time, the initial pilot and subsequent production rollout were received very positively by the end users. The most commonly cited benefit was real-time access to e-mail and the productivity gains enabled by being able to respond to messages immediately.

# Case Study 3

Organization: Multinational investment bank.

User base: Employees.

Geographic location: North America.

Application: Wireless e-mail for mobile executives.

Business requirement: Enable wireless access to existing e-mail infrastructure and other applications securely.

Solution: Blackberry interactive e-mail pagers on Mobitex networks.

Background: This organization possessed similar requirements as the previous organization but selected a different wireless architecture. Although the company considered utilizing WAP enabled cell phones, the company wanted to expand the wireless project to additional applications beyond e-mail. For these reasons, the organization required a device with more capabilities than the average WAP mobile phone.

Ultimately, the company deployed over 3,000 Blackberry wireless handhelds from RIM to their user base, making it one of the world's largest Blackberry deployments.

Following successful deployment of the Blackberry wireless e-mail solution (for further details on the Blackberry architecture, please see Chapter 6), the company began investigating how to utilize the deployed Blackberry devices to access other corporate data, in particular market data information that traders and brokers could receive on the Blackberry devices. Given the slow network throughput and reduced computational capabilities of the Blackberry device, data with the simplest user interfaces and minimal throughput requirements were given first priority.

The organization evaluated the various browser products available for the Blackberry device and ultimately selected a browser-based application that could be launched from the Blackberry device and connect to a secure server residing behind the corporate firewall. This solution provided a significant benefit end-to-end security. By placing a proxy server behind the corporate firewall, the organization retained secure network access without any of the WAP Gap issues. Furthermore, in leveraging the symmetric key encryption available in the Blackberry devices, the organization ensured that the market data did not get decrypted until it reaches an authenticated BlackBerry device. Figure 10-5 highlights the layout of this solution.

**Figure 10-5**

Extended wireless corporate e-mail and application solution

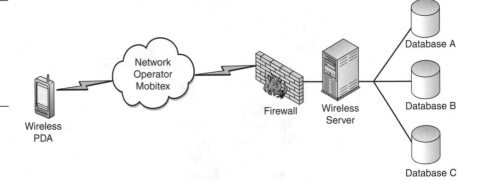

Wireless PDA

Network Operator Mobitex

Firewall

Wireless Server

Database A

Database B

Database C

# Case Study 4

Organization:  Large hospital.

Users:  Employees.

Geographic location:  United States, single geographic metropolitan area.

Application:  Wireless PDA access to patient clinical data.

Business requirement:  Enable doctors to access corporate securely.

Solution:  PDA-based solution accessing corporate network via a Mobitex network.

Background:  This organization was trying to provide access to critical patient data to an increasingly mobility workforce. PCs were not always immediately accessible to physicians, and given the importance of real-time response to information, the organization felt considerable pressure to develop wireless access to this information. Given the incredible sensitivity of this patient data, security was a paramount consideration. Furthermore, a new series of government regulations called *HIPAA* covered the U.S. healthcare industry. These regulations specifically dealt with patient confidentiality.

The organization ultimately selected the Palm VII wireless PDA. These devices access the Mobitex network and provide a large liquid crystal display (LCD) area that was more suitable for viewing the patient information than on a cellular phone.

On the application side, the organization's patient information was already accessible through a secure wired web interface. The next step was to modify the application to support wireless access. The Palm VII does not have a generic browser. Instead, access to applications is completely by Palm Query Applications (PQA). These are small programs that are installed and launched from the Palm device. The simplest analogy is in the wired world, a browser has a series of bookmarks. In the Palm VII, each bookmark is its own PQA. To support the PQA interface on the web server side, only minor modifications were needed. The main change was altering the web server content to a format that was compatible and viewable on the wireless device.

Once the application had been developed, the next step was developing a secure architecture. Like the wireless e-mail implementation in Case

Study 2, the web server hosting the Palm application was placed in an isolated DMZ with firewalls protecting access in and out of the DMZ. For data encryption, the organization relied on the encryption provided with the Mobitex network to protect the wireless interface. On the wired side, standard SSL was utilized. Figure 10-6 provides the overall architecture.

The only remaining security issues to consider was authentication. Because each Palm device contained a unique physical ID or serial number, the hospital decided to utilize that value for authentication purposes. Additional authentication measures were enforced at the application level with a traditional user name and password. A 90-day password renewal policy was also implemented.

The hospital also added two other important features to improve the security. First, the server side application tracks and logs usage by device ID. This can be used to disable access by individual devices if and when a device is lost or stolen. The second component was that the server application was configured to only accept connections from known IP addresses of the wireless service providers. Why is this so important? In enterprise settings where existing applications are being modified for wireless access, companies often mistakenly assume that the security threats are most likely from wireless environments. In fact, the vast majority of attempted hacks still originate in the wired world. This means that when

**Figure 10-6**

Wireless PDA access

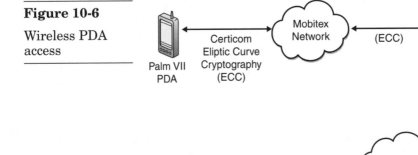

an existing application is wireless access, one needs to consider that threats can come from wired and wireless networks.

# Case Study 5

Organization: Industrial firm.

User base: Employees.

Geographic location: North America, single location.

Application: Wireless LAN in a campus environment.

Business requirement: Enable wireless LAN access securely.

Solution: Separate wireless LAN network accessible only via Virtual Private Network (VPN).

Background: This organization had developed a campus environment and was eager to utilize a wireless LAN to support their roaming employees, especially those in the engineering organization. Due to the highly sensitive nature of the data being transmitted on the network and the network resources, security was a key concern.

The solution to the problem proved to be easier than first anticipated. The company already had an infrastructure for providing access from a hostile network, the Internet, with the corporate VPN. The corporation decision was made to build a completely separate wireless network that would not have Internet connectivity, and the internal network would only be accessible through the corporate VPN.

The corporate VPN consisted of an IPSec appliance and a SSH gateway. One time password tokens were used for user authentication on the IPSec appliance and the Secure Shell (SSH) gateway.

The installation proved to be easy. Additional network cards were added to the IPSec appliance and the SSH gateway for connectivity to the wireless network. Only a few more machines were needed to make the network fully functional. A server was added to provide Dynamic Host Configuration Protocol (DHCP) and Domain Name Server (DNS) services to the wireless users because the VPN and SSH clients were configured to connect to a host name and not an IP address. Another server was added to the wireless segment to log activity and provide network-based intrusion detection. Figure 10-7 provides an illustration of this architecture.

**Figure 10-7**

Wireless LAN
deployment is
the same as
Figure 8-4.

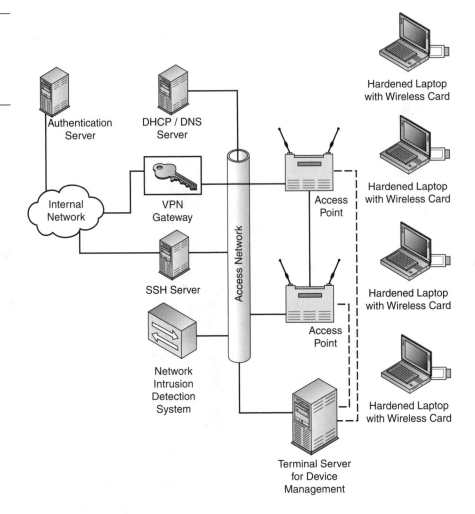

## Case Study 6

Organization: European bank.

User base: Consumers.

Geographic location: One single European country.

Application: Wireless banking and digital signing.

Business requirement: Enable wireless banking and signing of
transactions from mobile phones.

Solution:  Proprietary signing solution relying on short message service (SMS) and operating exclusively on a GSM network.

Background:  Like the organization in the first case study, this organization already had a presence on the internet with a web-based banking solution and was aggressively moving toward a wireless edition of the banking application.

In an effort to achieve product differentiation among its competitors, this bank wanted to offer digitally signing capabilities on various transactions. Digital signatures provide nonrepudiation and would provide another layer of security to certain higher level transactions. However, this architecture suffered from a major problem. Digital signing capable handsets were not available at the time of the initial rollout in 2000. Although the WAP Forum had already reached consensus on a general method for digital signing based on something called *wireless markup language (WML) Script*, there were no WML Script-compliant handsets yet on the market.

Undeterred, the bank moved forward with a solution that enabled digital signing on the current handsets. The bank and its supplier utilized a capability inherent in the GSM specification called the *SIM Application Toolkit*. This toolkit provides the opportunity for operators to interact with the user's individual SIM card in a proactive manner. For example, many of the settings related to configuring SMS services are managed between the operator and handset via the SIM application toolkit.

Because the current WAP phones could not support digital signing, this solution used the SIM Application Toolkit to provide signing capabilities. As Figure 10-8 demonstrates, it requires a multichannel interaction between the handset and web server. When a wireless user wants to conduct a transaction, the web server sends a unique block of data via a SMS

**Figure 10-8**

Wireless banking
with digital
signatures

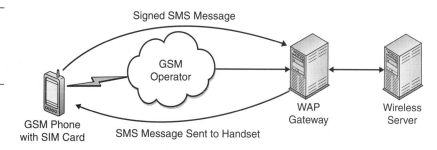

message to the user's handset. Upon receipt of the SMS message, the user's handset calls the SIM card via the SIM application toolkit. This process can access the private key on the SIM card that can be used to sign this SMS message and then returned to the web server for verification.

Although architectures like this will ultimately be phased out as handsets with native digital signature capabilities appear on the market, this case study is still a useful illustration of how certain functionality can still be achieved with today's networks. Table 10-1 also demonstrates the differences between the various case studies and reinforces the fact that there is no single recipe for wireless security.

# Case Study Wrap-Up: Key Characteristics

Although one could fill an entire book on assorted wireless implementations, these six studies listed here provide a good sense of both the underlying business problem and how solutions were developed that did not adversely increase the security risk to the organization. These case studies all shared five general characteristics that were crucial to the individual project's success.

## First Characteristic—Simplicity

In each case study, there was a clear, concise, and well understood business objective. Instead of broad strategies like access to "any data from any device on any network," these organizations identified the most crucial needs and only focused on those. Any IT project should start with the question, "What problem are we trying to solve?" If you cannot come up with a solid answer to that question, the project is likely to be unsuccessful.

Simplicity also means that goals are usually well understood and that metrics to track those goals can be easily applied and measured. In today's increasingly tight budget era, simple projects that offer a high probability of a positive return are always going to be given priority.

| User Base | Case Study 1 Consumers | Case Study 2 Employees | Case Study 3 Employees | Case Study 4 Employees | Case Study 5 Employees | Case Study 6 Consumers |
|---|---|---|---|---|---|---|
| Require new wireless devices? | Yes | No | Yes | Yes | Yes | No |
| Geography | Europe | United States | United States | United States | United States | Europe |
| Wireless data network | GSM | TDMA, CDMA | Mobitex | Mobitex | 802.11 | GSM |
| WAP compliant? | Yes | Yes | No | No | No | Yes |

**Table 10-1**  Comparisons of Case Studies

## Second Characteristic—Flexibility

Each organization covered in the case study demonstrated a willingness to modify plans or objectives based on technological or other external forces. For example, some tried to standardize on a single network bearer technology and device only to find out that in certain regions, coverage for different technologies varied differently. Rather than push a single standard through and risk certain dissatisfied end users, these companies' willingness to support multiple vendors paid off in the long run because it led to the creation of more robust solutions and compatibility with the widest range of users.

Flexibility also mattered on the security side. Many customers have tried to enforce equivalent wired security policies on wireless projects and then determine that wireless projects cannot meet these policies and therefore should be scrapped. In these case studies, the organizations made complete evaluations of risk and in some case, enabled special modifications to security policies for the wireless projects.

## Third Characteristic—Scalability

Scalability is increasingly becoming a must-have for any wireless project, but in the wireless world, the sheer volume of potential users (even within an enterprise) means that scalability is essential in the wireless world. The big difference is that in wireless projects, scalability needs to be developed at the onset. Many IT projects start out on a low scale and often do not encounter a scalability issue until considerably later in the project. Wireless projects could encounter massive demand within a few days or weeks. A classic example is NTT DoCoMo, which temporarily pulled all its promotional and advertising efforts in early 2001 because new users were growing so fast that the network was experiencing performance problems. Although these kinds of scalability problems are nice problems to have because they reflect success, inadequate handling of these problems can sap all the momentum out of a project permanently.

## Fourth Characteristic—Holistic

In all these case studies, the companies were providing wireless access to existing wired applications. Although the main security focus for these customers was protecting the wireless access routes, they did not view these wireless projects in isolation. Rather, they assessed them holistically as part of the overall infrastructure and applications. For instance, instead of just worrying about attacks against these applications from wireless attackers, these customers also considered whether these wireless projects increased the risk of attackers accessing these applications via traditional wired access routes. This will continue to be a critical success for any wireless implementation and will require close collaboration and communication between the various business groups in the organization to ensure that everything is considered on a broad scale and not just with wireless tunnel vision.

# Fifth Characteristic—Motivated User Base

In every instance cited here, the organizations possessed users who were keenly interested in participating in wireless projects. The high interest is directly correlated with the first characteristic because the motivated users were vocal and able to articulate their concerns. The wireless projects contrasted sharply with many IT projects that are conceived within IT and pushed out into the other departments. In this regard, wireless benefited from its obvious cool factor as people eagerly volunteered to participate in wireless projects so they could utilize the latest wireless devices. In these case studies, the organizations embraced the cool factor to drive demand and interest across the organization.

Another neglected side benefit of a motivated user base is that it requires considerably less training. Users are generally less intimidated by wireless devices than PCs and demonstrate a remarkable ability to test and experiment with the devices. This enabled these projects to scale much more rapidly than if users had to undergo lengthy training sessions.

Lastly, this characteristic also provides continual improvement and enhancements to the existing wireless project. The highly engaged user base is willing to offer feedback, which, if properly applied, can be used to extend the initial project to support incremental functionality and ensure that the wireless project remains at the core of the organization's IT strategy.

# Conclusion

Just like the automobile manufacturers state that the "mileage may vary," the expected results from any wireless project will vary. These case studies are not a guaranteed blueprint for success. Your organization could operate in the same vertical and same geographic region as any of the examples listed here and achieve vastly inferior (or superior) results with the same wireless architecture. This proves the continued complexity of wireless projects, but by identifying the key success factors and characteristics, these examples will hopefully provide a useful framework that can be used to deploy secure wireless access within your organization with a reasonable budget and positive results.

# CHAPTER 11

# The Wireless Future

Many technology presentations have quoted the ancient Chinese curse "May you live in interesting times" to reflect the rapid changes that technology is imprinting on our society. The wireless world has proven to be as complex and dynamic as any technology market over the last 20 years.

Although the Internet and dot-com craze of the late 1990s raised the bar for hubris and unabated positive expectations that will likely never be seen again in our lifetimes, the wireless wave of the twenty-first century still has some tremendous opportunity and momentum. The continued optimism surrounding wireless technologies despite the global macroeconomic downturn in 2001 and 2002 is a testament to wireless' resiliency and reflects that wireless technologies are here to stay. Although the manifestations of specific wireless technologies will vary greatly across technologies and geographies, wireless technologies will increasingly influence our lives.

As an example of the degree to which wireless is already pervasive in our lives, consider the daily activities of the average worker in the United States. In the course of a normal business day, this individual interacts with more than half a dozen different wireless technologies, including the following:

- **AM/FM radio**   At home and in the car
- **Infrared**   TV/VCR/DVD remote controls and to beam contact information between personal digital assistants (PDAs) in a business meeting
- **Wireless local area network (LAN)**   The home network for managing PCs, printers, and peripherals
- **Personal communications service (PCS) cellular services**   Cell phone for voice
- **General Packet Radio Service (GPRS) wireless data**   PC card for high-speed wireless access from laptop
- **Radio Frequency ID Tags (RFID)**   Remote car alarm starter and automobile transponders for automatic toll collection
- **Other**   A cordless phone in the home, a baby monitor, and so on

This is neither a comprehensive list nor are all these technologies covered in this book, yet the list illustrates how wireless technologies are already centrally involved in our daily activities. This will only continue.

Despite wireless' current pervasiveness, new technologies are still emerging that will influence daily activities in the future. Some of the new technologies are new and untested in the market (such as Bluetooth), whereas others are enhancements and upgrades to current technologies (such as 802.1x and 3G). There will also be entirely new technologies that have yet to be developed.

Ultimately, the marketplace determines which technologies are winners and losers. In most cases, the new concepts have significant momentum in the form of industry leaders supporting the new technologies, but it is often difficult to determine the relative level of commitment to these new ideas. Some companies may be merely hedging bets to avoid missing out if a technology takes off, whereas others are fully committed to seeing a new technology through to commercial success. Regardless of the outcome, all areas of wireless will continue to experience dramatic development in the future. The next sections provide some prognostication about what lies ahead in the wireless world.

# Third-Generation (3G) Networks

Of all the future wireless technologies, third-generation (3G) networks have probably generated the most significant amount of buzz and industry attention. In addition, 3G networks are probably the closest to being commercially launched, having already been rolled out in small pockets in Japan in late 2001.

Much like the initial Wireless Application Protocol (WAP) experience where operators overpromised and underdelivered compelling applications, initial press reports about 3G networks talked about throughputs of 2 Mbps to a handset, streaming video on cell phones, and a host of other tasks normally reserved for high-bandwidth-equipped PCs. Although these tasks are all feasible on 3G networks, the reality is that these services will not likely be part of the initial 3G content services. Throughputs will be considerably less than 2 Mbps and higher-bandwidth services will command a higher-price premium.

Nonetheless, the race for 3G is already well underway in Europe and Japan. The first step toward 3G was the licensing of the appropriate radio spectrum to support new higher-bandwidth services. Although the process varied from country to country (some held closed fixed-bid auctions, whereas others opted for so-called beauty contests where other non-monetary factors affected the results), most Western European countries had completed the necessary frequency auctions by the close of 2001.[1]

These auctions generated considerable debate because of the staggering prices paid for spectrum. Collectively, European network operators paid over $100 billion for the 3G spectrum. Although public-policy advocates applauded such auctions as a valuable process to line governments' coffers with badly needed funds for social programs, the high auction bids shocked people in the wireless industry because of the severe financial burden these fees placed on the winners. In some of the later auctions, some bidders either dropped out or joined forces with other carriers in the bidding process to minimize a company's individual financial exposure.

Despite the high license fees, operators have remained optimistic about 3G services. The Universal Mobile Telecommunications System (UMTS) Forum, an industry association for 3G networks, predicts that service revenue from 3G networks will represent a substantial market opportunity of $320 billion in 2010 alone and around $1 trillion over the decade as a whole. For this reason alone, operators have been unwilling to ignore 3G.

---

[1]The web site of the Universal Mobile Telecommunications System (UMTS) Forum, the industry association for 3G networks, is www.umts-forum.org.

# Worldwide Status of 3G Networks as of 2002

In the non-GSM regions (notably the United States), network operators are also preparing next-generation wireless networks based on Code Division Multiple Access (CDMA). The 2.5G equivalent for CMDA operators is a technology called CDMA2000 1xRTT (usually abbreviated as *CDMA2000 1x*), which will offer transmission rates in excess of 64 Kbps. These services do not require additional radio spectrum, but true 3G-based CDMA networks require additional capacity.

Figure 11-1 provides a map of the general evolution from 2G to 3G networks for both GSM and CDMA operators.

Having paid for hefty fees for the spectrum, network operators are eager to launch 3G services to generate revenues to help offset 3G costs. In each major global geographic region, 3G efforts are underway and all at various levels of deployment. Table 11-1 summarizes the current status of 3G networks worldwide as of the spring of 2002; the following section provides more detail on each region. Table 11-1 is not all-inclusive of every operator in every region. It merely highlights the most significant activity and differences from region to region.

> **Japan**  Japan is the undisputed worldwide leader in deploying 3G services. The runaway success NTT DoCoMo i-mode service has given Japan a key edge over every other geographic region —a large user base willing and demanding wireless data services. NTT DoCoMo first launched its 3G service in October 2001 in limited metropolitan regions. Called Freedom of Mobile

**Figure 11-1**

Path to 3G for GSM and CDMA operators

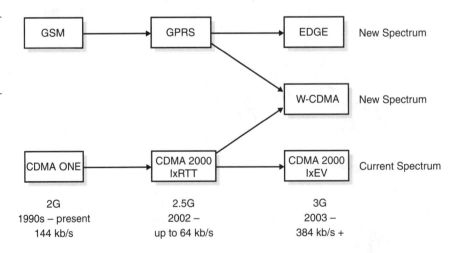

**Table 11-1**

Global 3G Network Deployments (2002)

| | Japan | Asia | Europe | North America |
|---|---|---|---|---|
| Commercial launch | Fall 2001 | Spring 2002 (Korea) | Fall 2001 (U.K.) Winter 2002 (Scandanavia) | Spring 2002 |
| Bearer technology | W-CDMA | CDMA2000 1xEV-DO | | CDMA2000 1xRTT (Verizon and Sprint PCS) and EDGE (Cingular and AT&T Wireless) |
| Network operators | NTT DoCoMo | SK Telecom | Sonera (Finland) mm02 (U.K.) | Verizon Sprint PCS, Cingular, and AT&T Wireless |

Access (FOMA), this service has been plagued with periodic glitches and problems with the handsets. Nonetheless, DoCoMo plans to continue its network expansion and expects its 3G network footprint to cover 60 percent of the Japanese population by the summer of 2002. Although the FOMA service has attracted less than 50,000 paying subscribers, it is still a key milestone for the industry in proving 3G's technological feasibility. For the foreseeable future, Japan will continue to be the lead region for the deployment and development of 3G technologies.

**Europe** The 3G license process was untimely for many participants as the global economic recession of 2000 and 2001 forced many operators to scale back previous aggressive plans for 3G launches. Nonetheless, there are already two trial 3G networks online in Europe, and more are expected throughout 2002. British mobile operator mm02 (the wireless subsidiary of British Telecom) created a separate venture called Manx to launch a 3G network on the Isle of Man off the coast of England. Much like the Japanese experience, the trial has experienced various technical glitches, but it is operational. Manx hopes to translate the Isle of Man trial into commercial success in

England and the European continent. Finnish wireless operator Sonera launched its 3G network in January 2002, but compatible handsets were not yet available.

**North America** Due to the different bearer technologies in operation in the United States, the status of 3G networks varies. Generally speaking, the United States suffers from a significant spectrum shortage that will hamper the long-term deployment of 3G networks. The spectrum shortage is considerably more pronounced in the United States than in any other region of the world and this spectrum issue will increasingly become a major public-policy issue for the U.S. government.

The CDMA operators are already launching CDMA2000 1x services in major U.S. cities. Verizon Wireless, the largest U.S. carrier, plans a nationwide footprint by the end of 2002 and has announced expected throughputs of 40 Kbps to 60 Kbps. Verizon is also offering CDMA2000 1x services for handsets and PCs (via a special wireless PC card). Sprint PCS, the other major CDMA carrier, plans to launch a CDMA2000 1x network nationwide by the summer of 2002.

Neither Verizon nor Sprint PCS has announced plans for migrating beyond CDMA2000 1x to true 3G capabilities with CDMA2000 1xEV-DO.

The other major operators in the United States are deploying GPRS- and EDGE-based networks. Cingular Wireless, the second largest wireless operator, is actually migrating from CDMA to GSM-based networks and plans to complete the migration by early 2004. Because of the migration, Cingular will offer GPRS and EDGE services. AT&T Wireless plans to complete its GPRS network by the end of 2002 and will add EDGE services in limited areas by the end of the year as well.

Voicestream, the current GSM operator in the United States, launched a GPRS service in late 2001 with throughputs approaching 56 Kbps. Voicestream has announced its intention to start deploying W-CDMA sometime in 2003, with actual deployment to follow within another year.

## What about EDGE?

Some wireless vendors (notably Ericsson) envisioned the possibility of some operators losing out in the auction process and sought to develop high-speed wireless alternatives that could be utilized on existing spectrum. The result was the Enhanced Data Rates for GSM Evolution (EDGE) standard. As the acronym implies, EDGE was designed as a mechanism to evolve current 2G and 2.5G networks to support faster throughputs. EDGE offers several significant benefits:

- **Utilizes existing radio spectrum**   This means that existing Global System for Mobile communications (GSM) operators can proceed without purchasing UMTS spectrum.

- **Relatively low infrastructure requirements**   Supporting EDGE is much like supporting GPRS; it only requires minor software upgrades to the existing base stations. This means that EDGE can be implemented for a fraction of the cost of pure 3G networks.

- **Baby step to 3G**   Although EDGE was originally conceived with the losers of the 3G auctions in mind, EDGE works equally well for the auction winners because it provides a relatively low-cost test bed upon which to launch initial high-bandwidth applications. On a technology level, EDGE also relies on a new frequency modulation scheme that is the same as that used by 3G networks. Thus, the EDGE upgrade gives operators the opportunity to understand the new technology in advance of a complete 3G rollout.

# What Lies ahead for Wireless Operators?

As the entire wireless industry evolves toward these next-generation networks, several key issues confront the industry. The wireless industry's ability to confront these challenges will ultimately determine the overall success of 3G services:

- **Financial**   Not surprisingly, financial considerations are the first challenge. Although the majority of the discussion has focused on network operators' ability to pay the hefty 3G spectrum license fees, many have overlooked that the cost of building a 3G network is equal to or greater than the $100 billion in license fees. This means that the network operators face considerable pressure to launch 3G services quickly in order to start generating revenues to offset the 3G expenses. Financial pressures affect every vendor in the 3G network value chain, not just the network operators. For instance, developing 3G compatible handsets and applications requires substantial investment and, in some cases, radical changes to current designs.

- **Revenue diversification** Wireless technologies continue to be dominated by voice, which accounts for 90 percent plus of network operators' revenues. Instant-messaging services like short message service (SMS) are making inroads, but voice remains the killer wireless application. Success in 3G will require the development of new wireless applications that can drive new revenue streams. These new services are required to attract users to sign up for 3G services. At the same time, operators must also ensure that current 2G/2.5G networks continue to function since the majority of wireless users will continue to be using those networks for the foreseeable future.

- **Technical challenges** 3G represents a quantum leap in wireless technologies and vendors must be prepared to adopt existing products to operate in these environments. For instance, given that the underlying bearer technology for 3G systems is CDMA based, the traditional GSM carriers will need to adapt from the current architecture, which is based on Time Division Multiple Access (TDMA). Although many suppliers have been actively preparing for this transition, it will still need to be monitored. On the handset side, technical challenges include a more compact design, better display sizes, and a stronger battery life and power management.

- **Expectation management** Everyone involved in the 3G space will need to tone down much of the marketing hype surrounding 3G in 2000. Yes, 3G will offer much faster wireless data, but delivery of 2 Mbps throughput to a wireless phone is still a long way from reality. Thus, the industry needs to focus on promising capabilities that can be reasonably delivered. This is already happening in the United States where the marketing campaigns for the initial 2.5G networks have toned down the hype considerably.

- **Closer collaboration** The wireless industry will need to work even closer together to make 3G a commercial success. A perfect example is Sonera's 3G launch in Finland in the winter of 2002. Despite being home to the world's largest cell phone manufacturer (Nokia), Sonera's 3G service could not occur because there were no compatible handsets available. The handset vendors, like many others, have been cautiously optimistic about 3G, but must collaborate across the value chain to ensure that the proper product mix is available at the time of the commercial launch. This also holds true for security capabilities that are developed in standards bodies such as Third-Generation

Partnership Program (3GPP) or industry associations such as WAP or Mobile Electronic Transactions (MeT). As new security architectures are ratified, it is imperative that these new specifications get into new products as quickly as possible.

# But Wait, There's More—Introducing Fourth-Generation (4G) Networks

To further prove the continuing evolution of wireless technologies, people are already discussing fourth-generation (4G) networks before 3G networks have even achieved significant global deployments. The discussion about 4G does not foretell 3G's untimely demise; rather, it indicates that the wireless industry is continuing to drive technology evolution to support even greater data throughputs and network capacity than those offered by 3G. However, 4G is closely linked to 3G. In fact, interest in 4G increased immediately following the 3G radio spectrum auctions in Europe as carriers began considering alternative and potentially cheaper methods for high-speed wireless access. In Japan, wireless pioneer NTT DoCoMo announced in March 2001 that they plan to offer 4G services by 2006, several years ahead of previously announced plans.

The main driver behind the interest in 4G networks is faster data throughput. In fact, 4G networks are not necessarily entirely new technology, but a combination of existing 2G/2.5G/3G technologies to attain faster data throughput. In a 4G environment, Bluetooth, 802.11, and 2G/2.5G technologies could all coexist and provide the necessary capabilities for high-speed wireless Internet access. This leads to the creation of so-called hotspots, confined areas in high-profile locations such as airports or hotel lobbies in which a wireless LAN network is installed and users connect to that LAN with a PC or handset and achieve high-speed access. See Figure 11-2 for more details. When users are removed from these hotspots, they essentially function as if they were on a 2G or 2.5G network.

The 4G approach has several significant advantages, notably to carriers:

■ **Lower cost** The 4G approach requires a new wireless infrastructure, but only in those areas supporting hotspots. Thus, network operators have to deploy high-speed switching stations in a fraction of the overall network footprint.

**Figure 11-2**

4G environment

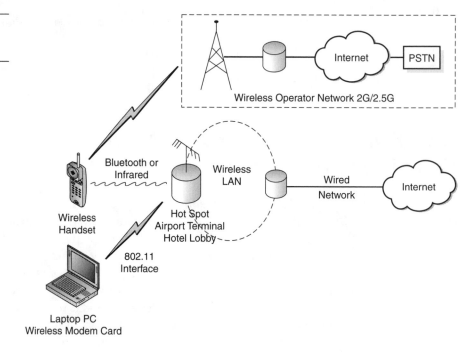

- **Utilizes existing technologies**   Although 4G still requires some infrastructure and software components, it can function with today's wireless equipment and handsets. This makes 4G considerably cheaper to deploy and also means that network operators may actually be able to deploy 4G sooner.

- **Simpler financial model**   The hotspot concept appeals to network operators because it will generate a significant return on investment (ROI). Enabling an entire network footprint with 3G services is not likely to be economically viable in the short term because some areas of the network will not generate enough usage to justify the cost. Hotspots are attractive because they can be located in the areas most likely to attract revenue-generating customers, particularly business users.

The renewed interest in 4G is reassuring because it indicates that the wireless industry is seeking to become more proactive in technology deployments, rather than having to react suddenly to new changes. If NTT DoCoMo's experiences are any guide for the rest of the world, over-capacity is a serious consideration for any wireless networks. In 2001,

DoCoMo actually temporarily suspended all marketing, advertising, and promotional activities for the service because so many new users were signing up for service that the network's bandwidth was maximized. It is worth noting that this happened on a 2G network with limited content. As content increases and improves, and as the wireless form factor improves in functionality, it is not inconceivable to envision similar overcapacity issues occurring on 2.5G and 3G networks within the next five years.

Some preliminary 4G network technologies have already been demonstrated. All of these demonstrations have focused on methods to increase throughput to the wireless device, particularly to enable capabilities like streaming audio and video. A common term used in both 3G and 4G architectures is *downlink performance*. This refers to the throughput *to* the device. Because the wireless devices are not expected to send large amounts of data to the network, uplink performance is not as important. Thus, the focus has been to design asymmetric networks that offer considerably faster throughput from network to device rather than vice versa. This is parallel to the concept behind Digital Subscriber Line (DSL) technology in the wired world in which download speed is much faster than upload speed.

The reality of 4G is that it has significant challenges. Given the asymmetric nature of the data flow, the wireless device's functionality must be increased significantly. With DSL, the standard PC is easily capable of handling the asymmetric requirements. Wireless devices do not have the same luxuries as PCs, such as high-powered processors, significant memory and storage, and ample power supply. For these reasons, some of the biggest hurdles for 4G will revolve on the capability to increase the wireless device functionality in areas such as battery life and processing power without significantly increasing cost.

4G has also renewed interest in a concept called *software-defined radio (SDR)*. SDR traces its roots to the ongoing radio frequency spectrum issues and was conceived as a method to enable network operators to reprogram base stations.[2] This functionality is important for better spectrum efficiency. Although interest initially concentrated on programmable base stations, the continuing advancements in silicon semiconductor technology have also opened the possibility of reprogrammable wireless devices. A reprogrammable wireless device could enable a

---

[2]The official website for the Software Defined Radio Forum is www.mmitsforum.org.

CDMA-based device to switch on the fly to GSM. This has some obvious benefits to operators, handset vendors, and users who currently cannot roam between different bearer technologies without multiple handsets. SDR is equally important in 3G/4G environments, where the capability to program individual cell sites or handsets helps the network operate more efficiently.

# What Lies Ahead—Wireless Networking?

Security advances in wireless networking gear will continue to evolve at a rapid pace over the next couple of years. Functional security standards are likely to be available soon. However, vendor interoperability is likely to take a while. An example of the lack of interoperability around an industry standard is IP Security (IPSec). IPSec is an Internet security standard that is discussed in other chapters of this book. The IPSec standard was approved years ago and its implementations have been deployed in many corporate environments. However, interoperability is still minimal at best. Many IPSec appliances and software will only talk to other IPSec appliances and software by the same vendor. The reason for the lack of interoperability is that many of the desired features are not included in the standard, such as user authentication using one-time passwords (OTPs). That leaves it up to the vendors to implement nonstandard features at their discretion. Vendors have taken advantage of adding proprietary features as market differentiators.

Wireless security will likely take this route, and many network designers are likely to choose vendor proprietary solutions. Proprietary solutions are not a bad thing per se. A responsible network designer must weigh the limitations of a proprietary solution against the advantages of the solution. The cost of upgrades and the life cycle of the proprietary solution need to be considered.

As wireless standards continue to develop, many manufactures will offer software updates to their equipment to allow new security features. However, very soon the security standards are likely to grow beyond the capabilities of the hardware. This will force existing installations to upgrade with new hardware. With hardware upgrade decisions, reverse compatibility is likely to be key decision-making criteria for the purchase of new equipment. Hardware vendors will make upgrades attractive by including advanced security features, greater speeds, and functionality.

With each evolution of wireless devices, they become easier to use, drop in price, and thus are more widely adopted. Currently, network designers are facing a "to buy or not to buy" decision. With the current security concerns, many have opted not to buy. However, with the cost and performance constantly getting better, network designers are not going to procrastinate implementing wireless networks much longer. Wireless networks are going to be everywhere.

Standards have pushed the rapid adoption of wireless networking and we will continue to see the standards mature. Weaknesses in early standards are being addressed and we are likely to see progress made in the following areas:

■ **Security improvements**   Security will continue to be the driving force behind purchase decisions. Advanced security features, such as the Temporal Key Integrity Protocol (TKIP), Message Integrity Check (MIC), 802.1x, and Advanced Encryption Standard (AES), are not likely to work in existing equipment because there is a limited amount of processing power and memory. Therefore, existing network equipment will be upgraded to take advantage of new security standards and features.

# Wireless—To Implement or Not to Implement? That Is the Question

Some companies are reluctant to install wireless networks citing security concerns. However, these companies do not realize that if the company does not install a wireless network, some users may purchase low-cost equipment and set up an unofficial wireless network. This installation is not likely to be secured. Therefore, in many cases, the company network is likely to be more secure if an official wireless network is installed using even the most basic of security precautions. Companies with or without wireless networks should have written policies about the proper use and installation of wireless networks.

■ **Higher speeds**   Data communications have continued to increase in speed every year. Just a few years ago, having a multimegabit connection in your home would have been a luxury for the super rich, but today many of us have broadband connections offering fast speeds. Technological advances will continue to push wireless speeds up. Soon we will see network designers opt for using wireless technologies instead of their wired equivalents. This will lead to cost savings because wiring can be very expensive. Wireless is also much faster to deploy and can be used in areas where wired networks are not practical.

■ **Low costs**   Standards will help to reduce the research and development costs of new technologies. The economies of scale of a highly adopted technology will help keep the cost down. Low costs will encourage more people to adopt the technologies and make network upgrades more frequent. Many devices will have wireless networking capabilities.

■ **Compatibility**   Reverse and international compatibility will continue to be a driving force behind technology advances. Many of the technology winners are going to be those with support for the older implementations. 802.11b will likely be the baseline by which the new technologies will be measured for compatibility.

■ **Increased availability**   Wireless cards and access points can already be purchased at most electronic stores, but in the future we are likely to find wireless functions built into many devices. Some laptops today come with built-in wireless LAN cards. Soon desktops, PDAs, and printers will all come with integrated wireless features, beyond the currently supported infrared.

■ **New applications**   As programmers and product designers become more familiar with wireless technologies, new ideas on usage are inevitable. Just as remote controlled televisions sets and cordless phones are now a part of life, wireless networks are likely to exist in every house. New wireless applications will lead to new wireless products.

# New Wireless Products

Wireless networking technology is still in its infancy and is continuing to grow. As the technology becomes richer with features, less expensive, and easier to use, we will see many new uses. Many existing cordless phones digitally transmit conversations, and voice over IP (VoIP) is starting to find a place in the corporate environment. The next likely evolution of wireless networking is the addition of voice services. With the speed of wireless networking increasing and progress being made in setting standards around quality of service (QoS) for wireless networking, voice services will be part of the next evolution. The addition of QoS will enable time-sensitive services such as voice or video to take full advantage of the available bandwidth and less time-critical services such as basic data transmissions to use the left-over bandwidth when it is available.

Virtual LANs (VLANs) are commonly used in many corporate environments. VLANs give network administrators the ability to logically group users for performance, management, or security reasons. With the adoption of voice or video on wireless networks, we will see more use of VLANs. Newer access points will support VLANs. VLANs will make it easier for network administrators to implement advanced security and QoS features.

# New Wireless Networking Markets

One market that is currently struggling is wireless-network-based wireless Internet service providers (WISPs). One problem for WISPs has been that the widely deployed wireless standard is too much like Ethernet. Ethernet does not have billing or authentication like the Point-to-Point Protocol (PPP), which is commonly used for traditional ISP services. The new security standards for wireless Ethernet are helping in this matter. Specifically, 802.1x used in conjunction with Remote Access Dial-In User Service (RADIUS) will provide those badly needed billing and authentication mechanisms and integrate into current ISP billing and authentication infrastructures.

Many ISPs resell their modems to other ISPs or wholesalers. This is very common among ISPs that offer international access to their users. Instead of having to establish a point of presence (POP) in a foreign country, which may involve licensing and administrative costs, the ISP wanting to provide service can just resell and use an existing ISP's POPs. This is a mutually beneficial arrangement that enables an ISP with unused modems to attract customers that would otherwise not use the service. The RADIUS protocol has evolved to enable ISPs to proxy authentication requests to other ISPs for authenticating users and billing purposes. This use of RADIUS has reduced the overhead for reselling modems and can be used for wireless applications.

After the adoption of 802.1x, the existing RADIUS infrastructure that enables ISPs to resell modems will also enable different ISPs to resell wireless services around the country or the world. That will help the existing WISP services that are largely regionally based and do not have a standards-based authentication scheme interoperate for the growth of the WISP industry.

Vulnerabilities with 802.1x have been published and need to be considered when choosing an authentication mechanism for an ISP. One problem allows an attacker within a wireless range to hijack a user's session. Using encryption with dynamic keys helps to mitigate this problem. We are likely to see more problems with the new wireless security standards.

# Two Worlds Collide

The world of traditional mobile providers and that of the WISP are going to collide. North American GSM operator Voicestream recently acquired Mobilestar, adding wireless-network-based services to more traditional services. Other providers are currently testing GPRS and wireless network hybrid products that will enable users to have the best of both worlds. Combining these two technologies is like other services that mobile providers have offered in the past. Many handsets today can be purchased with dual-mode capabilities that enable users to take advantage of multiple networks based on different technologies.

The convergence of wireless networks is one of the reasons why this book has addressed both the mobile provider and wireless network security issues. The security vulnerabilities and solutions are not substantially different between the technologies. Understanding both areas will better equip us to make the correct wireless security decisions.

# Looking Ahead—Key Issues

We thought it worthwhile to conclude this book with a list of some of the key issues and trends that will influence the wireless market in the years to come. Some are specifically security related, whereas others are not; however, all of them will undoubtedly shape the wireless industry landscape.

- **Location-based services and privacy**   Just like the wired world, privacy is a big issue in the wireless world and it is a double-edged sword. In the wireless world, the very nature of the technology means that it is possible to triangulate a wireless signal and determine the caller's physical location within a few hundred feet. In the United States, the government actually enacted legislation for network operators to support location-based services in order to enable public safety officials to locate individuals in distress. Although this is indeed a legitimate use of wireless technology, operators and application vendors quickly realized that this same location data could be utilized for more commercial means. For instance, if a restaurant knew an individual was walking by, wouldn't they be interested in sending him or her an SMS message offering a 10 percent discount off a meal if he or she came in right now? Some users may find this system very useful, but others are increasingly worried about potential abuses of that location data. Although every operator says that location services will require active participation by the user, location services will be a key security issue to watch in the years ahead.

  In February 2002, Japan's NTT DoCoMo said it would open its i-mode location-based system to more content providers, changing a previous policy in which only specific DoCoMo-approved providers could use the service. Although DoCoMo's service is not fine-grained (it can only transmit information about which of the network's nearly 500 separate calling areas the user is in), it reflects the commercial viability of location services.

■ **Device considerations**   The wireless form factor will continue to evolve. Where there were once separate voice and data devices, vendors are combining the two. Initial efforts to do so were not commercial successes. The Ericsson R380, Palm PDQ phone, and Nokia 9110 Communicator were all examples of devices that attempted to combine wireless voice and data into a single device. These devices' commercial failures did not deter manufacturers, and the fruits of those labors are starting to appear in the market. In the United States, the Handspring Treo, the RIM 5810, and Palm m705 are all examples of new multifunction form factors. This trend will only continue.

■ **Software considerations**   Directly correlated to the evolution of the wireless form factor is the advancement of the underlying software and applications that run on these devices. Unlike the wired world, where Microsoft® Windows operating system and Intel compatible PCs have emerged as the dominant platforms for client computing, the wireless world offers a variety of alternatives. In the coming years, these various technologies will battle against each other for dominace. Among the current contenders is Symbian, an industry consortium (Ericsson, Nokia, and Psion are among the members) that has developed an operating sytems for multifunction wireless devices. Other emerging alternatives include CDMA pioneer Qualcomm's Binary Run-time Environment for Wireless (BREW), which is being adopted by CDMA operators in the United States, Java 2 Platform Micro Edition (J2ME), and Microsoft, which has already co-developed some wireless software with Ericsson. In the immediate future, these various alternatives will likely coexist, but in the extended future, there will likely be two to three dominant wireless operating systems.

■ **The priority of security**   Wireless vendors are going to discover the necessity of implementing security into products. To date, much of the wireless weaknesses have been too arcane to the average user, but as the usage of wireless technologies increases, there will be new security threats such as wireless viruses (possible spread via SMS), denial of service (DoS) attacks (against base stations and individual handsets), and other new eavesdropping techniques. The rapid adoption of wireless technologies will increasingly make wireless security a high priority in the same manner in which the growth of the Internet raised awareness about information security.

■ **Security needs to be enabled as the default**  Amazingly, many of the initial WAP implementations actually turned off wireless data encryption to improve performance. Even more amazing was that users often had no knowledge that security capabilities were actually turned off. Fortunately, the security criticism against WAP generated considerable awareness so users now expect and demand that security be enabled as a default. This also means that security must continue to be unobtrusive to the user and not affect performance significantly.

# Wireless Wrap-Up

In the 100+ years since Guglielmo Marconi's first wireless transmission, wireless technologies have moved from a specialized communication vehicle for select constituencies like the military to a mass-market medium for communicating and disseminating information on a global scale. The continued innovations in wireless technologies are a testament to the continued importance that wireless technologies are playing in our lives. In some instances, wireless is no longer simply supplementing wired technologies, but actually replacing them altogether. For example, in the United States, many consumers have stopped using wired phones, relying exclusively on a wireless phone for communication. Network operators have encouraged this trend by offering free nights and weekends in the calling plans and even promoting the concept of disconnecting one's traditional home wired phone. As wireless networks mature and improve in areas like bandwidth and coverage, the trend toward favoring wireless over wired communications will only continue.

Unfortunately, the rise in usage of wireless technologies has been accompanied by an equivalent rise in wireless security threats and hacks. Due to the virtual medium over which wireless communication occurs, the potential for intercepting and eavesdropping on wireless communications has existed for as long as the wireless technologies have existed. Yet, as this book has shown, advances in wireless security countermeasures have not advanced as rapidly as have advances in core wireless technologies. This is not dramatically different from the wired world where security weaknesses are often discovered within weeks of a new product introduction.

The main difference between wireless and wired security issues is that wireless security issues have proven to be a more significant barrier to the wider adoption of new wireless technologies than have the wired counterparts. In the wired world, global incidents like computer viruses and DoS attacks have not had a significant long-term effect on the overall adoption of the PC and Internet technologies. In fact, the continued successful propagation of new viruses is further evidence that prior attacks have not significantly affected views toward security because users continue to ignore prior warnings or apply appropriate patches and third-party software to fix previously discovered weaknesses. By comparison, in the wireless world, high-profile security weaknesses such as those in the original WAP architecture and the 802.11-based networks have had a significant effect on eroding confidence and demand for these technologies.

Although these wireless security weaknesses have affected deployments of these technologies, these same weaknesses have helped raise security awareness within the wireless community. This is a positive development. Rather than shying away from wireless technologies because of security concerns, vendors and suppliers should capitalize on this development to design, build, and launch new wireless products and services that effectively address these security concerns. Doing so will help remove security as an obstacle to further deployment and will also increase the probability of greater commercial success.

Vendors and customers alike must also realize that wireless security is an iterative, ongoing process. Software and algorithms that are deemed secure today may not be secure in two years as people continue to refine hacking techniques and cryptographic analysis. This requires constant vigilance from everyone involved with the wireless industry. In fact, this book has contained numerous excerpts of architectures that were initially viewed as secure, only to have serious flaws uncovered in later years, which is further proof that you cannot assume that a given architecture will remain secure. Only by monitoring trends and technologies over time (and adapting to them) can the wireless industry hope to keep wireless deployments safe from emerging hacks and threats.

The other key point in the wireless market is that technology developments and potential security weaknesses cannot be viewed in a vacuum. IT managers and other people involved with wireless projects also need to understand overall wireless market trends and how they relate to security. Is a published wireless security weakness a theoretical one or can it be executed today? What does this weakness actually enable a hacker to do? Keeping a sense of market trends is a difficult process since it requires you to understand the true substance behind a press release or article in the trade press to determine between the hype and reality.

The perfect example of the need to understand a wireless security issue within the true market context was the furor over the WAP Gap security issue. At the time, the industry press was full of stories about WAP security and press releases from vendors offering solutions to address the proposed problems. Unfortunately, few vendors (or the press) focused on this issue within its larger context—namely, that this security issue was not particularly relevant for low-value information services like weather, and secondly that the WAP specification was an evolving specification with future releases aiming to address the security issues. By not focusing on the overall long-term picture, many vendors did the industry a disservice by utilizing the WAP security problem as a vehicle to sell more products, but in the process, these marketing campaigns turned many users away from WAP altogether. The WAP example only emphasizes the need to understand all wireless security issues in a broader market context.

# Conclusion

This book aims to combine relevant wireless market data with a broad understanding of wireless security threats and weaknesses. In doing so, we hope that we have provided an appropriate framework necessary to develop and implement a successful wireless security strategy and policy for any organization. By combining the best practices outlined in this book with an ongoing vigilance and awareness of wireless market trends, you will be best positioned to achieve success in any wireless project or application.

# CHAPTER 12

# Assessing Wireless Local Area Networks (LANs)

Wireless networks are here to stay. Whether your campus has a deployed wireless network or not, regular wireless assessments should be conducted at your campus. To the surprise of many network engineers and network security professionals, users often install wireless networks without consulting the proper channels. The low cost of wireless gear and the tremendous convenience that wireless enables make unofficial wireless network common. Therefore, network and security professionals need to know how to perform wireless assessments. This section is designed to give network and security professionals enough information so they can conduct wireless network assessments. The techniques discussed in this section are specific to 802.11, but the principles can be applied to any wireless networking technology.

## Getting Started

A good wireless network assessment starts with the correct equipment. The equipment needed to assess wireless networks is very similar to the equipment used by attackers as described in Chapter 2. The following is a comprehensive list of the necessary equipment:

- **Laptop**   A laptop with a moderate central processing unit (CPU), memory, and storage is needed. You may want to find a light laptop because you may cover a lot of ground, and a lighter laptop will save your back.

- **Wireless card**   You will need a good quality wireless card for your assessments. Most professionals have a number of cards because much of the popular software requires specific cards. Having at least one card that can be used with an external antenna can be very useful.

- **Global Positioning System (GPS) (optional)**   GPS receivers can be used to gather location information on wireless devices. This information can be very useful when evaluating the data gathered during the information-gathering phase or during follow-up assessments.

- **Building plan**   If not using GPS or when indoors out of the range of GPS, having a building plan can help you note where wireless devices were discovered for follow-up action.

- **Batteries**   Good batteries with a long life are extremely important to minimize the time needed to conduct wireless assessments. Having extra batteries is highly recommended.

- **Sniffing software**   Commercial and open-source sniffing software can be used to perform wireless assessments.

- **Antennae and cables (optional)**   Antennae can be used to increase the range of wireless cards for information gathering. Having an omnidirectional and directional antenna provides flexibility for information gathering. Make sure to get the proper connectors to hook up the antenna to the cards with the minimum amount of connectors and cable.

- **Amplifiers (optional)**   Antennae can be used to extend the range to find wireless devices. Amplifiers are used in conjunction with antennae.

- **DC inverter (optional)**   If your campus is spread out over many buildings, driving around the buildings can save time. A wireless inverter that provides power for equipment from a car's cigarette lighter is recommended.

# Wireless Policy

Most companies have information security policies. If you have a security policy, check to see if it addresses wireless networks. Wireless networks may be covered under the section involving connections to public or third-party networks. If you do not have a current information security policy or if your policy does not cover wireless networks, you may want to refer to Chapter 8 and create a policy that meets your business needs.

Some companies have found out that their network is vulnerable to wireless attackers by a rogue network that users set up. After discovering the wireless equipment, long political battles ensue because proper use of wireless networks was not specified in the security policy. After experiencing the convenience and mobility of a wireless network, most users are reluctant to part with it. So before you attempt to have rogue access points removed, be prepared to defend your reasons for removing it and have support from policy or executives.

When writing a policy that applies to wireless networks, make sure to appoint someone to be in charge of the radio frequencies on campus. Most wireless networking technologies use frequencies that may be used by other devices, such as security cameras and cordless phones. The person in charge of the wireless frequencies may be able to resolve performance problems and assist in planning wireless networks. If you are installing the wireless network in a facility that is not owned by the company, such as a mall or airport, you may want to check with the building owner to see if there is someone in charge of radio frequencies.

# Process

The wireless network assessments can be broken down into three phases. Depending on your environment, there may be many steps in each phase, but all tasks fall into the following phases:

- **Information gathering**   Physically walk or drive to look for wireless devices, including access points and stations. Active and passive information-gathering techniques are used during this phase. Location information should be gathered during this phase. (GPS can be used.)

- **Data analysis**   Now that you have all the data, it is time to make sense of it. Organizing the data by plotting it on maps, exporting it into a database, or putting it into tables assists with the analysis. The wireless policy can be used to determine what steps may be needed.

■ **Follow up**   Take the needed action on discovered wireless devices. This may include gathering additional information to validate findings or taking action to remove devices. This phase involves finding specific location information about wireless devices and sometimes using directional antennae or tracing wirers to locate wireless devices. After action is taken, conducting follow-up scans is recommended.

This general process can be used for any wireless technology, but the most widely available and deployed technology is 802.11b. 802.11a is also starting to be deployed. Additional equipment or software may be needed to search for equipment with different technologies.

# Information Gathering

Thereare two categories for gathering information on wireless devices: active information gathering and passive information gathering. In order to maximize the effectiveness of a wireless assessment, both methods should be used when gathering information about wireless devices.

Active information-gathering methods involve sending frames and watching for responses. My favorite active information-gathering tool is NetStumbler (www.NetStumbler.com). NetStumbler actively searches for access points by sending out probe request frames and listening for the probe responses. The probe responses include information about the access point; access points can be configured to not respond to probe requests so additional methods need to be used. NetStumbler and other active information-gathering tools can be configured to scan through spending a short period of time on each channel looking for access points. Not all access points are configured to respond to broadcast probe requests, so additional techniques need to be used to find access points. Additionally, some access points may be hidden stations to the assessing laptop, but additional methods can be used to learn about the existence of these hidden stations.

Passive information-gathering tools receive frames but never send any frames. When used by an attacker, these tools are very difficult, if not impossible, to detect. Passive information-gathering tools are the greatest tools used for wireless network assessments. My favorite information-gathering tool is a passive tool called *AiroPeek* by WildPackets. AiroPeek is a commercial sniffer and has a lot of features to assist in gathering and organizing information. Like NetStumbler, AiroPeek can be configured to scan through the channels. AiroPeek also supports the creation of filters for capturing or reading data and includes summary reports that greatly decrease the time needed to analyze data.

GPS receivers can be added to a number of information-gathering tools, including NetStumbler, for recording location information. Most war drivers, as discussed in Chapter 2, use programs like NetStumbler with GPS receivers and antennae to search for access points.

## What to Look For

When assessing an 802.11 wireless network, the following information will either provide specific information about wireless devices or clues about the existence of these devices:

- **Beacons**   Beacons are management frames that are sent out by most access points at regular intervals, advertising the existence and the capabilities of the access point.

- **Probe responses**   Active information-gathering tools, such as NetStumbler, send out probe requests and record information learned from the probe responses.

- **Probe requests**   Wireless stations send out probe requests, searching for the existence of access points. These management frames include information about the requested wireless network. The information contained in the probe requests can be used for investigation.

- **Basic Service Set ID (BSSID)**   802.11 data frames contain more addresses than standard Ethernet frames. One additional address field contained in data frames is the BSSID, which normally contains the Media Access Control (MAC) address of an access point.

- **Service Set Identifier (SSID)**   The SSID, which is included in beacons and probe requests and probe responses, may contain descriptive information about the wireless device.

- **MAC addresses**   Record the MAC addresses of all wireless devices encountered. These address are vital to data validation.

■ **GPS information**   Location information of wireless devices can help to organize data for analysis. Some information-gathering tools automatically record location information. Mapping software can be used during information gathering, and triggers can be set to plot information.

# Data Analysis

Large amounts of raw data can be gathered in a short period of time. The gathered data is only as good as the sense that can be made out of it. In order to prevent information overload when gathering data in a large or highly populated area, data needs to be properly organized. In many cases, the data from multiple tools can be exported into a common format for organizing.

## Organizing the Data

Before data analysis can begin, the information gathered must be organized into a manageable format. There are no rules for organizing data—whatever works for the individual analyzing it is sufficient. However, this section will include suggestions on how it can be organized. The most common ways of organizing the data are plotting on a map, organizing into a table, or exporting into a database.

Having the data in an easily accessible format makes the follow up easier, which may involve checking the wired network for MAC addresses to see if the wireless devices discovered are actually on the network. Many times, discovered devices are part of a wireless network installed in a nearby building. In a metropolitan situation with buildings in close proximity, this data validation step is important because it can save a lot of unneeded follow-up work.

## Mapping Out Coverage Areas

You can either use GPS information to map data after it is collected or the data can be mapped manually during information gathering using a building plan. This information can be useful in evaluating the risk of your deployed wireless network or during the follow-up phase.

Mapping programs, such as DeLorme's TopoUSA or Microsoft's Map-Point, can be used to plot data. Most information-gathering programs can export data into a text format that can be imported in these mapping programs. Many Internet sites have scripts that can be used to organize information from popular information-gathering programs such as Nets-tumbler or AiroPeek.

Mapping programs also have features that can be used plot data during capture by attaching a GPS receiver to a laptop running the software. In this situation, the person gathering the information would use a program, such as AiroPeek or a site survey program, and also run the mapping program. After seeing something that needs to be mapped, the mapping program could be used to read the GPS and plot the information.

# Follow Up

Following up after the information that has been gathered may involve taking action or gathering additional information to validate the results. The policy discussed in the beginning of this section will be used as the decision-making criteria for follow-up action. Regardless of the information gathered or follow-up action, a follow-up assessment should be scheduled and the data stored for this purpose. These follow-up assessments are normally conducted quarterly.

One large financial institution conducted wireless assessments and discovered that open wireless access points were installed on their network. Network and security staff wanted to remove the access points, only to have the top executives give approval for the access points. The access points were installed by a top sales representative for use by his staff. Eventually, a security consulting company was contracted to conduct a penetration test to demonstrate the risk that the company was exposed to. The security consultants conducted their penetration test from a hotel room located miles away from the company's building in a large city. The consultants compromised sensitive and proprietary information, including passwords, customer lists, and personal information of top executives without being detected. After the consultants delivered the report, the access points were secured. Securing the network was a long process that exposed the company to great risk. If a comprehensive wireless policy existed, many of these difficulties could have been avoided.

## Validating Data and Taking Action

Finding the exact physical location of access points and vulnerable wireless clients can be difficult. Radio professionals use directional antennae to triangulate wireless devices, and network professionals use networking gear to identify where these devices are installed and follow wires to discover the location of devices.

Radio professionals employ various techniques to locate wireless devices. This normally involves using different antennae and radio analyzers. Due to the multiple paths that wireless transmissions take, locating devices can be very difficult for an amateur. Therefore, having multiple ways to identify and locate the location of wireless devices is needed.

Network discovery techniques include checking switches' or routers' Address Resolution Protocol (ARP) tables to find out which device and port a wireless device is connected. Resolving MAC addresses to IP addresses allows the use of additional tools. MAC addresses of wireless devices are never encrypted. Packet sniffers can also be used on the wired network to find access points. Many access points send out management frames to other devices advertising their existence. Rogue access points may be set up to get the probe-requesting clients to connect. Network-layer reconnaissance techniques can be used to gather enough information to identify the machine.

Wireless sniffing software can be used monitor traffic, if it is not encrypted or if the encryption key is known, or can be cracked to reveal information about the users. E-mail traffic or Windows networking broadcasts are great ways to learn about the user. Or after IP addresses are discovered, network-based information-gathering techniques may be used. Many applications submit usernames in cleartext and identify the user.

Finally, if you need to locate a wireless device, just ask around. Using sniffing software, you can locate the general area that the signal is strongest and start walking around the area asking users. E-mail is a great tool that can be used to gather information. Send out an e-mail to users in the area and ask about wireless devices.

---

## Locating Wireless Devices at Different Layers of the Open Standards Interface (OSI) Model

■ **Physical**   Triangulation with directional antenna.

■ **Data link**   Trace wires based on information from networking gear.

■ **Network**   Network-layer information gathering.

■ **Transport**   Sniff network traffic to learn about the user.

■ **Application**   Use an application such as e-mail to ask users.

---

## Ongoing Assessments

Regular wireless assessments should be part of an enterprise wireless policy. Information gathered when assessing wireless networks is out of date immediately after it has been gathered because it only captures the current state. There is no way to know what the future will bring. Laptops are coming with integrated wireless devices, and new devices are continuously being added to the network. Therefore, regular wireless assessments are vital to the security of the network.

Hiring an independent third party to perform periodic wireless assessments is recommended. Depending on your environment, hiring a professional may cost less than training internal personnel to perform wireless assessments and buying all the needed equipment. A wireless security professional may also be able to detect wireless devices that may go unnoticed. Some companies elect to have quarterly assessments performed by internal staff and annual assessments performed by an independent third party. If these assessments can be scheduled in advance, discounts may be negotiated with the wireless security professionals.

# My Wireless Assessment Kit

The following items are in my personal wireless assessment kit:

- Toshiba laptop
  - Inverter for use in a car
  - Extra battery
- Wireless cards
  - Two Cisco 350 series cards—one with an internal antenna and one with external antenna connector
  - Lucent Gold World Card
  - SMC 2632W
- Garmin GPS
  - Data cable with DC connector for use in car
- WildPacket's AiroPeek software
- Netstumbler
- Assorted network tools
  - Ethereal/Tcpdump
  - Nmap
  - Dsniff
  - Linux with modified access point utility and tools
- DeLorme TopoUSA
- Yagi directional antenna mounted on a tripod
- Omni antenna on a magnetic mount
- DC inverter
- 2.4 GHz amplifier

# Emerging Markets

As discussed in Chapters 7 and 11, the wireless industry is in a constant state of change. Wireless assessment techniques, software, and hardware are going to constantly be changing. Therefore, there will continue to be a market need for additional tools and equipment. This includes tools for performing assessments across a wide range of wireless technologies. Many of the existing tools are specific to 802.11b, but we are starting to see 802.11a equipment installed. In the near future, 802.11g equipment will also be available.

Automating assessment techniques with passive tools that can installed throughout a campus would lead to cost savings. Research is currently being conducted around wireless intrusion detection systems (IDSs). Soon we will see products providing these capabilities, or some vendors may choose to add these features to access points. In addition to providing intrusion detection, these device would also be able to monitor the network for incorrectly configured devices.

# Conclusion

Wireless network assessments are vital to the security of your network. Security policies should contain detailed information on the proper use of wireless networking devices. Conducting wireless assessment is not extremely difficult, and regularly scheduled assessments should be performed. These assessments can be conducted by internal personnel and third parties. Training security and network personnel in wireless security issues can be very beneficial.

A good network or security engineer knows his or her network. He or she watches network traffic, routing tables, and logs to know how the network is being used. Now good network and security professionals also watch the airwaves and know about the wireless devices on his or her campus.

# PART 4

# Glossary

# APPENDIX A

# Glossary of Wireless Terms

**3DES** Triple Data Encryption Standard. A variation of DES that uses larger key sizes.

**3GPP** Third-Generation Partnership Project. A collaborative agreement defined in 1998 to manage standards for 3G networks.

**A3** Secret key algorithm used on GSM networks to authenticate an individual subscriber's handset to the network.

**A5** A 64-bit block cipher algorithm used on GSM networks to encrypt voice and data after successful authentication. Two variants of A5 are used: A5/1 and A5/2.

**A8** The algorithm used on GSM networks to generate symmetric encryption keys.

**Access point** Hardware or software that acts as a communication hub for users of wireless devices who connect to a wired LAN. Access points are important for providing wireless security and extending the physical range of service that a wireless user has access to.

**AES** Advanced Encryption Standard. A symmetric 128-bit block data encryption technique developed by Belgian cryptographers Joan Daemen and Vincent Rijmen. The U.S government adopted this as its encryption technique in October 2000, replacing the DES encryption it previously used.

**AH**  Authentication Header. An integrity component of IPSec.

**AKA**  Authentication and Key Agreement.

**AM**  Amplitude modulation. The first wireless technology capable of transmitting voice, which was invented in the early twentieth century. Technology that varies the strength or amplitude of a radio signal for transmission over a given frequency.

**AMPS**  Advanced Mobile Phone Service. A U.S. analog cellular voice standard.

**ARDIS**  Advanced Radio Data Information Service. A wide area wireless data network standard introduced in the 1980s.

**ARPU**  Average revenue per user. A key financial metric for wireless network operators that refers to the average monthly (or annual) revenue generated by each individual subscriber.

**ATM**  Asynchronous Transfer Mode. A network switching that transfers data in technology based on transferring data in cells or packets with a fixed size.

**Authenticate**  To reliably determine someone's identity.

**Baby Bell**  The term applies to the seven regional phone carriers that were created following the government-ordered breakup of the U.S. phone monopoly AT&T in 1984. Baby Bells are also known as Regional Bell Operating Companies (RBOCs).

**Beacons**  802.11 management frames advertising the existence and capabilities of an access point.

**Blackberry**  A wireless data hand-held device marketed and sold by Canadian-based Research in Motion (RIM). The device operates on Mobitex and GPRS networks, and interoperates with major e-mail applications to enable wireless e-mail forwarding.

**Bluetooth SIG**  Bluetooth Special Interest Group. A trade association comprised of various industry leaders interested in driving the development of a low-cost, short-range wireless specification for connecting mobile products.

**BSC**   Base Station Controller. A component of the wireless network that coordinates multiple base stations and communicates with the Mobile Switching Center (MSC) to place individual wireless calls.

**BTS**   Base Transceiver Station. Also known as a base station, this is the component of the wireless network that the wireless device first connects with to establish a call. There is one base station per cellular site.

**CA**   Certificate Authority. A trusted third party that issues and revokes digital certificates to end users to facilitate encrypted communications and digital signatures.

**Calling Party Pays**   The process by which a mobile subscriber pays to place a call, but is not billed for receiving a call. This is the dominant billing standard for wireless operators outside of North America. Placing a call from a mobile phone pays for the call.

**CAVE**   Cellular Authentication and Voice Encryption. The security algorithm used for voice encryption on CDMA networks.

**CCK**   Complimentary Code Keying.

**CDMA**   Code Division Multiple Access. A digital cellular technology in which individual conversations are encoded using unique numeric codes. Also known as ITU standard IS-95.

**CDMA 2000**   3G standard for Code Division Multiple Access. Also referred to as CDMA 2000 1X.

**CDPD**   Cellular Digital Packet Data. A wireless data technology that operates on standard cellular networks and offers transfer rates up to 19.2 Kbps.

**CEIR**   Central Equipment Identity Register. A database used by GSM carriers to track and maintain lists of known cloned or fraudulent wireless handsets.

**CEPT**   Conference of European Posts and Telecommunications Administrations. Pan-European organization responsible for defining initial GSM wireless network standard for Europe.

**CIA**   Central Intelligence Agency. The U.S. government agency responsible for international intelligence.

**CIFS**   Common Internet File System. A File Transfer Protocol based on Microsoft's common implementation.

**Ciphers** Secret writings.

**Circuit switching** The process of transmitting data and voice via a dedicated switch and connection.

**Cleartext** Refers to the passing of data without any protection or privacy. The data is "clear," or visible, to anyone who is listening on the network.

**CPU** Computer processing unit. The component of the computer that is responsible for all calculations. On individual PCs, the CPU is the same as the microprocessor; larger machines may have multiple CPUs.

**Cryptography** The process or skill of communicating in or deciphering secret writings or ciphers.

**CSMA/CA** Carrier sense multiple access with collision avoidance. The reliability method used with wireless Ethernet designed to avoid collision on a shared medium.

**CSMA/CD** Carrier sense multiple access with collision detection. The reliability method used with Ethernet designed to detect and recover from collisions on a shared medium.

**D-AMPS** Digital Advanced Mobile Phone Service. A U.S. digital cellular voice standard based on TDMA and is the successor to AMPS. Also known as ITU standard IS-136.

**DES** Data Encryption Standard. Data encryption standard adopted by the United States in 1976 that is to be replaced by AES. *See* AES.

**DHCP** Dynamic Host Configuration Protocol. The protocol that enables dynamic IP configuration.

**Diffie-Hellman** The first public/private key algorithm, named for inventors Whitfield Diffie and Martin Hellman.

**DMZ** Demilitarized Zone. Sanitized and secure area of network.

**DNS** Domain Name System (or Service). The process that translates web domain names into numeric IP addresses.

**DoS** Denial of service. A category of malicious attack that is designed to prevent a resource from providing a service.

**DSSS** Direct sequence spread spectrum. Binary encoding process that spreads the data by combining it with a multibit pattern or pseudo-noise code.

**EAP**   Extensible Authentication Protocol. An extension to PPP that provides support for multiple authentication methods.

**ECC**   Elliptic Curve Cryptography. A public key cryptosystem that derives the key material from selecting points on a given elliptic curve. Pioneered by Certicom Corp.

**EDGE**   Enhanced Data Rates for GSM Evolution. A standard for enabling higher-bandwidth applications on existing GSM networks.

**EEPROM**   Electrically erasable programmable read-only memory. A type of computer memory that retains memory even when power is off and can be erased through an electric current.

**Encryption**   The process of encoding data to prevent eavesdropping.

**ERMES**   Enhanced Radio Message System. A European standard for digital wireless mobile paging networks.

**ESA**   Enhanced subscriber authentication. The architecture utilized in 3G networks that offer simultaneous mutual authentication of both subscriber and network operator.

**ESN**   Electronic Serial Number. The unique hardware identifier placed on most computer hardware. In wireless networks, ESN is often utilized as part of the authentication process.

**ESP**   Encapsulated security payload. An encryption component of IPSec.

**ETSI**   European Telecommunications Standards Institute. A nonprofit standards organization that produces telecommunications standards for use throughout Europe. ETSI unites 789 members from 52 countries inside and outside Europe.

**ETSI BRAN**   Broadband Radio Access Network (HIPERACCESS). Task group working on HiperLAN/2.

**FBI**   Federal Bureau of Investigation. The U.S. government agency responsible for domestic law enforcement, including cyberterrorism.

**FCC**   Federal Communications Commission. An independent U.S. government agency responsible for establishing policies to govern interstate and international communications in television, radio, wire, satellite, and cable. The FCC regulates all forms of electronic communications both within and going out of the United States. The FCC works with the ITU, the ETSI, and other organizations to establish international regulation.

**FDMA**   Frequency Division Multiple Access. Wireless network bearer technology that transmits multiple communications over a single channel by varying the frequency of each individual communication. Not as efficient as TDMA or CDMA, which replaced FDMA.

**FHSS**   Frequency hopping spread spectrum. *See* spread spectrum.

**Firewall**   A hardware or software device that controls access to a given network.

**First generation (1G)**   The term for initial wireless voice networks. 1G networks are analog based and work exclusively with stationary users. The first 1G networks were launched in the late 1970s. *See also* AMPS.

**FLEX**   A North American wireless paging network standard initially created by Motorola. Recognized as an ITU standard.

**Frame**   Logical grouping of information at the data link layer.

**FTP**   File Transfer Protocol. The Internet protocol for transferring files.

**FUD**   Fear, uncertainty, and doubt.

**GGSN**   Gateway GPRS Support Node. The network node that connects the GPRS wireless network with other networks (such as wired voice networks and the Internet).

**GHz**   Gigahertz.

**GPRS**   General Packet Radio Service. A mobile wireless packet-data-based architecture for GSM-based networks. Often referred to as 2.5G.

**GPS**   Global Positioning System. A satellite navigational system that allows the calculation of geographic locations by performing calculations against signals received from these satellites.

**GSM**   Global System for Mobile Communications. A leading digital cellular system that uses narrowband with TDMA.

**Handset**   An end-user mobile phone device used for placing calls.

**Hash**   A function that takes a variable-length input and produces a fixed-length output.

**HIDS**   Host-based intrusion detection system. Software that will monitor the system for suspicious activity.

**HiperLAN/2 Global Forum (H2GF)**   HiperLAN/2 is an open industry forum created to be a global standard with complete interoperability of high-speed wireless LAN products. Its mission is to drive the adoption of HiperLAN/2 as the globally accepted, broadband wireless technology in the 5 GHz band, providing connectivity for mobile devices in corporate, public, and home environments. It is the European counterpart to WECA.

**HLR**   Home Location Register. The central database on wireless network that stores all relevant information about valid subscribers, including the mobile phone number, access privileges, and the current location of the subscriber's handset.

**HomeRF Working Group**   Leading companies from various industries formed to drive the development of interoperable wireless devices for voice, data, and multimedia. This group developed the SWAP protocol.

**HTTP**   Hypertext Transfer Protocol. Basic protocol for all World Wide Web traffic. Defines how images, files, and data are transmitted across the Web.

**IAPP**   Interaccess Point Protocol. The protocol used to exchange information between access points.

**iDEN**   Integrated Dispatch Enhanced Network. Wireless network adopted by the North American carrier Nextel.

**IDS**   Intrusion detection system. A system that allows for the detection of hackers or network intrusions by examining either network patterns (NIDS) or examining suspicious activity on individual computers (HIDS).

**IEEE**   Institute of Electrical and Electronics Engineers. The IEEE is a nonprofit technical professional association of more than 350,000 individual members in 150 countries. Much of its work involves technical publishing, conferences, and consensus-based standards activities.

**IEEE 802.11**   IEEE standards body designated to come up with wireless LAN standards.

**IEEE 802.15**   IEEE standards body designated to come up with wireless PAN standards.

**IEEE 802.16**   IEEE standards body designated to come up with wireless MAN standards.

**IETF** Internet Engineering Task Force. Responsible for forming and creating standards and protocols for the Internet.

**IMEI** International Mobile Equipment Identity. Unique numeric value assigned to each individual cellular handset.

**IMSI** International Mobile Subscriber Identity. Unique numeric value assigned to each individual cellular subscriber.

**Integrity** Cryptographic mechanism employed to guarantee that data has not been modified.

**IP** Internet Protocol. The protocol used for transmitting data across the Internet. The current version of the standard is IPv4.

**IPSec** Internet Protocol Security. A set of protocols designed to provide the secure exchange of packets at the IP layer. Encryption and digital signatures are used to provide privacy and data integrity.

**ISDN** Integrated Services Digital Network. A global standard for transmitting data and voice over digital or analog phone lines with throughputs of up to 128 Kbps.

**ISO** International Organization for Standardization. An international standards body made up of standards organizations from over 75 countries.

**ISP** Internet service provider. An entity that provides access to the Internet.

**ISV** Independent software vendor. Generic industry term applied to any vendor who produces software products.

**ITU** International Telecommunications Union. The ITU, headquartered in Geneva, Switzerland, is an international organization within which governments and the private sector coordinate global telecom networks and services.

**Jamming** Intentional or unintentional radio interference over powering a communications link.

**Kiosk** A small device that displays information.

**LAN** Local area network. A network combining multiple computers that is confined to a limited geographic area, such as an individual building.

**LEAP** Cisco's proprietary implementation of EAP.

**MAC**   Media Access Control. One of two sublayers that make up the data link layer in the OSI model.

**MAN**   Metropolitan area network. The term referring to a logical network serving a medium-sized geographic area that normally has a municipal designation.

**MD5**   Message Digest 5. Hash algorithm that was invented by MIT Professor Ron Rivest and is usually used for creating digital signatures.

**MITM**   Man in the middle. Refers to attacks in which a hacker intercepts a communication session and replaces the valid key material with other key material.

**MN**   Mobile node. The term used to refer to a wireless device without a fixed location.

**Mobile Party Pays**   Process by which a mobile subscriber pays to place and receive a call. The dominant billing standard for wireless operators in North America. The opposite of Calling Party Pays.

**Mobitex**   Wireless packet data network standard initially launched by Ericsson.

**Moore's Law**   The technology phenomenon in which the amount of transistors that could fit onto a single silicon chip would double every 18 months, leading to faster and cheaper computer chips. Named after Gordon Moore, one of the cofounders of Intel.

**MSC**   Mobile Switching Center. The network node that connects wireless networks with wired networks.

**NFS**   Network File System. A standard client/sever file system that runs over a network connection.

**NIDS**   Network-Based Intrusion Detection System. Detects intrusions based upon suspicious network traffic.

**NIST**   National Institute of Standards and Technology. The U.S. government agency involved in the development of a wide variety of technology standards, including cryptographic standards.

**NTT**   Nippon Telephone and Telegraph. Japan's incumbent phone carrier and the majority owner of the wireless carrier NTT DoCoMo.

**NVRAM**   Nonvolatile random access memory. Storage device whose contents are saved even when power is lost.

**OFDM**   Orthogonal Frequency Division Mutliplexing. A modulation technique for transmitting large amounts of data over a radio wave.

**OSI**   Open System Interconnection. A standard developed in the 1970s that defines a framework for developing networking protocols.

**OTP**   One-time password. A password that expires after its first use.

**Packet**   A logical grouping of data at the network layer.

**Packet switching**   The process of splitting data into separate blocks and transmitting these blocks over networks. Blocks are then reassembled at the receiving end.

**PCMCIA**   Personal Computer Memory Card International Association. Also used to refer to PC-Cards that are small, credit-card-size devices that provide a variety of functionality.

**PCS**   Personal communication services. 1.9 GHz.

**PCT**   Private Communications Technology. Designed by Microsoft.

**PDA**   Personal digital assistant. Hand-held computing device that offers multiple functions including calendar, contacts, messaging, and even wireless data and voice services.

**PDC**   Personal Digital Cellular. The wireless network standard utilized in Japan.

**PGP**   Pretty Good Privacy. A popular program used for encryption.

**PHY**   Physical. References the physical layer of the OSI model.

**PKI**   Public key infrastructure. An architecture that relies on the use of Certificate Authorities (CAs) to establish trusted and secure communications between multiple parties.

**POP**   Point of presence. The term used to refer areas services by a provider.

**Port forwarding**   The process of using a host to proxy network communications.

**POS**   Personal Operating Space.

**PPP** Point-to-Point Protocol. The most common protocol used to connect to the Internet.

**PQA** Palm Query Application. Applications developed for Palm VII handhelds to access web sites.

**Probe request** 802.11 management frame looking for access points.

**Probe response** Response to a probe request from an access point.

**PSTN** Public Switched Telephone Network. A traditional wired circuit-switched voice network.

**QoS** Quality of service.

**RAND** Random number.

**RBOC** Regional Bell Operating Company. *See* Baby Bells.

**RC4** Rivest Cipher 4. A stream cipher developed by Ron Rivest and utilized in the original IEEE 802.11 specification.

**RCP** Remote copy.

**RF** Radio frequency. Electromagnetic field used for wireless transmissions.

**RFC** Request for Comments. A formal document submitted to IETF to be reviewed and considered for becoming an Internet standard.

**Rogue access point** An access point set up to allow access to network resources or an access point set up by an attacker to impersonate ligament network resources.

**ROI** Return on investment.

**RSA Algorithm** Public key cryptographic algorithm invented in 1977 and named for the initials of the three founders: Ron Rivest, Adi Shamir, and Len Adelman.

**RShell** Remote Shell. A Unix program similar to telnet.

**R-UIM** Removable User Identity Module. A tamper-resistant cryptographic smart card that will be used on future 3G CDMA handsets and will equal the GSM SIM card in functionality.

**SAGE** Security Algorithm Group of Experts. An organization tasked with designing and evaluating security algorithms used on GSM networks.

**SHA-1** Secure Hash Algorithm. A U.S. cryptographic standard.

**SIM** Subscriber Identity Module. A small tamper-resistant cryptographic smart card used to store subscriber information and security algorithms on GSM handsets.

**Site survey** The process used to determine the characteristics of a wireless network.

**SMR** Specialized Mobile Radio. A wireless network technology originally utilized for mobile dispatch and law enforcement.

**SMS** Short message service. A service for sending short text messages (less than 160 characters) to mobile phones.

**Sniffing** Refers to the practice or equipment that is used to capture or view all of the packets that come across a network.

**SNMP** Simple Network Management Protocol. The protocol for monitoring and managing network devices.

**SOHO** Small Office Home Office. The term used to refer to the configurations common in home offices and small offices.

**Spread spectrum** A technique in which wireless data to be transmitted is dispersed over a wide bandwidth. CDMA utilizes spread spectrum techniques. *See* CDMA.

**SSH** Secure Shell. A protocol and program used to log into a remote computer, execute commands, and transfer files. SSH provides strong authentication and encrypted sessions.

**SSL** Secure Sockets Layer. The protocol for establishing encrypted communications between a web server and a web browser.

**STLP** Secure Transport Layer Protocol. The protocol used for encrypted transmission of data.

**SWAP** Shared Wireless Access Protocol. The protocol for voice and data transmission with data rates of up to 1.6 Mbps.

**TCP** Transmission Control Protocol. The IP protocol that enables hosts to establish connections and manage streams of data.

**TCP/IP** The term commonly used to refer to all protocols in the IP suite.

**TDM** Time Division Multiplexing. The method of sending multiple signals on a common medium by giving each signal a limited time to transmit.

**TDMA** Time Division Multiple Access. A digital cellular technology in which individual conversations are divided into time slots before transmission. Also known as ITU standards IS-54 and IS-136.

**Telnet** Terminal emulation for TCP/IP.

**TFTP** Trivial File Transfer Protocol. A lightweight file transfer protocol that is available on most systems.

**TIA** Telecommunications Industry Association.

**TLS** Transport Layer Security. *See* SSL.

**UDP** User Datagram Protocol. A connectionless protocol that runs over IP.

**UMTS** Universal Mobile Telecommunications Service. A set of international standards that define 3G wireless voice and data networks; also referred to as IMT-2000.

**UNII** Unlicensed National Information Infrastructure.

**URL** Uniform Resource Locator. The address used to locate information on the World Wide Web.

**UWB** Ultrawideband. The transmission technology that uses a very large frequency band.

**VLAN** Virtual LAN. LANs that are created through the configuration of software. This enables computers that may not be on the same physical network to appear as if they were on the same network.

**VLR** Visitor Location Register. A database on a wireless network that stores all relevant information about subscribers who are currently roaming on that network.

**VPN** Virtual private network. A secure network that connects remote sites and users over public networks like the Internet.

**WAN** Wide area network. The network connecting computers that are distributed over a large geographic area.

**WAP**  Wireless Application Protocol. A specification (not a standard) that enables the wireless transmission of data between a wireless phone or PDA and a content server. The specification is monitored and developed by the WAP Forum.

**WAP Gap**  A situation in WAP 1.x specifications in which encrypted data sent from a mobile device is decrypted and reencrypted at the WAP gateway, leading to data being exposed in cleartext for a brief millisecond.

**War driving**  The process of searching for open wireless access points by driving around.

**WBFH**  Wideband frequency hopping. Approved by the FCC in August 2000, WBFH permits channel bandwidths as wide as 3 and 5 MHz instead of the prior 1 MHz in the 2.4 GHz band. This increased bandwidth allows data rates as high as 10 Mbps per channel as compared to the original 2 Mbps maximum per channel (roughly 2 Mbps per 1 MHz of channel bandwidth). HomeRF 2.0 products and other FHSS products benefit from this.

**WECA**  Wireless Ethernet Compatibility Alliance. The organization that certifies the interoperability of IEEE 802.11 products and promotes WiFi and WiFi5 as global wireless standards.

**WEP**  Wired Equivalent Privacy. A security protocol defined in 802.11 that is designed to provide the same level of security as is found in a wired network. However, several security issues have been found with this protocol.

**WIM**  Wireless Identity Module. The secure storage location for information used in a WAP subscriber's transactions. WIM can either be a separate hardware module or a software component on an existing SIM card.

**WLANA**  Wireless LAN Association. A trade organization designed to foster market growth through increased awareness and understanding of networking technologies.

**WML**  Wireless Markup Language. Web programming language used to format web pages for viewing from wireless devices.

**WPAN**  Wireless personal area network. A logical grouping of wireless devices in a small area.

**WPKI**  Wireless public key infrastructure. The architecture that adopts existing PKI methods for use in wireless environments to enable secure mobile commerce. *See* PKI.

**WTLS**  Wireless Transport Layer Security. The security layer of WAP that provides privacy, data integrity, and authentication. It is based on TLS 1.0.

**Yagi**  A type of directional antenna.

# Index

# INTERNATIONAL CONTACT INFORMATION

## AUSTRALIA
McGraw-Hill Book Company Australia Pty. Ltd.
TEL +61-2-9417-9899
FAX +61-2-9417-5687
http://www.mcgraw-hill.com.au
books-it_sydney@mcgraw-hill.com

## CANADA
McGraw-Hill Ryerson Ltd.
TEL +905-430-5000
FAX +905-430-5020
http://www.mcgrawhill.ca

## GREECE, MIDDLE EAST, NORTHERN AFRICA
McGraw-Hill Hellas
TEL +30-1-656-0990-3-4
FAX +30-1-654-5525

## MEXICO (Also serving Latin America)
McGraw-Hill Interamericana Editores S.A. de C.V.
TEL +525-117-1583
FAX +525-117-1589
http://www.mcgraw-hill.com.mx
fernando_castellanos@mcgraw-hill.com

## SINGAPORE (Serving Asia)
McGraw-Hill Book Company
TEL +65-863-1580
FAX +65-862-3354
http://www.mcgraw-hill.com.sg
mghasia@mcgraw-hill.com

## SOUTH AFRICA
McGraw-Hill South Africa
TEL +27-11-622-7512
FAX +27-11-622-9045
robyn_swanepoel@mcgraw-hill.com

## UNITED KINGDOM & EUROPE (Excluding Southern Europe)
McGraw-Hill Education Europe
TEL +44-1-628-502500
FAX +44-1-628-770224
http://www.mcgraw-hill.co.uk
computing_neurope@mcgraw-hill.com

## ALL OTHER INQUIRIES Contact:
Osborne/McGraw-Hill
TEL +1-510-549-6600
FAX +1-510-883-7600
http://www.osborne.com
omg_international@mcgraw-hill.com

**SECURITY™**

**The Most Trusted Name in e-Security®**

# The Company

RSA Security Inc. is the most trusted name in e-security, helping organizations build secure, trusted foundations for e-business through its two-factor authentication, access management, encryption and digital signature solutions. RSA Security has the market reach, proven leadership and unrivaled technical and systems experience to address the changing security needs of e-business and bring trust to the new online economy.

A truly global company with more than 8,000 customers, RSA Security is renowned for providing technologies that help organizations conduct e-business with confidence. Headquartered in Bedford, Mass., and with offices around the world, RSA Security is a public company (NASDAQ: RSAS) with 2000 revenues of $282.7 million.

# Our Markets and Products

With the proliferation of the Internet and revolutionary new e-business practices, there has never been a more critical need for sophisticated security technologies and solutions. Today, as public and private networks merge and organizations increasingly expand their businesses to the Internet, RSA Security's core offerings are continually evolving to address the critical need for e-security. As the inventor of leading security technologies, RSA Security is focused on three core disciplines of e-security.

**Authentication**   RSA SecurID® systems are a leading solution for two-factor user authentication. RSA SecurID software is designed to protect valuable network resources by helping to ensure that only authorized users are granted access to e-mail, Web servers, intranets, extranets, network operating systems and other resources. The RSA SecurID family offers a wide range of easy-to-use authenticators, from time-synchronous tokens to smart cards, that help to create a strong barrier against unauthorized access, helping to safeguard network resources from potentially devastating accidental or malicious intrusion.

**Web Access Management**   RSA ClearTrust® web access management software is a unified privilege management solution that helps enable secure access to Web-based resources. It is designed to work within intranets, extranets, portals and exchange structures—all while providing users with transparent, single sign-on (SSO) within or across multiple sites and domains. This easy-to-deploy, rules-based solution integrates with existing infrastructures and provides scalability to support growing e-business requirements.

**Encryption**   RSA BSAFE® software is embedded in today's most successful Internet applications, including Web browsers, wireless devices, commerce servers, e-mail systems and virtual private network products. Built to provide implementations of standards, such as SSL, S/MIME, WTLS, IPSec and PKCS, RSA BSAFE products can save developers time and risk in their development schedules and have the security that only comes from a decade of proven, robust performance.

**Digital Signatures**   RSA Keon® solutions are a family of interoperable software modules for managing digital certificates and creating an environment for authenticated, private and legally binding electronic communications and transactions. RSA Keon software is designed to be easy to use and interoperable with other standards-based PKI solutions and to feature enhanced security through its synergy with the RSA SecurID authentication and RSA BSAFE encryption product families.

## Commitment to Interoperability

RSA Security's offerings represent a set of open, standards-based products and technologies that integrate easily into organizations' IT environments, with minimal modification to existing applications and network systems. These solutions and technologies are designed to help organizations deploy new applications securely, while maintaining corporate investments in existing infrastructure. In addition, the Company maintains active, strategic partnerships with other leading IT vendors to promote interoperability and enhanced functionality.

## Strategic Partnerships

RSA Security has built its business through its commitment to interoperability. Today, through its various partnering programs, the Company has strategic relationships with hundreds of industry-leading companies—including 3COM, AOL/Netscape, BEA, AT&T, Nortel Networks, Cisco Systems, Compaq, IBM, Oracle, Microsoft and Intel—who are delivering integrated, RSA Security technology in more than 1,000 products.

## Customers

RSA Security customers span a wide range of industries, including an extensive presence in the e-commerce, banking, government, telecommunications, aerospace, university and healthcare arenas. Today, more than 11 million users across 8,000 organizations—including more than half of the Fortune 100—use RSA SecurID authentication products to protect corporate data. Additionally, more than 500 companies embed RSA BSAFE software in some 1,000 applications, with a combined distribution of approximately one billion units worldwide.

## Worldwide Service and Support

RSA Security offers a full complement of world-class service and support offerings to ensure the success of each customer's project or deployment through a range of ongoing customer support and professional services, including assessments, project consulting, implementation, education and training, and developer support. RSA Security's Technical Support organization is known for resolving requests in the shortest possible time, gaining customers' confidence and exceeding expectations.

## Distribution

RSA Security has established a multi-channel distribution and sales network to serve the enterprise and data security markets. The Company sells and licenses its products directly to end users through its direct sales force and indirectly through an extensive network of OEMs, VARs and distributors. RSA Security supports its direct and indirect sales effort through strategic marketing relationships and programs.

## Global Presence

RSA Security is a truly global e-security provider with major offices in the US, United Kingdom, Singapore and Tokyo, and representation in nearly 50 countries with additional international expansion underway. The RSA SecurWorld™ channel program brings RSA Security's products to value-added resellers and distributors worldwide, including locations in Europe, the Middle East, Africa, the Americas and Asia-Pacific.

For more information about RSA Security, please visit us at: www.rsasecurity.com.

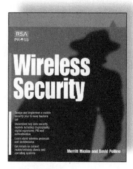